NIGHT
FIGHTER
ACE

TO

Joan Braham, and the many others who came to love and respect her husband

NIGHT FIGHTER ACE

TONY SPOONER

SUTTON PUBLISHING

This book ws first published in 1997 by
Sutton Publishing Limited · Phoenix Mill
Thrupp · Stroud · Gloucestershire · GL5 2BU

This new paperback edition first published in 2003

British Library Cataloguing in Publication Data
A catalogue record for this book is available from the British
Library

ISBN 0 7509 3473 5

Typeset in 9.5/12.5pt Nimrod.
Typesetting and origination by
Sutton Publishing Limited.
Printed and bound in Great Britain by
J.H. Haynes & Co. Ltd, Sparkford.

Contents

Foreword

I first met Bob Braham by proxy. It was at Bentley Priory, Stanmore, in the county of Middlesex – the headquarters first of Fighter Command and then, as the invasion of Normandy approached, of the Allied Expeditionary Air Force and the Air Defence of Great Britain.

Basil Embry – later to become Air Chief Marshal Sir Basil, with four DSOs and a DFC and much else besides to his name – stood proxy. The circumstances were rare.

I had just finished my second tour of flying, leading a Spitfire wing in East Anglia, and was at the start of my second stint as a 'resting' staff officer at HQ. Told by Leigh-Mallory, the Air Officer Commanding-in-Chief, Tactical Air Forces in Europe, that at 29 I was 'too old' for a third tour on fighters, I was waiting instead to join 2 Group and its Mosquitos where Embry was soon to become AOC. My future AOC was then also on the staff at Bentley Priory and was looking round for 'likely operational types' to join him when he assumed his new command.

One morning, he walked into my office for a talk, a familiar habit which I always regarded as a compliment. As I stood up in deference to a hugely respected senior officer of air rank, Embry advanced towards me until his nose was no more than six inches from mine. Looking straight at me with those piercingly direct eyes, he shot out an unexpected question. 'Have you ever met Bob Braham?'

'No, sir,' I said, 'I haven't, but I know all about him.'

'So you ought to,' said the Air Vice-Marshal. 'Bob Braham is a magnificent officer, an exceptional leader and a first-class pilot. He's the greatest intruder pilot of the lot. But there's something else which is compelling about him. He's happiest when he's looking for Germans to kill.'

Still looking me straight in the eye, Embry allowed himself one of his theatrical pauses designed for the maximum effect. He then revealed what he had obviously come into the room to say.

'Bob will be joining my staff at 2 Group as Wing Commander, Night Ops. That'll shake 'em in the Group when they hear about it!'

His satisfaction at the capture of Braham was manifested by the look on the predator's face. 'I like,' he said decisively, 'to have fully operational officers on my staff.'

With that, Embry launched into his oft-repeated diatribe about staff officers who 'sat on their backsides' and weren't prepared 'to go to war'. On the other side of the coin was the face of Bob Braham. By the time Basil had finished I felt I had known the legendary Wing Commander for much of the war.

When eventually I did meet him – one day at lunch with the AOC at a 2 Group HQ at Wallingford on the River Thames, he was quite different from the character I had conjured in my imagination. Quiet, almost reticent, and content to listen and keep his judgements and opinions to himself, it took the provocation of the AOC to prod him into a comment.

But it was his strikingly blue eyes, set below a fine crop of very fair hair, with a parting – unusually – straight down the middle, which stuck in my mind.

I did not see Braham again before he was taken prisoner. Nor, I think, was I truly aware of his total dedication to the fight until I had myself taken over 613 Squadron, with its day and night Mosquitos in 2 Group, based at Cambrai Epinoy, in northern France. Then, one evening in the Mess, our Engineer Officer recalled that, a month or two before Braham and his navigator had been shot down by FW 190s in daylight over Denmark, Wing Commander Braham had 'nicked' – that was the word used – one of 613's aircraft, SY–H for Harry, and taken it on a day Ranger* operation to Denmark, flying first

---

* A free-ranging, low-level daylight intruder, flown deep into enemy territory.

from Lasham to Coltishall in Norfolk to refuel. He had come down from Group HQ for the day accompanied by some unsuspecting and 'resting' navigator also from Embry's staff. Off the two had gone 'to seek out and destroy the enemy'. It transpired that, while Braham was doing his time on the staff, he had reached an understanding with his AOC that, once a week, he could find a navigator, borrow one of the squadron's aircraft and go off in daylight at low level and hunt over enemy-held territory for something to shoot up or down. It was, claimed the intrepid staff officer, 'the only thing that keeps me sane'.

On this particular day, 24 March 1944, Braham and his navigator found their reward. The pilot's log-book entry after the operation was revealing:

Grove – Aalborg: 950 miles. Saw Ju 52 and Ju 34 four miles south of Aalborg. Came up astern of Ju 34 (which had its wheels down) and shot it down in flames from 800 feet at 50–100 yards range (2 seconds cannon fire). Then chased Ju 52: one attack astern at 150 yards . . . E/a crash-landed in a marsh . . . and turned on its back. Shot it up on the ground. Landed back at Swanton Morley.

Embry probably had a point about Braham being 'happiest' when he was 'looking for Germans to kill'.

P.B. 'Laddie' Lucas CB DSO DFC
London
March 1997

Acknowledgements

The following persons have kindly helped me to prepare this biography. My sincere thanks are given to:

Mike Allen, a brilliant AI operator who knew Bob Braham when both were in 141 Squadron. Mike was awarded the DFC & 2 bars; *Harry Ashworth*, who knew the teenage Braham in Blackburn; *'Barney' Barnard*, an airman fitter who aided Bob in 29 Squadron; *Roy Bartlett*, who knew Bob when both were in the same sixth form; *John Brownbridge*, a 29 Squadron airman with fond memories of Bob; *Jack Bushby*, a fellow inmate of Stalagluft III; *Jim Carter*, an AI operator who knew Bob at both 51 OTU and 141 Squadron; *J.F. Claxton*, a 141 Squadron armourer; *Ron Dabney*, a fellow POW who later became Bob's brother-in-law; *Dr Jimmy Dougall*, affectionately known as 'The Mad Irishman' in 141 Squadron, and with whom Bob enjoyed pranks and friendly fisticuffs; *Norman Franks*, a fellow aviation author who supplied anecdotes and information; *Bill Geddes MBE*, a groundcrew sergeant who remembers strapping Bob into a Mosquito prior to a Ranger operation; *G/Capt. P.W. Gilpin CBE, DFC*, who was in the next cell to Bob during their interrogation at Oberursel; *Ernest Gouldsborough*, a sergeant engineer who knew Bob in 29 Squadron; *Doug Gregory DFC*, a fellow night fighter pilot of 141 Squadron; *W/Cdr W.J. 'Sticks' Gregory DSO, DFC*, DFM*, a brilliant AI operator who, from the rank of sergeant upwards, knew Bob Braham well at 29 Squadron, OTU, 141 Squadron, 2 Group TAF and after the war. 'Sticks' assisted Bob during twenty aerial combats in both Beaufighters and Mosquitoes. He was as highly decorated as any AI operator; *Jim Hartley*, an NCO pilot who flew alongside Bob after the war; *A. Haydock*, who supplied information about young Braham when both were living in Blackburn before the war; *R.M. Holdsworth*, who served Bob as a fitter after the war, at the Central Flying Establishment, West Raynham; *W/Cdr D.M. Holliday AFC*, who helped me to contact others; *W/Cdr Jack Hoskins DSO, DFC*, who knew Bob in Paris when both were assigned to SHAPE; *A. 'Baron' Humphreys*, a pilot of 613 Squadron, who remembers Bob Braham arriving to 'borrow' a Mosquito for a Ranger; *AVM E. 'Jimmy' James*, who saw quite a bit of Bob Braham at the Ministry of Defence after the war; *R.H. 'Jimmy' James DFC*, who was Guy Gibson's AI operator and contributed useful information about Bob and Guy during the period when both were scoring successes with 29 Squadron; *George Jones*, a navigator of 141 Squadron with a high regard for Bob Braham as his squadron commander; *Dr B.A.J. Kurrie*, who offered helpful advice from Australia; *David Lowe OBE*, the Bursar at Taunton School, who supplied details of Bob Braham as a schoolboy; *P.B. 'Laddie' Lucas CB, DSO, DFC*, who served under Basil Embry alongside Bob Braham prior to D-Day, 1944; *Eddie 'Tosh' Marsh*, an airman who knew his flight commander at 29 Squadron as 'S/Ldr Bob', and who had good stories to tell; *AVM F.R.L. 'Togs' Mellersh CB, DFC*, who, as a young pilot joined 29 Squadron and was inspired by Bob Braham's leadership; *Bruce Micklewright*, who used to go flying with Bob when he was working for SHAPE in Paris; *Freddie Newton*, who was warmly welcomed by Bob when he joined 141 Squadron; *Brian O'Reilly*, who knew Bob with SHAPE in Paris; *Fred Pedgeon*, a flight mechanic of 29 Squadron who had memories of both Bob and Guy Gibson; *Harry Powell*, a fellow pupil at Taunton School who knew Bob and his father; *C.H. 'Buster' Reynolds*, who was Bob Braham's friend, counsellor and Intelligence Officer when both were with 141 Squadron. Buster also got to know Braham's wife and family; *Andy Savill*, of 613 Squadron, who remembers the shock of Bob Braham being reported missing; *Ronnie Sherwood*, who offered useful advice; *Arthur Smith*, who flew with Bob Braham on 29 Squadron; *Margaret Snashall*, a WAAF at Duxford who kindly sent cuttings from her scrap book; *Derek 'Steve' Stephens DFC*, Doug Gregory's 141 Squadron AI operator; *Taunton School*, for unearthing Bob's school records via its bursar, David Lowe OBE; *Ian White*, who has supplied useful AI information relating to aerials, etc; *William White*, an armourer with memories of Bob and Guy Gibson when both served on 29 Squadron; *A/C Charles Widdows CB, DFC*, who was CO of 29 Squadron when Bob was his young 'anchor man'; Charles also scored at night; *Eric Webster*, an experienced researcher at the Public Record Office, Kew; *AM Sir Peter Wykeham KCB, DSO, OBE, DFC*, who knew Bob at 2 Group TAF. He also agrees that Bob rates greater recognition.

I must also express special thanks to Don Aris and Joan Braham. Without *Don Aris* this book could not have been written. A devoted 141 Squadron armourer, Don has spent years researching the life of Bob Braham and produced his own detailed biography specifically for members of Bob's family. It is his personal tribute to a man whom he greatly admired. He most kindly made me a copy and it constitutes the backbone of this biography. Don also gave me names and addresses of others who knew Bob and this has enabled me to add colour to fact. The consideration that Bob Braham always showed to others has clearly rubbed off on Don. He even made time to check through an early draft of this book. No thanks of mine could ever be enough.

Joan Braham and her son Michael have cooperated from the start. Both live in Canada and we have had to work via correspondence. However, from the warmth and kindness shown in her letters I feel that I can claim to know both Joan and her Bob (John to her). Also I can appreciate why Bob, from his first glimpse of her, knew that 'she was the one'. From Joan, it becomes very clear that Bob Braham was not just Fighter Command's most highly decorated pilot of

ACKNOWLEDGEMENTS

the Second World War but also one who greatly loved his country and whose understanding and common touch inspired many of his colleagues. In addition, Joan has given permission to quote, as I occasionally have, from *Scramble*, the autobiography which Bob wrote after the war and of which she holds the copyright.

Abbreviations

AFC	Air Force Cross. A decoration given to aircrew for outstanding non-operations flying.
AI	Airborne Interception. A type of radar used to detect other aircraft.
AOC	Air Officer Commanding. The commander of a RAF Command, Group, etc.
ASR	Air Sea Rescue. The service which picked up downed crews from the water.
ASV	Air to Surface Vessel. Airborne radar used to detect vessels at sea.
BAF	Belgian Air Force.
BEF	British Expeditionary Force; this went to France in 1939 and was evacuated, in part via Dunkirk, in 1940.
Blip	Name given to an echo or response visible on a radar screen.
CH	Chain Home. The first British ground radar defence system.
CHEL	Chain Home Extra Low. As CHL, but even more effective.
CHL	Chain Home Low. A subsequent radar defence system designed to be more effective against low-flying enemy planes.
CO	Commanding Officer of a Wing, Squadron or Flight.
CRT	Cathode Ray Tube. An essential part of all radar sets.
D-Day	6 June 1944. The day when Allied troops first went ashore for the recapture of France.

DFC	Distinguished Flying Cross. Decoration for gallantry awarded to RAF officers on operations.
DFM	Distinguished Flying Medal. Decoration for gallantry awarded to aircrew other than officers.
Do	Dornier. German aircraft manufacturer.
DSO	Distinguished Service Order. A high decoration awarded to officers of all fighting services engaged on wartime activities.
FAA	Fleet Air Arm. The flying service in the Royal Navy.
Freya	German early warning radar system.
Fw	Focke Wulf. German aircraft manufacturer.
Gee	British device to aid navigation.
He	Heinkel. German aircraft manufacturer.
Himmelbett	German system of radar-controlled searchlights and AA guns, used also by fighters.
IFF	Identification Friend or Foe. British device which triggered responsive echoes on British radar. It enabled our own planes to be differentiated from enemy blips on radar screens.
IO	Intelligence Officer. Sometimes called 'spy'.
Ju	Junkers. German aircraft manufacturer.
LMF	Lack of Moral Fibre. Euphemism for cowardice.
MC	Military Cross. Gallantry award given to Army Officers.
Me	Messerschmitt. German aircraft manufacturer.
MOD	Ministry of Defence.
Mother	British radar homing device on airfields.
MTB	Motor Torpedo Boat.
OTU	Operational Training Unit. The final stage of aircrew training establishment.
Radar	Original code name for Radio Direction And Range.

RDF   Range and Direction Finding. An early name for radar.

Ranger   Freelance operation over enemy territory looking for targets of opportunity.

SASO   Senior Air Staff Officer.

SHAPE   Supreme Headquarters Allied Powers Europe. A postwar military organization with HQ in Paris.

Stuka   Ju 87 single-engined dive-bomber.

TFU   Telecommunications Flying Unit which did much to perfect the use of radar for the RAF.

TRE   Telecommunications Research Establishment which carried on the work started by TFU.

U-boat   German submarine.

USAAF   United States Army Air Force.

USAF   United States Air Force. Later in the war it incorporated the USAAF and other US air forces.

VAD   Voluntary Aid Detachment. A nursing auxiliary force.

Wings   The badge given to a Service pilot after passing his initial flying tests.

RAF Structure and Ranks

STRUCTURE

The RAF is composed of a number of Commands. In the UK the most prominent in the Second World War were Bomber Command, Coastal Command and Fighter Command, although there was also Training Command.

Each Command consisted of a number of Groups with separate headquarters. Each Group contained a number of Wings, and each Wing contained a number of Squadrons. Each Squadron had a number of Flights, usually only two.

RANKS

Officers:
Marshal of the Royal Air Force (MRAF)
Air Chief Marshal (ACM)
Air Marshal (AM)
Air Vice-Marshal (AVM)
Air Commodore (A/C or Air C)
Group Captain (G/Capt.)
Wing Commander (W/Cdr or W/Co)
Squadron Leader (S/Ldr)
Flight Lieutenant (F/Lt)
Flying Officer (F/O)
Pilot Officer (P/O)

Others:
Warrant Officer (WO)*
Flight Sergeant (F/Sgt)

Sergeant (Sgt)

Corporal (Cpl)

Leading Aircraftsman (LAC)

Aircraftsman (AC)*

* These are divided into first and second class.

Introduction

Among the many groundcrew who appreciated Bob Braham's humanitarian touch was Willie White. He knew both Bob and Guy Gibson at West Malling when both were scoring victories for 29 Squadron. Willie White writes: '. . . the man I most admired was Bob Braham. He disliked "bull" and used to tell us when we were on night duty with him on dispersal that we should address him as "Bob", but that if we saw him around SHQ we should salute him and address him in the correct manner. In my opinion, if ever a man deserved to have a book written about him, that man is Bob Braham DSO, DFC.'

John Randall Daniel Braham's operational record during the Second World War rates a biography. The surprise is that it has not been written before. At the time when W/Cdr Braham's war came to an abrupt end in June 1944, he could have claimed the following distinctions: first, that he was the equal top-scoring night fighter of the war; second, that, his earlier appointment to 141 Squadron probably made him the youngest Wing Commander to command an operational squadron in the RAF; third, that he was, and would remain, the top-scoring ace of all twin-engined fighter pilots of the war, and one whose twenty-nine confirmed victories place him fifth top-scoring ace of all (see Appendix A); and fourth, that he was about to become the most highly decorated RAF fighter pilot of the whole war.

Not that he would have made any of these claims because J.R.D. Braham was essentially a modest man who shunned publicity. To all who knew him in the RAF in wartime, J.R.D. Braham was simply 'Bob', although this name has no association with any of his three Christian names. The explanation is simple. As a young Pilot Officer before the war Braham was posted to a squadron where, it so happened, there were several others also christened 'John' (the name by which he was known to his family). Accordingly, to avoid the inevitable confusion, all the 'Johns' drew lots to determine which of them would remain 'John' and also to find names for the others. John Braham drew 'Bob' and it stuck. This is the name that will normally be used in this biography.

The reason why no biography of Bob Braham has been written before is less simple. Biographies of all the other top fighter aces of the Second World War were written long ago. In the main these biographies concern pilots whom the wartime Press, and hence the public, seized upon. They praised their accomplishments literally 'to the skies'. Yet both Press and public remained ignorant about Bob Braham. His name is largely unknown even to those who served in the RAF during the war. Although the author served in the RAF throughout, and despite having studied and read extensively about the RAF (this being his sixth book to feature the RAF), it was only on a visit to his publishers in 1986 that he first came across the name of Bob Braham. He wished to say of the hero of his *Warburton's War* that W/Cdr Warburton was the most highly decorated pilot of the war, but the publishers drew his attention to Bob Braham's superior awards. Ever since, the author has had the desire to bring from the shadows the great accomplishments of Bob Braham.

Bob Braham and his unsurpassed wartime record have remained largely unknown for a number of reasons. Foremost is that Bob and the Press remained at loggerheads. Bob much disliked the aura of glamour which the Press created for other wartime aces and for this reason he would have nothing to do with them. On one occasion when they called on him in order to get a story and build up his image, he refused to meet them in spite of the pleadings of colleagues. On another occasion he physically ejected them from his home. Thereafter the Press chose to ignore him.

It is also relevant that, from 1940 onwards, night fighting depended upon a top secret device. Known as AI (Airborne Interception), it was an early application of the military use of airborne radar. So even if Braham had agreed to be interviewed by the eager Press, he would not have been permitted to explain to them how he was able to track down enemy aircraft at night. It suited Bob Braham to rebuff the Press, who consequently turned their attention to other aces. The name of Bob Braham remained unknown.

Although postwar analysis has placed him only fifth in confirmed victories, the four ahead of him were all pilots of single-engined fighter planes, as were the next dozen or so behind him. As nineteen of Bob's confirmed victories were at night, this puts Bob equal with the highly publicized John ('Cat's-Eyes') Cunningham.

This is the story of one man and his rise to fame as told to the author by Bob's family, friends and many acquaintances who had the pleasure of knowing him before, during and after the war. His friendly meetings with the German pilot who had shot him down are well covered both during his time as a POW and after the war. Sadly, Bob Braham died when he was still quite young. Thankfully he leaves behind a legacy of skill, determination and courage almost unmatched even in wartime RAF.

It is to be hoped that this tale may serve to inspire others. It is an example of what a person blessed with sound, but not outstanding, natural gifts is able to achieve by putting his whole being into a project. Bob Braham loved his country and its institutions. He had a fierce hatred of everything that Nazi Germany stood for. From 3 September 1939, from that eleventh hour when Britain declared war upon Hitler's Germany, Bob's single aim was to see that what he regarded as right would prevail. Could Bob Braham have been inspired by Neville Chamberlain's words delivered over the air to the British peoples on that memorable morning? 'This country is at war with Germany. . . . It is evil things that we shall be fighting against: brute force, bad faith, injustice, oppression and persecution.'

It would seem so.

1
Early Days

There was nothing in Bob Braham's early life to indicate that he would become the great air ace that he did. His education was affected by his father's occupation. His father was the Reverend Doctor Ernest Goodall Braham and, during Bob's early childhood, he was a Methodist Minister: one who was moved around England from time to time. There is no information regarding which schools, if any, Bob attended during his first ten years. During this period, his father moved from Shepton Mallet to Bristol, then to Bolton, Lancs and then to London. However it is known that Bob Braham attended the Preparatory School, Belmont, from 1930 onwards. This is the Prep School for the Public School Mill Hill, and Bob was attending as a day boy. His parents then were living at 139, Hendon Way, London.

The probable lack of an earlier schooling may not have been to the boy's disadvantage. His father, who was proud of having come from good Yorkshire working man's stock, was a believer in self-education. While ministering at Bristol, although he had earlier graduated from a Manchester Methodist Theological college, the Reverend E.G. Braham obtained a BA from Bristol University with a first in Philosophy. Later, while at Bolton, he obtained his Bachelor of Divinity Degree from Liverpool University. He clearly believed that learning did not cease with schooldays. It is inconceivable that his only son was not either sent to school or taught at home from an early age. After three years at Belmont School Bob, who by then must have passed the

Common Entrance examination, became a boarder at Taunton School. His parents were still living in London where the Rev. Braham was further educating himself at Kings College, London University in preparation for the PhD which he obtained in 1935 with a First in Theology.

A curious comment appears on an early school report: 'can go short runs only'. This implies a physical weakness and is in strict contradiction to all that followed. Joan Braham (wife) was most surprised when informed. In her words 'I never knew him to have any serious illness, in fact until the year of his death I never knew him to have a headache – unless it was of the hangover variety'. It is mere speculation but could this curious comment on a school report have been significant? Could it be that the young Braham, having at an impressionable age once been stigmatized as only 'fit for short runs', spent the rest of his life determined to show that, physically, he could outlast all around him?

At Taunton School the signs are that Bob Braham more than held his own scholastically as he finished up in the Classical VIb form. He was powerfully built and reached a height of 6 ft 1 in. All his photographs show the strong neck of the good rugger player and a pair of big hands to match. It has been estimated that he weighed 12–13 stone quite early in life. At the age of 15 years and 8 months, he successfully passed his School Certificate – then the entrance exam which opened doors to a University. However he was almost at once moved again as his father, in late 1935, took up the appointment of Minister of Trinity Methodist Church, Blackburn, Lancs. Between London and Lancashire the family had also lived for a while at Weston-Super-Mare. There may have been some upheavals or sickness in the family during John R.D. Braham's middle years at Taunton as, during this period, his school record refers to a total of 37 days' 'absences', 33 of which occurred during the summer and winter terms of 1934. Not too surprisingly, the boy did not receive especially good reports for those two terms although one report does refer to 'A good intelligent worker but exam results disappointing'. This constant moving of home, due presumably to his father's ministerial appointments, could hardly have produced much stability in the household.

The stipend of ministers was never generous – especially those of the Methodists, and it can be imagined that, as soon as his son had successfully passed the School Certificate hurdle, it made sense and eased the family budget to remove him from boarding school. Back in Lancashire, Bob Braham again became a day boy: this time at the Queen Elizabeth Grammar School, Blackburn. Here he was in the Upper Sixth, Modern: an indication that he was above the average scholastically. The year by then was 1936 and Bob, although only 16, left school for good after only a few months at the Grammar School. Although he was at this good Grammar School for only a brief time, he is remembered there by one of his contemporaries as a well built chap with a forceful personality and a good boxer.

The Britain of 1936 was lacking in resolution. The country's power and prestige was clearly on the wane. Europe was being torn apart by the conflicting claims of the Fascists and the Communists. Both claimed to be the panacea to the world's ills. The Great Depression of the 1930s had left unemployment queues in most lands. A sound and solid future in England for a young man with good health and education was hard to imagine. The threat of war was overhanging most of Europe. The Spanish Civil War was already aflame, with both rival ideologies attempting to prove that 'Might is Right'. It was a period of uncertainty and confusion, with the German Nazis taking every advantage of the situation to increase their stranglehold over their country and its neighbours.

It is not too surprising, in that uncertain atmosphere, that Bob Braham, aged 16, set his sights on a career outside his native country. The once mighty British Empire had decreased in size but was still a powerful influence in many foreign lands. There were big colonies in Africa, the Far East, the Caribbean and elsewhere. Many a young man of his background and physique thought likewise; rubber planting in Malaya; cotton growing in the Sudan; tea estates in India or in Burma. In such places, the prospects of a full and meaningful life still seemed possible . . . and preferable to life in an England divided by political beliefs and riddled by uncertainty with her traditional industries already under threat from cheap labour in emerging countries.

As the war years were later to show, Bob Braham firmly believed that his country still had an important role to play. He was a patriot who was prepared to give his all to preserve his country's way of life. This may well account for the decision which he made at the age of 16, to prepare himself for a career with the Colonial Police. He had also considered the Merchant Navy but his father was dead set against this. Naturally he would have wished his only son to be a doctor, or a minister like himself, but Bob was clearly not built for such scholarly and sedentary occupations.

In order to pursue his Colonial Police aim, Bob Braham obtained a position as a clerk in the nearby Wigan Lancashire police. He reckoned that this experience would stand him in good stead when later he would be old enough to apply for the Colonial Police; where the pay and prospects would be more promising and a life spent in preserving the British way of life, more self-rewarding.

By 1937, when the young man had worked for a year or so at the often boring routine jobs which are inevitably part of a policeman's lot – especially, no doubt, for its junior clerks – the clouds of war were more ominous. The German and Italian Fascist dictators were becoming ever more arrogant and demanding. While the rest of the world stood by or made ineffective protests, Italy and Germany were using the huge armed forces which they had built up to claim more and more 'living space' for their enthusiastic followers. Their arms industries had been built up. This had reduced their unemployment queues. The new territories that both countries had seized had brought their dictators enhanced prestige. To almost all in Britain, France and elsewhere in

Europe, a showdown was becoming almost inevitable. Either the Fascist dictators would overcome the rest of Europe or they would have to be stopped by war. Words, and the League of Nations, had failed.

One of the actions which a slowly awakening Britain had taken was to expand, as rapidly as possible, an Air Force which had been cut to a minimum by politicians of all shades unwilling to spend money on National defence. A major decision was to institute a Short Service Commission scheme under which adventurous youth, with fairly demanding physical and educational qualifications, could join the RAF for flying duties as officers, but only for a five-year term. Thereafter they would be released with a sizeable gratuity. It was a scheme that attracted a large number of the dissatisfied but eager young men of the country and, incidentally, one which probably did more than any other to save the country from being overcome in the air during the war years which were soon to follow.

To the young bored police clerk in Wigan, it seemed an answer to his many doubts.

The fact that his father, unusually for a minister of the Church, had joined up to become an officer pilot in the Royal Flying Corps during the first Great War of 1914–1918, may have been an additional incentive. Although only aged 17, he applied and, rather to his surprise, Bob Braham's application was one of those to be accepted. His commission was dated 7 March 1937. His service number was 40667. He must have been one of the youngest officers in the Royal Air Force. As was to be proved later, the RAF had made a sound choice.

Another curious anomaly arises. All who came to serve with Bob Braham in the RAF comment upon his aggression. Every picture of him also attests to this. With legs apart and a look of determination on his face he personifies a bull-dog attitude. Yet, as Joan and others testify, he adored his gentle mother in preference to his ever knowledge-seeking father. It is also known that at home he was very fond of, and got on well with, his younger sister, the Brahams' only other child.

Roy Bartlett who was at Taunton School with the young Braham remembers chiefly his 'gentleness and lack of aggression'. Harry Powell, who was also a Taunton School contemporary, emphasizes that Bob Braham was not a physical weakling but mentions that he did have a temper and was treated by others with a degree of caution. Harry Powell – an acute observer who would grow up to become a professor of anthropology, was a close friend. He recalls noting during a visit with Bob at his parents home at Weston-Super-Mare that 'there was a considerable latent tension between Bob and his father'. He adds that 'both had strong, not to say, dominant personalities'. The Reverend Braham 'seemed to disapprove of their visit' even though permission had been granted and it had involved a long cycle ride. He also mentions that father and son used to spar (boxing) with one another and that 'it seems that the sparring sometimes got out of hand'. He also speculates that Bob may have taken up boxing to prove that his chest condition ('only short runs') was no handicap. The long cycle ride (25 miles each way) seems proof enough about his stamina at aged 14–15. Harry Powell's own father was also a minister and their belief was that Reverend Braham was under some strain because his many academic achievements did not get him the academic appointments he wanted. A frustrated man is not always easy to live with.

Although it can never be known what influence his father had upon the young Bob Braham and to what extent the father's earlier decision to fly and fight for his country as a pilot in the First World War did influence the son, there are indications that the Revd E.G. Braham was the dominant influence in that household. For one thing, Bob Braham's mother seems not to have been blessed with her son's good health. All that is known is that she died when young after contracting pneumonia during the early years of the Second World War. It is also learnt that the Revd Braham, although a man who was forever seeking more knowledge to such an extent that he became a renowned philosopher, was apt to be tyrannical at home. Clearly he was not a man cast in the normal mould. Not many ministers of a Church desert the pulpit for the cockpit of an aeroplane. Not many ministers find the time and patience to become chairmen of philosophical societies and a lecturer on the subject at universities. Even rarer still not many Methodist ministers later become Church of England priests and RAF chaplains. Yet the Revd E.P. Braham's career encompassed all these things before his early death at the age of about 60.

Considered along with the tyrannical behaviour at home, noticed by his grandsons and referred to by others who knew him there, a picture emerges of a most unusual man. One who was close to him had considered that he would have made an excellent Oxford Don. Could the Revd Dr Braham's working class background have prevented him from obtaining the academic appointments that he wanted and for which he had qualified himself so diligently?

It is possible to read into Bob Braham's desire first to go abroad as a Colonial policeman or to join the Merchant Navy and subsequently to seek an RAF Commission, a pressing need to leave home where, perhaps, all was not a bed of roses for a youth striving to assert himself? What is certain is that the young Bob Braham, well accustomed to discipline at home, took readily to the enforced discipline that a career in any of the fighting forces necessarily entails; especially when a raw recruit. Be that as it may, young Bob was soon thriving in the new environment outside his father's house. The RAF and he hit it off well.

Short Service entrants to the RAF began their training with a curious blend of civil and military flying. Although accepted into the RAF as a pilot officer and paid as such, a new entrant was still much on probation. Until the RAF could be assured that the entrant had the required ability to cope with an aircraft alone in the air, he was not put into Service uniform and his initial flying instruction would be given by a civil flying school operating under contract for the RAF. In short, it was left to the civil flying school instructors to sort out the sheep from the goats. A condition of the school's contract was that their flying instructors had to have been in the RAF or were on a RAF Reserve. It was a good way of increasing the RAF rapidly as it meant, since the pay of an instructor at an RAF contract school was above that which was paid to a similar instructor at a purely civil flying school, almost anyone capable of teaching flying became involved in the rapid expansion of the RAF.

2
Pre-war RAF

Thus it was that Pilot Officer-on-probation J.R.D. Braham, physically removed from the stresses of home, took his first flying lessons at the No. 7 Elementary and Reserve Flying Training School, at Desford, Leicestershire. The school used the DH 82 Tiger Moth which was then the standard elementary flying trainer both for most Flying Clubs dotted around the country and also for the RAF. At Desford, his instructors used their RAF (Reserve) ranks.

The normal period between the first lessons and being assessed sufficiently competent to be allowed to fly solo is about 8–11 hours of dual instruction. Some youngsters, usually those who are proficient at fast moving ball games such as squash and cricket where the ability to hit a moving ball is paramount, quickly master the essentials of flight. With their quick reflexes, they show the judgements and skills required to take off, fly, turn, recover from unusual situations and carry out the all important smooth landings almost at once. They might be sufficiently proficient to fly solo after as few as 6 or 7 hours of dual instruction although they are usually held back until later. On the other hand, there are those who lack the essential co-ordination between hands, feet and eye and who seem unable ever to possess the ability to fly. Among the young, such are rare. The accepted RAF maximum period of dual instruction, pre-war, was 15 hours. If the pupil had not by then impressed his instructors – and a pupil had to be checked by more than one such before being washed out – he would be dropped. Some, when failed, especially later when the demands of war were greater, would then be offered the alternative of training as navigators or air gunners, but in 1937 the demand in the RAF was principally for pilots.

Bob himself in his autobiography *Scramble* is the first to admit that, although many on his course were being sent solo after only about 8 hours dual, he and one or two others were being held back. It was a worrying time for him. One of his instructors was Bill Oliver who remembers him as being 'soft spoken, almost painfully shy and about average as a pilot without any manifestation of the greatness to come'. After his instructor was changed, better progress was made and, after over 13 hours of dual, the moment that all pilots will never forget arrived. Even then, he made rather a hash of his first attempt to land solo and had to open up and go round again. After that Bob Braham seems to have kept up with the others although he admits that his instrument flying 'under the hood' was weak. As any reader of *Scramble* soon finds out, Bob Braham's honesty regarding his faults and weaknesses shines throughout.

As might be expected, the young men on the course – and they came from all corners of the Commonwealth – soon came to regard themselves as the 'young bloods' of the town. Flying in 1937 was surrounded by an aura of glamour. It was the era of the record-breaking flights to and from America, to Africa and Australia. It was one of the few activities at which Britain still shone. Britons had won the Schneider Trophy. This was the high speed trophy of the world. With speeds of well over 300 mph, Britons, again flying the Supermarine seaplanes which had won the coveted trophy, also held the world speed record. It is also true that a young man who 'finds himself' in such a challenging occupation as flying, gains in self-confidence and expands in other directions. Limited only by money – a pilot officer received only about 11 shillings per day – the self-confidence generated prompted the students to visit the pubs, look for girls and indulge in wild games and pranks. Life was opening up like a flower in the sunshine.

Those who passed the tests at the EFTS, and most did so, were then fully incorporated into the RAF. The next stage of their induction was to attend a course of 'square bashing' at Uxbridge under the stern eyes of experienced drill sergeants. This was accompanied by lectures about Service life and the obligations that were implied. As Bob Braham writes in *Scramble*: 'This [drilling] smartened us up a bit'.

By the end of May 1938, Bob and his fellow students were deemed ready to progress to 'the real thing'. He and his particular friend Dave Blomeley were posted to No. 11 RAF Flying Training School at Shawbury, near Shrewsbury. This was no semi-civil school. Bob Braham had made it. He was now fully in the RAF. For the rest of his flying career he would be operating only military aircraft. Various Hawker-built biplanes – the Hart, the Hind and the Audax – were those on which most pilot recruits first encountered RAF aircraft as was the case at Shawbury. They were a good deal bigger, more powerful, faster and more complicated than the small Tiger Moths. Again Bob Braham found himself a mite behind some of the more gifted 'natural' pilots. But once having overcome this difficulty, he soon caught up. To fly light aircraft (and the Hawker types still came under this category), the pilot needs to be delicate with the controls. Bob's otherwise fine physique may well have handicapped him here. He was strong and rugged; not light and delicate of touch. Bob Braham's ability to apply himself with unusual singlemindedness probably accounted for the manner in which, after a slow start, he caught up those pilots more naturally gifted. In the end, after an absorbing period of flying the various Hawker aircraft by both day and night, during which he had been granted the coveted RAF Wings, Bob was assessed as Average in all categories: Piloting, instrument flying, aerobatics (which he loved to do) and navigation. The only comment was: 'A keen pupil who, although slow to learn at first . . . maintained satisfactory progress throughout the term'. This aligns with the 'unusual improvement, very good progress' noted by Taunton School. Bob Braham was one who never gave up.

Before leaving RAF Shawbury at the very end of 1938, Bob and others spent an enjoyable five weeks at the RAF Armament Training Camp at Penrhos in Wales. Here they learnt air-to-air shooting. Bob found himself scoring well at this. It was the nearest thing to actual combat in the air. The drogue targets would be trailed behind other aircraft. With war now very much 'in the air', it felt good to be firing live ammunition even if only at a towed drogue.

The fear among the young pilots was that war would break out before they were fully trained and eligible to join a squadron. The belief then was that if the war did break out, it would be a swift one. From start to finish, only a few of the young officers had failed to make the grade. By then, those who remained had become fully imbued with RAF traditions and fighting spirit. They were raring to be put into action. It is to be doubted whether many realized that the Luftwaffe, the German air force, their most probable enemy in the event of war, was both bigger and more battle-trained than their own. Nor was it appreciated that it was equipped with great numbers of modern front-line planes, far in excess of those of the 1938 RAF.

The Luftwaffe had learnt much from the period 1936–1937, when it fought in Spain on the side of the Fascists, and it was only during the late 1930s that Britain began to produce comparable aircraft. The Hurricanes were starting to arrive but the Spitfires were still under final development. By contrast the Me 109 was battle-proved and available in numbers.

In Bob Braham, now a fully fledged Pilot Officer and a proud wearer of the RAF Wings, the RAF had turned out a fine example of the kind of courageous optimistic youth, eager and ready for war; to defend what he regarded as right; to defeat what he regarded as evil. At Shawbury, the pupils were asked to give their preference. There was a choice. They could opt to move, after graduation, to one of three fighting Commands of the RAF: Bomber, Fighter or little-known (and relatively new) Coastal. Many, with their sights upon a civil airline career at the end of their Short Service Commission, elected for Bomber or Coastal Command. There they would be flying the larger twin-engined planes with characteristics akin to the airliners of the time. Bob Braham, however, with his love of aerobatics, opted for fighters. His father had fought as a pilot in the First World War. Then it had largely been a single-engined struggle. There was something about flying fighters which appealed to him. It bespoke of glamour too. The performance of the Hurricanes and Spitfires was already making headlines. In a giant leap, the RAF was replacing obsolescent 200 mph bi-planes with sleek streamlined monoplanes capable of nearly twice that speed. Later Bob Braham was to eschew glamour but that wasn't the mood of the eager 18-year-old pupil who was graduating from RAF Shawbury.

To the chagrin of many who had opted for the twin-engined aircraft, it was decided that most of those on Bob's course would be sent, along with Bob, to fighter squadrons. Tension in Europe, with the ever more threatening Hitler now firmly in charge of Germany, dictated events in Britain. If Britain was to stand up to Hitler, who by then had seized the Saar Basin from France, had marched into Austria and, having already over-run parts of Czechoslovakia, was now laying claim to parts of Poland, the RAF's first need was to build up her fighter force.

By then Bob Braham had already experienced examples of the need to treat aeroplanes with respect. In experimenting with a novel aerobatic, he managed to 'bend' a Hawker Fury – another of that manufacturer's biplanes but a single-seated one. He almost had to bale out, so severely had he 'bent' the Fury by his violent manoeuvre. Honest as ever, he confessed to his error and was punished by having to wash down other planes with soap and water. He had also on another occasion failed to negotiate a cross-wind when landing and had put another Fury on to one of its wing tips. The damage was slight but again Bob found himself with the unpleasant chore of having to wash down another plane.

Over-confidence has killed many a pilot at about the stage that Bob had reached. These salutary lessons probably helped to induce more caution in Bob at a meaningful time. He was lucky to escape from these misfortunes unscathed . . . and, one hopes, wiser too.

Although Bob Braham had reason to congratulate himself that he, almost alone of the course, had *chosen* to be posted to a fighter squadron, he was in for a big disappointment. In the way of the world in general, and in Service postings in particular, it so turned out that it was he, and not those with their sights on heavy aircraft, who found himself posted to a *twin*-engined squadron. It *was* a fighter squadron but one of the very few which was being equipped with twin-engined machines. The unit was 29 Squadron which was about to convert from biplane Hawker Demons to Bristol Blenheims. Although this latter was a monoplane of modern design, it was more suitable as a bomber than as a fighter. That it was being used as a fighter – albeit a slow one – was perhaps indicative of the urgent need to build up a fighter force comparable to that of the Luftwaffe. It was a much less glamorous type than the Hawker Hurricane that others of his course would soon be flying. Bob would not have objected even if the fighter squadron had still been equipped with the obsolescent Gloster Gladiators. They at least were single-engined fighters and, although biplanes, were superior in performance to the Bristol Blenheims.

Never one to conceal his feelings, Bob, as soon as he arrived at his new base, Debden in Essex, immediately put in a request to be transferred to one of the other squadrons on the same RAF Station since he had observed that they flew Hawker Hurricanes. This naturally got him off on the wrong foot with the hierarchy of his unit and he was icily informed that 29 Squadron was a proud one and that there was no way that he could opt out of the posting.

Probably because of his bad start, it took Bob several months before he was allowed to fly the Blenheim. He had not before flown a twin-engined aircraft and the Blenheim, with its retractable undercarriage, flaps, variable pitch propellors and other more advanced systems, was quite different from anything that Bob Braham had experienced before. However, he was a steady learner and he experienced little difficulty in flying the type when allowed to do so. Also, after his 'black mark' start, he soon proved to be a popular young officer and one who threw himself into the squadron spirit and games with unbounded enthusiasm.

It was with 29 Squadron that John Braham became 'Bob' Braham. It speaks well for the unit as not every squadron was so informal as to use Christian names when in the air.

With war growing ever closer, the pilots were lectured about the performance of the enemy's Me 109s. It must have been a sobering thought that, if ever it came to air-to-air combat, with their Blenheims pitted against the vastly swifter, more manageable and better armed Me 109s, there could only be one expected outcome. Fortunately, it never came to that as in August 1939 the squadron was re-equipped with Hurricanes. Being late to be so equipped, 29 Squadron had the advantage of receiving later models than those which had been supplied to the other two fighter squadrons at Debden. The 29 Squadron machines had the more efficient variable pitch propellors whereas 85 and 87 Squadrons had to make do with the fixed pitch ones which, by comparison, adversely affected the aircraft's performance.

Another event of that last month of peace was a week-long exercise during which the fighter planes of the three squadrons at Debden (and others) tried to intercept the 'invading' bombers of the RAF and French Air Force. The ground radar system which was to be so valuable in the war which followed had not been fully developed. With largely only a Ground Observer Corps to assist the fighters, most of the bombers got through. Also, when they did manage to intercept an 'invading' Wellington or Hampden bomber, it was reckoned that the Blenheims when employed as fighters would likely have been shot down by the rear gunners of those planes. The exercise gave the RAF much to think about:

much to learn. One good outcome (or was it just a coincidence?) was the immediate replacement in 29 Squadron of the vulnerable Blenheim by the far more deadly Hurricane fighter planes.

By the end of August all leave had been cancelled. Barring a miracle, or a climb-down by Hitler, war was now inevitable and the other Hurricane squadrons at Debden were dispatched to France. 29 Squadron was still learning to master their Hurricanes: an aircraft which posed no difficulties for P/O Bob Braham. By then he had already become a good average, or above average, pilot. His wish had come true. When on 3 September at 1100 hours Britain declared war against Nazi Germany, Bob Braham was fully trained as a fighter pilot and would be in the front line, if required, with a powerful single-seater eight-gun Hawker Hurricane under his control. He had timed it to perfection.

As he and others crowded around the wireless set to hear Prime Minister Neville Chamberlain's declaration of war, Bob Braham was raring to go: to fight those evil things that Chamberlain had spoken about: 'Brute force, bad faith, injustice, oppression and persecution'. Time alone would tell whether or not his self-confidence was justified but Bob Braham was fighting fit and ready for war.

3
War and Blenheims

Like most others in Britain, Bob Braham expected the worst
to happen immediately. It was known that the Germans had
ruthlessly bombed and ravaged Poland on the first day of
their war. Their towns, and especially their airfields, had
been hit hard. Hordes of bombers were expected to raid
Britain without delay. In preparation for this, a million or
more children had already been evacuated from in and
around London. The windows of all buildings in the cities
and on the RAF aerodromes had been plastered over with
paper strips. Sandbags surrounded all essential buildings.
Trenches were being dug in the parks. Anderson personal air-
raid shelters were widely distributed and the population
erected these in their gardens. The air alert system had been
tried out. Wailing sirens would announce each raid. However,
nothing whatever happened except for the false air raid alarm
warning which sounded minutes after the Prime Minister
had finished speaking to the nation on 3 September.

To meet the expected hordes of bombers 29 Squadron
moved half its aircraft daily to a forward base, Wattisham, in
Suffolk. The others were retained at Debden in a state of
readiness. Although the Squadron's Hurricanes were
scrambled on a few occasions, they all turned out to be false
alarms. However, the practice sharpened the pilots' skill, kept
the squadron on its toes and generally gave the pilots much
needed real practice on their new machines.

The euphoria of these pent up Hurricane pilots was short
lived. The war had barely been in existence a month when the

order came for 29 Squadron to hand over their Hurricanes to others and to revert to Blenheims. However, this time, it was to use this bomber type as a night-fighter; in consequence, the squadron's aircraft were painted over with 'Berlin black'.

The meagre armament of the Blenheim – One forward gun and a Vickers K gun in a turret at the back – was increased by adding a four-gun forward-firing pack under the aircraft's belly. It took the squadron quite a while to add this pack to each aircraft but fortunately few, if any, night raiders were then venturing over Britain. It was the period of the 'phoney war' with nothing of note happening either across the Maginot line of forts protecting the East border of France or over Britain. Poland was carved up: Russia had appeared on Germany's side and by prior agreement with Germany had seized the eastern part of that unhappy land. Only at sea, where the new U-boat menace was threatening, were Britons mostly at peril. Even over the French–German borders there were few serious air battles.

Neither 29 Squadron, nor indeed any other unit in the RAF, knew much about night-fighting. Airborne radar was in its infancy and the aircraft of 29 Squadron were not, initially, equipped with this useful device. It was vaguely understood that searchlights would illuminate night raiders and that fighters would then destroy them, but it had not been much practised. Even the Ground Control radar system was not fully developed. Night navigation in Fighter Command was also largely untried. The Blenheims were sent up to patrol certain lines at night in case the enemy might attempt to send bombers over the Channel and North Sea. Ground flares were used to help guide the aircraft but the principal hope of destroying an enemy at night lay in having him first caught in the beam of a searchlight; fortunately these were relatively numerous. Again a forward base was used. This time 29 Squadron moved to Martlesham Heath near Ipswich. In these circumstances it is not surprising that 29 Squadron recorded no kills until well into June 1940 by which time the war had begun in earnest.

During January, P/O Braham was able to show that he could cope satisfactorily with an emergency situation. He had taken off from Martlesham to return to Debden in conditions of snow. The snow much reduced the plane's take-off performance. As a result, the Blenheim scarcely cleared the airfield and, before climbing safely away, one leg of the undercarriage had hit the ground hard. This had damaged the hydraulic system so that the wheels could not again be lowered nor could landing flaps be used. It didn't help that, at that time, it was popularly believed that a Blenheim was liable to catch fire and disintegrate if landing with its wheels up. Bob Braham was in an even worse situation. One wheel was partially down and the other was firmly up.

Bob kept his head. He flew in this configuration back to Debden where the CO, S/Ldr Gomez, took off to fly alongside Bob in order to assess the damage and give advice. By flying to Debden Bob had deliberately reduced the plane's fuel load and weight. Meanwhile the observer/gunner had the offer made to him to bail out. However he decided to stick with Bob. In the end, with half the squadron and the ambulance and fire-tender crews watching, Bob Braham made a perfect, largely wheels up, flapless landing, with the aircraft slithering along in the snow without major damage to itself or its two occupants.

Perhaps this demonstration of a cool head and sure handling was responsible for Bob Braham being given an 'Above Average' rating when next assessed. Up to that point, Bob Braham's annual rating had been the more normal one of 'Average'. The pilot who had taken so long to first solo was learning fast. 'Unusual improvement' again.

As 1940 progressed, the Blenheims began to be equipped with AI sets. These were an early version of airborne radar. The device was still cloaked in tight secrecy, and it is therefore difficult to determine when exactly the Blenheims of 29 Squadron were so modified – if indeed all were eventually done, since 'AI' i.e. Aircraft Interception, were initials that were not to be mentioned. Instead, 'RDF', standing for Range and Direction Finding, was apt to be used, but even this was a term to be used with caution. RDF was also the basis of the ground control system which had, by 1940, been brought up to a good degree of efficiency. Later RDF came to be called radar. 29 Squadron records contain a reference to 'signals' on top of a word crossed out which appears to be 'AI'.

While the aircrews of 29 Squadron struggled to come to terms with night-flying, night-tactics, their Blenheims and, where fitted, an early version of AI – without much help from outside and certainly without ever threatening the few enemy aircraft which approached Britain – events of monumental significance were happening elsewhere. In April 1940, Norway was attacked and swiftly conquered. Narvik in the north held out for a while but the British Forces sent there, including a few fighters, were outnumbered and out-classed. Norway was soon entirely in German hands. The RAF had lost a number of planes and the Royal Navy a number of ships, without being able to achieve much. 29 Squadron had played a minor role in this campaign by carrying out convoy patrols from Drem, an airfield in Scotland.

Worse still was to follow swiftly. Even while the Germans were carrying all before them in Norway, their armies, most admirably supported by the Luftwaffe, launched their major attack in the West. Belgium and Holland were trampled underfoot within days, the bombing of Rotterdam being particularly devastating. Denmark, earlier, had capitulated without a shot being fired. Almost before they could grasp what was happening, the French found their much vaunted Maginot Line of forts bypassed and blasted. The French army floundered and the British Expeditionary Force (BEF) in France was also routed: not that it was anything like the 2,000,000-plus size of the French army.

The RAF force in France, again not over large, found that its Blenheim and Fairey Battle bombers were 'easy meat' to the Me 109 fighters which shot them down in large numbers. Only the few squadrons of Hurricanes could fight on anything like equal terms with the Messerschmitts. Spitfires at that time were few in number and none was sent to France. Quite determinedly, and against the pleas of others, the C-in-C of Fighter Command, Air Chief Marshal Sir Hugh Dowding, realizing that the battle for France was already lost on the ground, preserved all the Spitfires he had for the later defence of Britain, which he believed would soon be a vital necessity.

While the Allies attempted to stop the invading hordes which had swept through the Netherlands and Belgium, the main German thrusts were gathering themselves in the forests of the Ardennes. This was south of the areas which the Allies were defending and south of the Maginot Line. When the Panzer divisions of General Rundstedt broke out of the Ardennes and raced across central France almost unopposed, panic broke out. Within days Paris had fallen and the rest of France lay open to the invaders. By mid-June France was asking for surrender terms. The battered remnants of the BEF, along with a number of French units, managed to escape back across the Channel from the Dunkirk beaches. To many, the war seemed over. Germany stood victor with all Western Europe in her grasp.

As a desperate measure, Parliament put aside Party differences and banded behind the ageing Winston Churchill who alone seemed to be keeping his head and who continued to broadcast defiance against the victorious Nazis. A National Government under his firm leadership decided to fight on. Hitler, while laying plans for an invasion of Britain, was really biding his time. In his mind, the war in the West was won. Britain would soon have to realize the futility and impossibility of carrying on alone. If necessary, he would invade Britain: in which event, his army chiefs were confident of victory. They did, however, mention one proviso. In view of Britain's known superiority in numbers of warships, the German generals advised that, before any invasion across the English Channel could be launched, it would be necessary to destroy what was left of the RAF. The German bombers would then be able to take care of the surface ships.

Hitler did not regard this as a major proviso since Goering, his colourful Air Force Chief, assured him that his Luftwaffe had shot down the RAF Blenheims, Wellingtons and Battles with ease. They had also been fairly successful against the Allied fighters. It was not thought that Britain, which had already lost over 500 Hurricanes, would have many of this worthy type remaining. Few encounters with Spitfires had taken place. It was true that, in all, the Luftwaffe had lost about 1,000 planes, mostly bombers, but they had another thousand or so to throw into battle if Britain obstinately continued to fight on. Their bombers, especially the Ju 87 Stukas, had terrified both the civilian population and much of the vaunted French army as well. Hitler and Goering saw no reason why the same medicine should not be inflicted upon the already battered British Forces, especially as those which had escaped via the Dunkirk beaches had lost all their armour in France.

Even the superiority of the British Navy had been reduced. Due to the vain efforts made at Narvik and elsewhere in Norway and the considerable losses during the Dunkirk evacuation, Britain had lost a large number of naval vessels, principally destroyers. Moreover, the success which Admiral Doenitz's U-Boats were achieving in the Atlantic against Allied convoys required Britain to employ in those waters almost all her remaining destroyers. This was to counter the growing threat of being cut off from supplies from America and from the sources of oil in the Middle East. The fact that Britain also had a great superiority in numbers of battleships, aircraft carriers and cruisers was not considered all that important. These big ships would be of limited use in preventing an invasion across the narrow Dover Straits. They would, in German eyes, be easy targets for the Luftwaffe bombers. Furthermore, U-boats had already sunk both battleships and aircraft carriers.

On the day after the French asked for an armistice, 18 June 1940, 29 Squadron shot down its first night raider. By then, Hitler, always a great believer in terrorizing his enemies, had begun to send over large numbers of bombers each night: up to 100 or so when the weather conditions were favourable. Britain at that time had no adequate answer to such raids. The Blenheims, especially those machines which had not been fitted with AI radar sets, were not either fast enough or deadly enough to catch and destroy the Luftwaffe's well-defended and armour-plated bombers: i.e. the Heinkel 111s, the Dornier 215s and 217s and the growing number of even better machines, the Ju 88s. Apart from the ineffective Blenheims, Britain depended for night defence upon a small number of Bolton & Paul single-engined Defiants. A single-engined day fighter with a four-gun rear turret, the Defiant had proved a disaster as a day fighter and was being used, more in hope than expectation, as a night fighter. The RAF at that time had no aircraft which had been designed as a night fighter and therefore resorted to using a number of Hurricane day fighters. Both Defiants and Hurricanes depended solely upon Ground Control, aided by searchlights. Except in conditions of good moonlight, neither type was likely to be able to locate a raider in the dark unaided. Both types were single-engined with only a short endurance.

What the RAF wanted was an aircraft with an endurance of several hours, with a good excess of speed over the attacking bombers and with the devastating fire-power of cannons rather than machine-guns to destroy the enemy bombers almost as soon as it sighted them. Above all, such a machine needed to be equipped with a device which would enable it to find its enemy in the dark. Such an aircraft, if working closely with Ground Control, which by the summer of 1940 had become a well tried and proven system, would set the enemy a problem: especially if flown by pilots who had become proficient at night flying.

29 Squadron had such pilots. The Bristol Beaufighter was about to arrive. It came, not too soon, as an answer to their prayers.

4
29 Squadron Learns its Trade

Before 29 Squadron received its Beaufighters, and thereafter became an effective night-fighter unit, the Battle of Britain had raged overhead. This affected 29 Squadron on the ground as much as in the air. The Blenheim was not capable of assisting the hard pressed Hurricanes and Spitfires in their heroic daylight battles against the huge raiding formations of bombers protected by Luftwaffe fighters. The squadron, therefore, continued with its assigned role of night fighting. In retrospect, the importance of this was that the pilots became proficient in night flying. Prior to the outbreak of war, pilots of Fighter Command were not trained to fly at night. A few night flights were part of their overall initial training as, until actually assigned, it was anyone's guess whether a trainee would end up in Bomber, Coastal or Fighter Command. Most of those who ended up in Fighter Command had flown as little as ten or fewer hours at night and only on elementary training aircraft. Once in Fighter Command, there was normally no incentive to perfect night flying techniques. Yet night flying was, and still is, much more hazardous than daytime flying.

Losses during night flying training were high and would continue to be so throughout the war. Even in peacetime, landing at night was never easy. The pilots had in the first place to identify the airfields in the dark and they had to locate accurately the specific landing area. (Only a few RAF airfields then had runways.) They needed to approach at the correct angle in the right direction before accomplishing a smooth touchdown in near darkness. The principal landing aid was the Chance Light, a small floodlight which was switched on to illuminate part of the desired landing area. As war progressed, a guiding circle of lights around the airfields was later introduced; also glide slope indicators. However, against this, war also produced the blacking out of all lights in Britain making it all the more difficult to locate the home airfield or, indeed, any airfield.

It didn't help that, as soon as an approaching enemy raid was confirmed by the Ground Control stations via their radar detection systems, all lights at all airfields in the area were doused. These included lights at airfields where pilots, such as those of 29 Squadron, might be attempting to land. Add to all these difficulties the ever present threat of a fog, often totally unforecast, suddenly blanketing the airfield and the dangers of night flying in wartime can readily be appreciated.

As 29 Squadron struggled to get to grips with this new form of operational aviation, the great daylight battles in the air overhead meant that *all* RAF airfields in Britain, especially those facing the North Sea and English Channel, were now in a new 'Front Line'. To a raiding Luftwaffe pilot, any airfield was liable to be an enemy fighter base and, as such, was an obvious target during those periods of the Battle of Britain when the orders of General Goering were to attack Fighter Command on the ground at their bases.

By this time 29 Squadron had been moved to Digby, in Lincolnshire, and had become part of 12 Group Fighter Command. However, much night flying took place from the small satellite field at Wellingore. Digby was attacked on four occasions by enemy aircraft bent on attacking all RAF airfields and Wellingore on no fewer than ten occasions. Even their decoy dummy airfield was bombed three times. These many raids caused little real damage and had a negligible effect upon the outcome of the Battle of Britain but they must surely have disrupted 29 Squadron training and operations, at least to some extent.

Attempts were made to make the Blenheim a more acceptable night fighter. A new Frazer-Nash twin gun turret was fitted. More significantly AI (Airborne Interception) Mark III sets were gradually being added. Although a few Special Signals radar officers arrived, there was no one with operational experience to tell the crews how best to use this new device. Lessons had to be learned by personal experience.

AI was also apt to fail. An idea of the shortcomings and of the errors made by the squadron during this learning period can be gauged from the following instances.

On 30 June 1940, one crew went after an enemy aircraft caught in the beams of a searchlight. They themselves became dazzled by the searchlight. They lost control and crashed. Both crew members were killed. A few days earlier another crew had caught up with an enemy aircraft, had signalled that it was attacking and succeeded in bringing down a twin-engined bomber. Return fire had been experienced and this was the last seen or heard of the Blenheim crew until the pilot's body was washed up on a beach some weeks later. One Heinkel 111 destroyed but also one Blenheim.

At about the time that the pilot's body was washed ashore, the Blenheims were modified to have their fuel tanks protected by self-sealing compounds. This solved one major weakness. Unless so protected, even a single enemy bullet could lead to a disastrous explosion and fire aboard as the highly inflammable fuel escaped. In July, one of the squadron's Blenheims shot down an RAF Battle by mistake. This was another lesson to be learnt and digested. In the dark, it was always difficult to tell friend from foe. Both defender and attacker would be blacked out as thoroughly as possible. Ground Control usually, but not always, knew which was which. Home aircraft had an electronic identification signal, the IFF, but, like all else that was new on board, this was not 100 per cent reliable nor was it necessarily always switched on. Some form of visual identification was therefore a prerequisite before opening fire.

If nothing else, the destruction of the Battle emphasized that Ground Control was not infallible. In this case it had given the OK to open fire. In August another crew sighted an aircraft and gave chase. For nearly an hour the Blenheim could not gain on the enemy. It did eventually catch its quarry and may have destroyed it but it showed up the aircraft's performance limitations. Nor was the Blenheim itself a 100 per cent reliable aircraft. Bob Braham upon returning one night at Wellingore had to crash land because the undercarriage could not be lowered; a chafed hydraulic pipe was the cause. However, Bob, by then already assessed as 'Above Average' as a pilot, coped with this difficulty without harm to himself or to his crewman observer. This individual was Sgt Gregory, always known as 'Sticks' because, before the war, he had played the drums in Debroy Sommers's well known jazz band. Much more will be heard of Sticks Gregory later.

By the summer of 1940 and into the autumn, AI became progressively used. Hitherto, in the Blenheim, the other occupant had simply been an Observer/rear-gunner. With AI on board, he soon became quite a different specialist and an absolutely essential one if the crew were to score successes. However, he had been neither recruited nor trained in AI which, like every other form of airborne radar, had one serious drawback.

The principle of radar is simple. A stream of electronic pulses are continuously being transmitted, mainly forward. If they encounter anything solid, they are bounced back and reappear on a screen, which is little more than a cathode ray tube – something that we all know today as a TV screen. The solid object hit by the pulses appears on the screen as a tiny tick or 'echo'. The distance between the plane and the solid object 'hit' is calculated by timing the short period it takes for the electronic echo to bounce back. The snag is that the pulses also bounce back off the ground and that the ground echoes are therefore also continuously being recorded. Electronic interference from electric circuits on board, and other impulses in the atmosphere, also provide flickering false returns. To interpret correctly the echo returns on the screens of the Mark III AI sets required almost a sixth sense. Some operators never acquired the art. Others did much better. In every case, it required a lot of actual experience to sort the sheep from the goats, i.e. to detect the one extraneous blip, or minute extra return, from the plethora of returns being continuously presented from the ground or from interference. Some observers or air gunners mastered this art. They, as much as their pilots, were henceforth responsible for their crews' success. To pay tribute to the new skills that they had to master, they will be referred to henceforth in this book as radar operators. Various official titles were given to these crewmen at different times e.g. 'Observer (Radio)', 'Radio Observer', 'Nav/Rads'.

Radar operators also had to perfect another new skill: that of calmly directing their pilot after having first correctly detected an aircraft on their AI set. The pilots were generally senior in rank and certainly in status to their radar operators. It was not every RO who had the required nous to direct the pilot firmly towards their quarry. In effect they had to assume an unfamiliar command role in the aircraft. Some AI training was being carried out at the airfield of St Athan, South Wales. This was the scene of another tragedy. One of the squadron's air gunners-cum-radar operators had gone there and was carrying out a stalking exercise in a Blenheim aided by the radar operator's AI set. However, the chasing aircraft closed too swiftly upon the other Blenheim which was acting the part of the enemy. The two collided and both aircraft crashed with loss of life of all on board. Another lesson to be digested: keep cool and close *gradually* upon any aircraft picked up on AI.

I can write about this with some feeling. Towards the end of 1940 I was posted to a Wellington squadron which was the first of that type to be equipped with another early form of airborne radar. This was ASV (Air to Surface Vessel), and the task before me and others in 221 Squadron was to detect enemy U-Boats in the broad waters of the Atlantic. As with the Blenheims of 29 Squadron, the device was so surrounded by Top Secret edicts that scarcely anyone in the squadron, certainly none of the operating crew of which I was in command, knew the first thing about radar, its principles, its limitations, etc. All had to be learnt the hard way. At first, therefore, the radar operators quite naturally tuned out all the 'fuzz' which was cluttering up their tiny screens, the 'fuzz' being either electrical interference or the massive ground returns. This presented the operator with a nice clean screen but, as eventually was realized, it also reduced the sensitivity of the set to a totally ineffective zero.

Also, as was the case with the night fighter aircraft, the ASV set had been hastily added into an already restricted space. The operator was left to get what use he could out of the new device in extreme discomfort and cramped conditions.

The responsibilities thus added to the shoulders of the former observers or air gunners were very heavy and if some never really came to terms with AI Mark III, allowances should be made.

Another limitation imposed on 29 Squadron during the Battle of Britain period was that many of their pre-war trained pilots had departed. New squadrons were being formed fast. Fighter Command's losses in pilots had been severe. By September the Command was almost desperate. Test pilots were being roped in. Fleet Air Arm pilots were hastily being put into Hurricanes and Spitfires. The wonder is that 29 Squadron was left with any experienced fighter-trained pilots. The replacement pilots were mostly those who had been hurriedly trained since the outbreak of war. Some were excellent; others were not.

As a result, the pre-war trained Bob Braham now found himself both one of the more experienced pilots of the squadron and, at the age of 20, one of its most senior in rank. Soon he was to be given the rank of Flying Officer (F/O). He was also appointed a deputy Flight Commander. Hence a situation developed in 29 Squadron whereunder some crews were being commanded by pilots who could barely fly their aircraft (due to the need to rush through all forms of pilot training) and were being manned by Radar Operators who were ill equipped to master the strange new device which had been foisted upon them with only the barest of instruction on how best it should be used. In many respects it was a case of the survival of the fittest. Those Blenheim crews which did overcome all these difficulties and shortcomings and also proved themselves capable of operating safely at night and did survive unscathed were, by October 1940, by which time the Battle of Britain had been won and the invasion of England indefinitely postponed, ready and raring to fight at night. The date is significant because it was in September 1940 that the mighty Bristol Beaufighter began to replace the inadequate Blenheims of 29 Squadron.

None was more raring to go than F/O Braham. Also, by then, he was one of the very few in the squadron – indeed in the entire RAF – who had tasted success at night. This had come his way on the night of 24 August 1940.

It is significant that on that occasion, his crew consisted of *three* persons. There was, as usual, an air gunner Sgt Wilsdon. The extra crewman, Aircraftsman N. Jacobson, is described as a 'Special Equipment Operator'. He was clearly a ground radar set operator but the security arrangements surrounding anything to do with AI then prevented him from being described as such. Bob and his crew had departed from Wellingore at night as usual. Although it was one of the few occasions when operating with Blenheim aircraft that Bob Braham did have a specialist radar operator on board, that person appears to have played no part in the action.

Bob Braham was on patrol in the Humberside area when he was directed towards an aircraft being held in searchlights. He hurried northwards after it. Although it was twisting and turning to get out of the dazzling beam, it was not escaping. Closing to within 500 yards Bob opened fire. In all he gave the aircraft several sustained bursts. He then closed up all too rapidly. However, this allowed his gunner to get in a few bursts from his position aft. The range by then was within a

100 yards or less. The gunner's shots were, according to Bob's modest combat report, the ones which were the most effective. Although the enemy plane did not catch fire or explode, it was last seen with smoke and sparks emanating from it as it dived down. No return fire was noted. In all probability the crew of the bomber was being blinded by the brilliance of the searchlights focused upon it and never saw its enemy. Bob Braham, in his reports of the engagement, does not seem to know if the enemy was a Heinkel 111 or a Dornier. However the searchlight crew reported seeing the enemy fall in flames into the sea, something that the Blenheim crew flying above the clouds could not have seen. Although there was a dispute whether Bob or an AA battery had been responsible for the 'kill', this was eventually resolved in Bob's favour.

Several points seem to be of some significance. Two are the failure to identify the enemy type and the 500 yard range at which Bob originally opened fire: also his error in closing up too rapidly and almost overtaking the enemy. In future combats, Bob Braham was at pains to identify more positively the aircraft at which he shot: in future attacks, he would also close up less rapidly and withhold his fire until within more deadly range. It all points to F/O Bob Braham carefully analysing the attack and applying the lessons he had learnt from this first success.

That Bob Braham did not positively recognize the plane at which he was shooting, and the fact that he opened fire at a range at which success with machine-guns was unlikely and which would also give away his position and therefore his tactical advantage, and then overshot his target, was no surprise.

Bob Braham had by 24 August 1940 been searching for his enemy for the best part of a frustrating year. The frustration was general to the pilots of 29 Squadron. All during the Battle of Britain, the national newspapers were full of little else other than the heroic feats of RAF Fighter Command. The publicity given to successful pilots such as 'Sailor' Malan, Paddy Finucane, Stanford Tuck and the legless Douglas Bader had made them national heroes. Pilots were obliged to wear their RAF wings on their uniform even off duty and in public, and the euphoria generated by the RAF during the Battle of Britain induced complete strangers to approach and enquire, with almost breathless awe: 'Are you a fighter pilot and how many have *you* shot down?' If the wearer of the pilot's wings badge had to reply 'none', it was bad enough; if, as clearly was the case with Bob Braham, they had been trying as hard as anyone could to do so, then it was all the more galling. Little wonder therefore that when sighting an enemy for the first time Bob, like others in similar circumstances, went almost berserk.

It was exactly the same when a Coastal Command pilot, perhaps after years of searching in vain for elusive U-boats, did at last manage to catch one on the surface. He would throw all caution to the wind and attack with almost demoniacal fury, regardless of all else. It was not that all pilots wished to become national heroes. Bob Braham most certainly had no such publicity-minded ambitions. It was simply that the weeks and months of trying his hardest in a plane unsuited to the task had built up inside him an absolute determination to get to grips with the enemy. It was a determination that never left Bob Braham.

To become a successful deer stalker, night fighter, U-boat attacker from the air or even submarine commander requires that the attacker approaches with cunning: a mixture of stealth, care and caution. The target must be correctly identified as the one sought. It must, for as long as possible, be left unaware that it is being stalked. When at last within lethal range, it must be despatched with swift and sudden finality. All this has to be learnt and there is no substitute for actual experience. With experience, the great killers learn to control their natural excitement and learn to go about their deadly business with calm but lethal detachment.

29 Squadron was fortunate to have a couple of keen commanding officers: first the New Zealander 'Mac' McLean and, after an interlude, Charles Widdows. Charles Widdows

was an ex-Cranwell trained Regular, an experienced day fighter and a test pilot. By coincidence he had in 1931 been posted to 29 Squadron upon leaving the RAF Officer's College at Cranwell. Charles Widdows managed to keep up the unit's spirits in spite of its very limited success which hardly matched the losses it was experiencing either in training or in its few combats with the enemy.

Charles Widdows had arrived to find 29 Squadron at a rather low ebb. His immediate predecessor had lasted only eight days, mostly spent in hospital. To Charles, there seemed to be too much drinking and a general feeling of frustration. The inadequacies of the Blenheim were all too apparent. The crews understandably had little faith in the aircraft as a night fighter. They also found AI, the supposed panacea of their difficulties, even when working well, was of little help as, at that time, the Lincolnshire area which they guarded was barely covered by Ground Control. AI Mark III needed the help of Ground Controllers if it was to work as planned. The air crews, therefore, mainly had to depend upon the assistance that wavering searchlights might provide. Such positive illumination was seldom available.

Under Charles's direction, a number of key inefficient personnel were posted away and some of the less keen crews were replaced by an intake of six new pilots. What these youngsters lacked in experience they made good by enthusiasm. The likes of Lovell, Graham-Little, Robin Miles, Ken Davison and Dave Humphreys brought a new zest to the unit. With Bomber Command soon to allow such experienced pilots as Guy Gibson and Don Parker to switch from night bombing to night fighting, spirits were further raised.

Charles Widdows personally boosted morale by borrowing a Hurricane and making attempts to use this as a night fighter: all in vain, alas. If searchlights could pinpoint a Heinkel or Dornier for him he, at least, had the fire power to destroy it: also the speed rapidly to overhaul any night enemy. However, it was good for squadron morale that the CO was prepared to risk his own neck.

It had not helped to forge a squadron spirit that, to assist in defending Liverpool or Coventry, the crews would be scattered to distant airfields far from Wellingore. Wellingore's barely long enough runway – only 650 yards with an overshoot extension of another 150 yards – was also an ever present threat.

A particularly sad loss was when P/O Barnwell was killed. He was not only much liked and had been the first to register a victory in a 29 Squadron Blenheim (June 1940), but was known to be the son of the man who had designed Bristol aircraft including the Blenheim. Barnwell was not lost entirely in vain. He was the pilot who had shot down the Heinkel 111 before losing his own life in that same night engagement.

Soon other night fighter squadrons would be equipped with the far more deadly Beaufighters and one pilot at least, John Cunningham, commonly dubbed 'Cat's Eyes', was by early 1941 receiving the same kind of public adulation, thanks to the Press, as was being given to the day time fighters such as Bader, Tuck, Malan *et al*. This made the burden for 29 Squadron, with its very limited success, all the more difficult to bear. It may also have given Bob Braham a very jaundiced impression of the Press and the manner by which it attempted to glamorize those pilots who were having the most successes, almost to the exclusion of others who were also doing their utmost but with less good fortune.

While 29 Squadron was awaiting delivery of its Beaufighters, it was sent a few other types. Some like the Fairy Battle were even less suited than the Blenheim for night action but the unit did officially get hold of a number of Hurricanes. They were also not really suitable as night fighters, but as Bob Braham recalls in *Scramble*, it was nice to be flying a more modern type, and the Hurricanes came in handy for daylight airfield defence as the enemy was still raiding RAF airfields. Wellingore seemed to be one of their favourite targets and by then the Squadron had moved from Digby to there on a more permanent basis.

The unit was required on occasions to send a few aircraft to Ternhill airfield in order to be able to patrol at night over Merseyside, whenever, as was not infrequent, Liverpool/ Manchester were expected to be attacked.

Bob Braham was at Ternhill when a single Ju 88 dived out of the clouds and delivered a skilful attack. It swept across the field and planted its bombs on a hangar. 29 Squadron's Blenheims were not seriously affected but the hangar and 13 training twin-engined Ansons were destroyed; with another 20 damaged. It showed that, although the Battle of Britain was not going their way, the Luftwaffe was still a powerful, well organized force with determined and courageous pilots.

Generally, as the Battle of Britain waned after 15 September 1940, the RAF began to pay more attention to defeating the night attacks which then followed. Its chief instruments in this new struggle were the Bristol Beaufighter, more effective Mark IV AI sets and a further ground radar chain to back up the original chain which quite naturally concentrated upon detecting the enemy planes before they could cross the East and South Coasts. The later chain of radar stations meant that for the first time Ground Control could continue to track enemy planes well after they had crossed the coast.

This provided a system which enabled an enemy aircraft which had been detected over the sea to be followed as it flew inland and which, in theory at least, could then direct night fighters swiftly to the enemy until their own AI could continue the tracking process. When the enemy aircraft had been sighted and visually identified, the awesome firepower of aircraft like Beaufighters was capable of doing the rest.

The system needed above all pilots who were proficient at flying at night and radar operators who could cope with AI sets. The many, largely ineffective hours, which the pilots and radar operators of 29 Squadron had put in, now came into play. And none made greater use of the system than the recently promoted Flying Officer Bob Braham.

5
The Beaufighter Era Begins

Although other squadrons had received their night fighting Beaus, by which name the Beaufighters were known, in which John Cunningham and his expert AI operator Jimmy Rawnsley were scoring a number of successes (with the Press acclaiming the former and virtually ignoring the latter), 29 Squadron did not receive their first Beau, and in effect their first genuine night fighting aircraft, until September 1940. By October it had still only received a couple. These were used chiefly as training aircraft to enable the pilots to get themselves familiar with the type and to get the ex-air gunners or observers familiar with the AI device which, henceforth, would be their principal responsibility. The Beaufighter deserves a description.

The prototype flew for the first time in 1939, shortly before the outbreak of war. For a fighter it was exceptionally large. It must have weighted about three or more times the weight of a Spitfire. It was a twin-engined aircraft with two Bristol Hercules engines each of approximately 1,600–1,750 hp. As war progressed the output of engines increased in the light of experience and development. The first Hercules were no more than 1,450 hp. This gave it about three times the power of the Spitfire. However, due to its size and weight, it was never as fast as that famous fighter. Possibly it may have been, if stripped down, about as fast as a Hurricane. The Beau had a pilot up front, with excellent vision over the short nose, and a rear seat amidship for another crew member but the two positions were not normally physically connected internally, except via intercom. An armour-plated door separated the two positions but this could be swung back and bolted in the open position. Some crews flew like this. For night fighting, the rear position was the Radar Operator's position and it was he who had the two small radar screens to tune and decipher. As used by 29 Squadron there were no rear, or turreted guns. The initial deliveries had only the four 20mm cannons fixed to fire forwards. This was firepower enough but it was soon augmented by adding six .303 machine-guns; curiously two in one wing and four in the other. When so equipped the Beau possessed the greatest fire power of any fighter aircraft of the Second World War. Due to its power and considerable wing area, the Beau seemed, throughout the war, to be able to take without difficulty whatever extra equipment and weight was added: also to operate satisfactorily, despite some extra drag from the additional aerials that AI, and all subsequent devices, required. It was big, strong and rugged.

It was designed as a long-range day fighter and it served as such in those areas where its considerable range and endurance were most required. It was never the swift light fighter aircraft comparable to the competing Spitfires and Me 109s. It served the RAF well as a relatively long-range day fighter and also as Britain's principal night fighter until the peerless Mosquitoes arrived.

The Beaus also served Coastal Command well; both as a fighter to accompany the daylight torpedo bombers on their daring daylight attacks and, later, as the torpedo carrier itself. With an 1,800 lb torpedo slung underneath, the TorBeau, as it came to be called, was to strike terror into enemy sailors wherever it was used. The Japanese nicknamed it 'Whispering Death'. With bombs and/or rockets under the wings, the Beau also later became a fast and deadly low-level daylight strike plane against both shipping and land targets.

All in all the Beaufighter was a versatile and memorable plane: far more successful than the same manufacturer's Blenheim. The pilot's compartment was ample and there was room for another to sit on a step behind the pilot. However it only had seats for the pilot and rear crew member. When used as a long-range fighter, the observer in the back was, at times, given hand-held machine-guns.

It is known that in the Middle East, when a panic evacuation of the Cairo HQ was started at the time when Rommel was within 60 miles of Alexandria, at least *four* WAAF at a time were carried to safety as extra passengers in a few Beaufighters! It was also in the Middle East that the Beau was used successfully as a photo-reconnaissance aircraft. In this role, with all guns and armour removed, it proved to be almost as fast as the Me 109s. Approximately a ton and a half, including armour plate, had by then been removed.

The two radar screens, or cathode ray tubes, for the AI were fitted side by side within a single visor hood, to provide the radar operator, who operated the sets, with an indication of both the azimuth and elevation of the enemy. Within fairly narrow limits these enabled the operator, via the intercom between the two crew positions, to advise the pilot approximately how far he was behind the enemy aircraft and whether he was above or below it and whether it was to his left, right or dead ahead. The effective range, especially in the early Mark III and IV sets, was short. Range was basically a function of the height of the aircraft: i.e. at 10,000 ft, it was a theoretical 2 miles, at 15,000 ft about 3 miles. It was therefore necessary for the Ground Controller to direct the Beau to within about a mile or two of the invading plane. Ground Control, however, could never give more than an approximation of the enemy's height. Much therefore depended on the skill of the two-man team aloft.

On many occasions, although put on the scent by Ground Control, the crew saw nothing either visually or on the AI screens.

The pilot also had an electrically illuminated gun sight. Because it was necessary for the pilot to have his flying instruments and his gun sight illuminated at night, this made it difficult for him to see extraneous objects in the dark. It takes time for the pupil of the eye to adapt from even dimmed illumination to darkness. Pilots such as Bob Braham reduced cockpit and ring-sight illumination to a minimum as soon as Ground Control and/or their RO advised that they were on the trail of an enemy aircraft. In respect of night vision, they were at a disadvantage compared to the rear gunners of the Heinkels, Dorniers and Junkers bombers who had no lighted instruments which required constant attention. Consequently the enemy gunners had no night-adaptation problems and were constantly on the look out for tell-tale signs of fighters which might be chasing them in the dark. On the other hand, the night fighter pilots only needed to concentrate on peering into the outside darkness at times when it was known that there was something worthwhile to look for but against this the pilot in the chasing plane might catch a glimpse of the enemy's engines exhausts. These would be shrouded by a flame damper to avoid detection but some dull red glow was apt to remain visible.

Generally the chasing pilot had a slight advantage in lookout especially if he manoeuvred his aircraft below his foe although there were several occasions when both aircraft opened fire upon the other more or less simultaneously. As always, it depended upon the skill, eyesight, experience and dedication of the individuals concerned.

From the approaching fighter's point of view, a good powerful first burst of fire was all important. Once any burst was fired, there could be no doubt in the German air gunner's mind. He then knew where the enemy stalker was and would return fire at once, often with accuracy. If, however, the first burst of fire from the chasing plane killed or otherwise incapacitated the bomber's rear gunner, then the German plane would be very much at the Beaufighter's mercy. In experienced hands the Beaufighter could out-turn and overhaul every type of German night bomber. However, some Ju 88s, having dropped their bombs, could just about match a Beau in level speed and even exceed it at some favourable heights.

The massive fire-power of the Beau gave it a great advantage. Against its four 20 mm cannons and six .303

machine-guns, the enemy bombers could usually only muster a couple of rearwards-firing machine-guns. This advantage in weight of fire outweighed the enemy gunner's advantage of being able to swing his guns in order to hit the fast-moving target of the Beau. The guns of the Beau, by contrast, were fixed to fire forwards. The aircraft itself had to be aimed directly at the bomber.

Most successful 'kills' came after the attacker managed to get his aircraft into a position at close range without the enemy being aware of it. To capitalize upon this initial advantage, the fighter pilot then needed to press the firing button for a sustained first burst of fire from all guns.

After his first experience of opening fire too soon and of closing the distance between the two planes too rapidly, Bob Braham was quick to learn from these mistakes. He also deduced quite correctly that his best chance of achieving the all important surprise was to manoeuvre his Beaufighter not just close to and behind the enemy before opening fire but also slightly below it. He considered that it would be more difficult for the rear gunner of the enemy plane to see him or to hit him there.

Bob had noticed that one of the first visual indications of an enemy plane occurred when a patch of stars would inexplicably be eclipsed. This showed that there was something solid between him and the night background. That something had to be the plane which he was stalking.

To be able to concentrate on the attack, the pilot had to be the complete master of his aircraft: to be flying it within precise limits without any conscious effort or need to look at the aircraft's many instruments, giving complete attention to the directions which the Ground Controller and his own AI operator were giving him. He also needed to act upon this information with complete trust. At night it is all too easy to be misled by such things as a wisp of cloud crossing the moon path: to see things which are not there. Eagerness to catch a glimpse of the enemy could lead to wishful thinking taking over. In the final stages of the chase, the radar operator was in effect in control. Until actually obtaining a sufficiently clear visual picture of the enemy to be able to identify it as such, the pilot had dutifully to be obeying the instructions coming to him through his earphones while holding his fire and containing his mounting excitement.

For one as keen as was Bob Braham to destroy his country's foes, that was a supreme test. Bob Braham's determination to get at his enemy was a strictly impersonal thing. It was his machine against theirs. If *he* didn't get in the first deadly burst of fire, then the enemy might shoot *him* down. This impersonal attitude was soon to be put to the test. His new CO Charles Widdows had shot down a Ju 88. It crashed inland and was not too far away to visit. A number of squadron personnel crowded into a few cars to drive to the scene of the wreck. They were looking for a suitable souvenir with which to decorate their messes: perhaps an enemy prop to hang on the walls? They found the wreck of the plane and decided to extract from it a large-calibre gun which had caught their eye. As they tugged at it, they also uncovered a German leg. If it caught Bob off balance temporarily, he soon recovered.

Although Bob Braham was among the first in 29 Squadron to test and fly the Beaufighter which had been delivered in September 1940, that flight became his last for a month or so. This was because he spent nearly all of September in hospital recovering from injuries sustained in a car accident.

Bob was ever ready to join in whatever high-spirited venture was offered. The car accident was, no doubt, one which had occurred late at night. Most of the young officers had got hold of some rather ancient but vaguely sporty cars. Wartime restrictions, and the strictly rationed petrol allowance for cars, meant that, to keep them going at all, their owners usually had to run them on worn-out tyres and dubious spare parts. Also, in the RAF, many were run on unofficial 100 octane petrol, somehow obtained! These cars would be driven home from the pubs late at night with half a dozen or more inside or clinging on. The roads would be unlighted and the car's only permitted headlights were heavily masked so as to remain concealed from above. The blackout throughout Britain, especially during the winters of 1940 and 1941 when the enemy night raids were most frequent, was all embracing. Under these circumstances, car crashes involving RAF aircrew after the pubs had closed were all too frequent.

Although it is doubted that any official count has ever been made, the total number of young aircrew officers or NCOs hurt or even killed on such occasions must run into the hundreds; or even thousands. It is hard to think of any unit which did not lose personnel, at times ace personnel, in this manner. A young man brought to a high pitch of life as never before by the thrill of flying, in his prime of youthful health and living a life without normal home or feminine comforts, finds much relief and satisfaction in the enjoyment of a fast car and a riotous alcoholic evening out.

Bob himself had an open Wolseley Hornet small sports car: probably several years old. Whether he was driving this or was a passenger in a similar vehicle for this particular crash is not known.

Most understanding COs and Station Commanders did not frown too severely upon the antics that the aircrew got up to off duty. They recognized the need for the individuals to unwind and let off steam. This kind of wild behaviour was not even a wartime by-product. Pre-war, the young RAF pilots were notoriously fast and often incoherent drivers. Drinking and driving was not then frowned upon as now. There were no breathalizer tests nor automatic driving bans for those found over the limit.

Some Blenheims were still being used in October 1940 and Bob Braham, out of hospital, did his best to catch a raider in one. He was flying with a P/O Wilson who is described as an air gunner, not a radar or AI operator. By then the Blenheims had been provided with AI but, due to its many failures and a lack of instruction on how to use the device, it seems (as is confirmed by Charles Widdows) that they had little faith in their new equipment. On 25 October Bob Braham made a valiant attempt to catch an enemy raider. He had been guided to it by Ground Control. He thought that he saw two exhaust flames and, after being assured by Ground Control that he was chasing an enemy plane, he fired at it and thought that he saw sparks fly from his quarry before he lost it in the clouds. It would seem that, if AI was used, he and P/O Wilson got very little aid from it. Otherwise October 1940 is chiefly notable for the number of times that Bob and the others were attacked by enemy bombers when at their airfields. However, it was only the aforementioned Ternhill attack which caused other than light damage.

November 1940 was a more memorable month for 29 Squadron. More Beaufighters arrived and Bob Braham carried out the first night patrol for the unit in a Beau on the 17th. A few days earlier, a S/Ldr Guy Gibson had been posted in to command one of the squadron's two Flights. This was an unusual move as Gibson was a Bomber Command pilot who had just completed a tour of operations with 83 Squadron in Hampdens, where he had shown great drive and skill. It was Gibson's own idea of an 'Operation Rest' period. Somehow he got his own way. He was a pilot already beginning to make his mark. Later, as Wing Commander Guy Gibson, back again in Bomber Command after yet another splendidly completed tour as a CO, it was Gibson who led the Lancasters of 617 Squadron on the now famous Dambuster raid. For this he was able to add the Victoria Cross to the DSOs and DFCs which he had already gained.

It was not easy to arrive fresh from one RAF Command and immediately take over a Flight of a squadron in another Command, but Guy Gibson soon impressed all with his determination and skill. Charles Widdows especially welcomed Gibson. He may even have asked for a pilot of his high calibre. In his view the squadron was in need of new leaders with these qualities. The squadron also took part in some experimental operations with Fairey Battles which towed flares behind them. These, in theory, illuminated the enemy planes for the Blenheims and Beaufighters to destroy them. The scheme shows that the Command was trying a number of ways by which the enemy could be positively identified and attacked in the dark. It also suggests that they were having doubts about the effectiveness of AI. These experiments with Battles proved to be futile; as were others which used a powerful airborne searchlight.

It was during November 1940 that the Germans carried out their very devastating raid upon the city of Coventry. Much of the city and its ancient cathedral were destroyed. It aroused great anger among the British people; none more so than with Bob Braham. It increased further his absolute determination to shoot down as many of the hated Huns as was humanly possible. Did he feel the loss of the cathedral more keenly than most because of his father's calling? His father by then had become an RAF chaplain.

As was almost inevitable, the new faster and more powerful Beaufighters gave the pilots fresh problems to solve. Some engine failures led to the loss of aircraft and crews. Charles Widdows himself nearly had to bail out on one occasion: indeed the order to do so was given but his crewman, P/O Wilson, found himself trapped, whereupon the CO managed to get the damaged plane down safely. Generally the squadron used November to solve the teething troubles of the new type with its new more powerful engines: but at a cost. It did not help that the Beaufighter was, more than some new types, plagued by technical and engine failure problems.

Of the Beaufighter operations – a total of 75 in all – carried out by 29 Squadron during November 1940, Bob Braham flew nine of them. This shows that he had by then become acknowledged as an above average pilot: one who had rapidly mastered the new and more powerful type of aircraft. Charles Widdows has written that: 'Bob Braham was one of my anchor men upon whom to rebuild the squadron.' Widdows also attests: 'The Beaufighter arrived and that changed the whole scene. . . . we all loved the Beau.'

Bob Braham's usefulness to the Squadron was further enhanced by the decision to send him on a blind-flying course at Watchfield, Oxfordshire. Here, flying Ansons, he was taught to land in low visibility conditions using a beam system which shortly would be fitted to the unit's Beaufighters.

Meanwhile Guy Gibson was fast learning to become a night fighter. He was already an accomplished night-time pilot and this was at least half the battle. However, like most others, S/Ldr Gibson did not get right his first night attack. On 11 December, although chasing and shooting at a Ju 88, he lost it in the clouds. Another pilot, Flight Sergeant Munn, also failed to destroy the contact which he had picked up on his aircraft's AI. He committed the over-enthusiastic beginner's error of closing too quickly and overshooting his target. He was also flying a Beau. However, the squadron history shows that, during December 1940, about half their operations were still being flown by the less effective Blenheims.

Bob Braham and F/Sgt Munn were selected by the CO to accompany him on a special operation to Middle Wallop aerodrome to reinforce the night fighters of 604 Squadron when it was known that a raid upon the city of Bristol was about to be made. (Ultra intelligence?)

It would appear that F/Sgt Munn was also recognized as an especially keen pilot. As will be seen later, Bob and he were the first two in 29 Squadron to receive gallantry medals. Probably F/Sgt Munn was a pre-war Sgt Pilot and a recognized 'old hand'. Later, as the war progressed, a large number of young pilots were indoctrinated into the RAF and immediately granted that once prestigious rank.

By the end of 1940 the RAF had already expanded enormously. Also, during that year Britain, by some near-miracle of production despite having her factories bombed, caught up and overhauled the Germans in numbers of aircraft produced. Before the war, Nazi Germany had far outstripped a peace-minded Britain and had been producing many times the British number of military aircraft. By 1938, the deficit had been reduced to about half (Germany 5,235: Britain 2,827). Yet, despite the bombing and wartime difficulties experienced during 1940 by Britain, its aircraft workers produced 15,049 aircraft to Germany's 10,247. In order to operate these machines a vast pilot expansion scheme had been initiated. Thousands of young men, having first passed the stringent RAF educational, fitness and aptitude tests, were enrolled as pilots and immediately given the rank of sergeant.

Training losses on both sides throughout the war were high and it was rare that the enemy, although producing thousands of aircraft annually, could mount a raid upon Britain by as many as 500 aircraft. After their Russian campaign started, this figure was probably never once exceeded.

The Battle of Britain had been a 'close run thing' and pilot losses had become critical. Also during 1940 our aircraft-producing factories had been hit and damaged; yet, generally, by the end of 1940, the RAF, as well as 29 Squadron, was well on its way: and that was literally upwards. 'Per ardua ad astra', the motto of the RAF, was proving to be no idle boast.

6
Progress at Last

The early months of 1941 were quiet but not uneventful. Group made a decision – one which showed that night fighting was of increased importance to them – that night fighting squadrons, such as 29, should be commanded by wing commanders rather than squadron leaders. This meant promotion for Charles Widdows. Also in January, as part of a further boost to the night fighter squadron, Bob Braham was awarded an unexpected DFC. It was unexpected as he had only destroyed one enemy aircraft. 29 Squadron, like other night fighting units, had to bear many losses due to the difficulties of night flying, flying in poor weather and having to cope with their new more powerful Beaufighters. As F/Sgt Munn, a pilot who had not even shot down any enemy aircraft, was at the same time awarded a DFM, it would seem that both awards were given to the most keen officer and NCO pilot of a unit which, although trying its best, was in reality losing more aircraft and crews than it was destroying enemy. The desired effects of such awards was to raise the squadron's morale and to show the crews that, although they were achieving little, their efforts were being noticed and appreciated. It is known that other squadrons in similar circumstances had also been encouraged by similar awards, likewise given to their most persevering and popular pilots.

There are signs that during both January and February 1941, the crews were coming to terms with both their new aircraft and, perhaps more importantly, with the Mark IV AI with which all the Beaus were equipped. On several occasions crews, including both Bob's and Guy Gibson's, all but caught up and destroyed enemy aircraft after having first been vectored towards them by Ground Control and then closing further by making use of their aircraft's internal radar. Several were fired at but none could be claimed as destroyed.

By mid-February all operations were being carried out in Beaus with the inadequate Blenheims, at last, phased out for good.

Bob Braham had rightly decided that, if AI was to be the valuable aid that, in theory, it was supposed to be, then it depended upon team work between the RO at the rear with his face pressed against the visor of his two tiny screens and the pilot up front obeying the directions coming to him from his radar operator over the intercom via his headset. Bob and a Canadian radar operator, Norman Ross, teamed up together and henceforth he tried always to fly with this same crew member in the rear compartment. Although Ross had been among the first to get to grips with AI, he was a wild character on the ground with a taste for alcohol which exceeded most. Bob was never one to pull rank or pilot-in-command attitude over those who flew with him. Neither was it his nature to do so nor, aged just 20, had he the authority of years behind him. He invariably used first names in the air and did not mind if he was called 'Bob' by his NCO helpmate in the aircraft. Canadians, in any case, were always apt to be less conscious of such rank demarkations. This degree of matiness between pilot and radar operator undoubtedly aided teamwork.

It was with Ross that F/O Braham scored his first success in a Beau. The date was 13 March 1941. Bob had digested a lot of lessons from his earlier operations in Blenheims and also from the chases which Ross and he had experienced with their new aircraft and the more effective Mark IV version of AI. Thus it was that when Ross began to direct him towards the contact which he had detected on his AI and enquired from his pilot: 'Where do you want him Bob?', the swift reply was: 'Dead ahead and about 100 feet above us.' From an initial 4,000 yd, Ross gradually brought Bob closer and closer.

At about a range of half a mile, Bob had a first glimpse of something between his straining eyes and the night stars. He kept his cool and again checked with Ground Control that there were no friendly planes in his vicinity. At about 700 yd, the twin tails of a Dornier bomber could be made out. Again he kept calm and continued to urge his radar operator to keep calling out the range and relative height of the enemy.

It is significant that one of Ross's first instructions to Bob had been 'throttle back: slow down'. Several of the squadron's pursuits which had been made using AI had resulted in the powerful Beau overtaking the enemy too rapidly and then not being able to regain contact. Ross and Bob had digested those mistakes. Three times Ross had to direct Bob to 'turn another ten degrees starboard'. This is further indication that the two of them, working in concert, were taking things gently, bit by bit. Excitement had to be mastered if a successful controlled approach was to be made.

When certain of the correct visual identification of the enemy as a Dornier bomber, Bob told Ross to abandon his AI and to act as an additional look out. At a range of only about 250 yards Bob fired a long burst from all four cannons. (Only later Beaus had the six machine-guns as well as these cannons.)

An ineffective short burst of return fire came from the Dornier. More surprising than this was that it made little effort to take avoiding action. A white flash was seen to come from the starboard side of the Dornier but this soon died down and the aircraft flew on. The only change was that it began a slow turn towards the south.

The early version of the Beaufighter, as well as having no machine-guns to back up its cannon fire, also had no long belts of cannon ammunition. Drums of 60 rounds were fitted to each cannon. (A single round of 20mm cannon weighs 4.59oz, about twelve times more than a single round of .303 machine-gun ammunition.) After these had gone, the radar operator would have to remove the drums and replace them. The drums were heavy and, in the cramped and dark space, this was a difficult task. Bob had expended the contents of all drums but, unknown to him, the port outer cannon had jammed after only two rounds. As Ross struggled to fit the new drums, Bob kept the enemy in sight. Twice Ross reported that the drums had been changed but each time when Bob pressed the firing button, nothing happened. They were flying at about 13,000 feet on a cold clear winter's night. According to *Scramble* it was later discovered that the oil in the cannon's mechanism had become frozen, but the combat reports made no mention of this.

Bob Braham, after so long a period of not being in a position to destroy a hated enemy (and perhaps conscious that he had done relatively little to deserve the DFC ribbon sewn on his tunic?), was not going to allow this enemy to escape. For reasons which were never explained, the Dornier flew on without taking any marked avoiding action. With the Beaufighter's guns silent, did the enemy pilot think that he had shaken off his pursuer? Was it even possible that the pilot was dead and the plane was continuing by itself on an auto-pilot?

With such a sitting target – and one which was not firing back – so clearly in his sight, Bob Braham decided, since his guns would not fire, to try to ram the Dornier bomber instead. He figured that if he could place one of his big robust wings under the tail of the Dornier and then bring it up smartly, that might knock off the rear end of the bomber; without, he hoped, doing too much harm to the Beau. Ross, meanwhile, was down below his feet trying to work free the firing mechanism of the guns.

By now, the Beau was within about 60 yards of the Dornier and when Bob once again pressed the firing button, the three good guns erupted with such a blast that the Dornier literally blew up in Bob's face with bits flying past his aircraft. What was left of it went plummeting down in a ball of flame into the sea. It was a strange contest in that there was a duration of about 13 minutes between first burst of fire and final destruction.

Even Bob's second burst of fire had used up 36 rounds per gun. He was always a pilot who believed in sustained bursts of fire. One who knew him once surmised (wrongly as it turned out) that Bob would never be able to shoot down *two* enemy planes on the same sortie because, even with the belted ammunition which was soon to become standard, he reckoned that Bob's long first bursts would have expended it all! Bob, of course, was right. If a pilot could manage to close up into a killing position without being observed, that first burst of fire would be the all important one. Moreover, there was scarcely a plane built which could remain in the air after being hit by a sustained burst of fire from the (later) Beau's four cannons and six machine-guns. However, research shows that Bob Braham did *not* use unusually long bursts of fire. Indeed 'Sticks' Gregory, his brilliant radar operator of many later successful combats, considers that Bob was a first class shot, i.e. one who used up *less* ammunition than most in destroying enemy aircraft.

A few hours later, the CO, Wing Commander Widdows, shot down another enemy bomber and the very next day Guy Gibson scored his first night kill. The enemy seemed to resent this as, by coincidence, they promptly dropped bombs once again on Wellingore but, as usual, they caused only minimal damage. This was Wellingore's seventh attack.

It must not be imagined that all was deadly serious at Wellingore or at other RAF stations. The crews were young and high spirited and, even when there was nothing to celebrate, they found means of letting off steam either in their respective messes or in the local pubs. The latter were probably preferred as there the officers and NCOs could drink together. It can well be imagined the kind of 'thrash' which followed after both Braham and Munn received the squadron's first decorations. As Bob Braham admits in *Scramble*: 'This was an excellent excuse for a wild party and, in spite of our readiness commitments, some of us suffered thick heads for many days.'

Even before the victorious crewmen could get out of their Beaus they were surrounded by ground and aircrew who somehow had learned of their success. Doubtless again many had thick heads after the events of 13 and 14 March when, after such a long period of no official victories, the squadron had destroyed three enemy bombers within the space of 24 hours.

It is typical of Bob's thoroughness that, after having landed, he went to talk with the armourers to try to find out why *all* his guns had not fired and why for an annoying while they had become frozen up. He learned that a faulty bullet had been responsible for the failure of the port outer cannon and the freezing up problem was one which was far from unique. Modifications were in hand and the guns of future Beaus would soon be both better heated and fitted with belt-fed ammunition instead of the awkwardly located drums.

March was a lucky month for the squadron. Even when another crew was fired at by the rear gunner of a friendly aircraft – a risk that all night fighters had to endure, the Beau was not hit. Nor, happily, was the RAF Hudson when the Beau pilot had fired back! Not being able to see in the dark had many disadvantages when compared with the day fighters: being shot at by friendly rear gunners was one.

A quite different problem was how to get adequate sleep and food in the active and noisy environment of a RAF station which had a busy daylight schedule and which was not geared to a 24-hour restaurant service. The enemy's many daylight attacks upon Wellingore were also not conducive to rest and relaxation between operational night flights.

The difficulties of night fighting in 1941, even when supplied with a powerful well-armed aircraft fitted with more effective AI and when assisted by helpful directions from the new ground radar chains, were still considerable and proved to be beyond the capabilities of most. However F/O Bob Braham, with the assistance of Sgt Ross operating the AI set, was showing the way.

Would March 1941 prove to be the harbinger of better things to come?

7
Springtime All Round

April 1941 was a memorable month for Bob Braham. He scored another major success. He also got married after a truly whirlwind courtship!

If, as appears in *Scramble*, he met for the first time his Joan after his success of 13 March, then the period between their first meeting and his 'I do' at the altar was a bare month or less. By 15 April he was a married man.

It happened like this.

After having spent many an evening in the pubs of Lincoln, Bob Braham decided for once to venture further afield and see what in the way of drink and feminine company the town of Leicester had to offer. In his Wolsey Hornet he went in company with another pilot to the Grand Hotel, Leicester. They were in Simon's Bar with a couple of girls whom they had probably picked up. One, however, was soon to be quickly dropped!

Bob's eyes soon alighted on a beautiful young girl at a table with an older woman. Thereafter his eyes continued to stray in that direction.

Confirmation of the good looks of this young girl has lately been obtained from 'Buster' Reynolds – an RAF Intelligence Officer who later in the war was to know both Bob and his wife Joan well. 'She was like the young Elizabeth Taylor but a lot more lovely' is Buster's fond memory of her.

This is high praise indeed but Bob would not have disagreed for he had clearly become smitten – literally by love at first sight. Ignoring the 'popsie' at his side, he asked a waiter to go over and to invite the pair at the table across the room to take a drink with him. When they agreed he took leave of his companions and thereafter spent the rest of the session with Joan, the object of his roving eye, and the older woman who turned out to be her mother.

He quickly learned two things: that Joan Hyde was a nurse in the VAD on leave and that there was a dance that night at an adjacent hall.

Although he politely invited the mother, as well as the daughter, to the dance, he was relieved when she declined. After seeing that Mum was safely on her way home by tram, Joan and he spent the rest of the evening together.

What the girl with whom Bob had started the evening's drinking thought of it all is not recorded!

Before the evening was through, Bob Braham was truly a victim of Cupid's arrow. He arranged a date two days hence, again in Simon's bar, for lunch and during that meeting made plans for him to see her parents in her home and for her then to accompany him to his parents who by then had moved to Duxford – a few miles south of Cambridge. This was a highly ambitious plan. For one thing, Leicester is at least 30 miles from Wellingore and Duxford about 50 from there and about 75 from Wellingore. It all added up to a whole month's petrol ration. Bob had also, on his return to Wellingore, immediately written to his parents to advise them that he would be coming home for a couple of days complete with girl friend to be put up. As Joan was under age (which then meant under 21), Bob was well aware that he needed her parents' consent before being able to whisk her away to his parents' home for the planned visit. He also recognized that if this whirlwind romance was to run its full course – as he already hoped – and was to end with Joan becoming his wife, an even more important permission would first have to be obtained from her father.

The couple met as arranged in Simon's bar a few days after their first wonderful evening together. Here they fortified themselves with some Dutch courage before tackling their first hurdle: the visit to Joan's father. However, Mr Hyde, a grocer by trade, gave Bob much the same welcome as had Mrs Hyde who from the outset had looked upon Bob with favour.

Soon thereafter, with the first hurdle overcome, they were off to Duxford to meet his parents.

Much had happened to the Revd Dr E.G. Braham since 1939. Even before the outbreak of war, he had made an unusual break. He had given up the Methodist Church, which he had served in fairly senior positions for many years, and become ordained in the Church of England, his first appointment in his new faith being as a mere curate in Tavistock, Devonshire. This must have been a very different appointment in all respects from the Methodist Church in Blackburn where, until joining the Church of England, he had been the minister in charge.

By 1940 the Revd Braham had obtained a Church of England living at St Peter's parish church at Duxford. Additionally, since there was a well established RAF base at Duxford, he had after the outbreak of war also become that base's RAF chaplain.

Bob and Joan spent two ecstatic days at Duxford by the end of which both had decided that 'This was it' and that the only logical thing to do was to get married as soon as possible.

Naturally both sets of parents considered that the couple were too young and had known each other for an insufficient length of time. However, the youngsters were obviously hopelessly in love and, with some natural misgivings, the Hydes gave their consent and the Brahams their blessings. Not wasting a moment, Joan immediately gave notice to resign from the VAD and went to live with Bob's parents at Duxford, so that the marriage banns could at once be read there. The Revd Braham agreed to marry his son in his parish church on 15 April 1941, only nine days after Bob's own 21st birthday: his official 'coming of age'. Several people from the squadron, including the CO Charles Widdows and his wife, attended the happy ceremony and, in typical RAF style, a formation of Beaufighters from 29 Squadron duly 'beat up' the church with a shattering roar during the service. The Revd Braham seemed not amused although, if he had cast his mind back to First

World War days when he had been a wartime pilot full of youthful bravado and bonhomie, he would have appreciated that it was a mark of his son's popularity and high standing in his squadron despite his slender years.

The path for lovers is never wholly free of obstacles – especially perhaps in wartime, with Britain still seriously threatened by a victorious enemy. The couple's plan of a two-week honeymoon in the more peaceful backwater of Minehead, Somerset, was to be disrupted. A signal from Charles Widdows demanded Bob's immediate return. 29 Squadron was being moved from the flatlands around Lincolnshire to a more vulnerable location in Kent. Here at West Malling, the squadron would be very much 'in the front line' and Charles naturally wanted to have one of his best pilots immediately available.

However, despite their advanced location, within a month or two of the squadron transferring to West Malling, the pilots found few enemy aircraft to chase because the number of German raids on Britain's towns and cities began to diminish steadily. The reason, which only became obvious in June 1941, being Germany's massive, and quite unprovoked, attack against her treaty ally, the USSR. Bombers which otherwise would have been positioned to attack Britain were used instead to pave the way for the rapid onrush of German armour into an unprepared Russia. Approximately 60 per cent of the Luftwaffe and most of its bombing force had been moved to look eastward.

However, before the raids over Britain slackened off, Bob Braham, again flying with Sgt Ross, destroyed another of the nightly invaders: this time a Heinkel 111. As before, Ground Control had initially directed his Beaufighter towards the target when, within a mile or so of the enemy aircraft, Ross in the rear compartment took over the chase. He soon established AI contact but at a range of about 2,000 yards the tell-tale blips on the aircraft's tiny radar screens split into two, indicating that they were stalking two enemy aircraft close to one another and flying at the same height. Bob elected 'to go first' for the one which was immediately ahead, he informed his radar operator. Clearly he intended, if possible, to bag the pair of them. The team in the Beaufighter worked in perfect unison. The visibility must have been poor as it was not until within 200 yards of the enemy that Bob obtained visual confirmation. By then he had, with Ross's assistance, reduced his speed so that it was approximately the same as that of the enemy he was pursuing. Not until he was almost underneath the nearer of the two enemy aircraft was a clear visual sighting made. Then Bob Braham saw them both simultaneously. Both were identified as Heinkel 111s. Their exhaust glows had given them away. Quickly, after first alerting Ground Control, he pulled up the nose of his aircraft and fired a short burst. Return fire with tracer went streaming over Bob's head. The Beau was not hit but neither was the enemy finished. Bob had been hoping that this Heinkel could be swiftly dealt a death blow. He had purposely preserved ammunition for the other enemy on his right. By then he was almost alongside the plane at which he had fired. Turning swiftly into it, he fired a long second burst. That did the trick. All return fire ceased and the Heinkel dived earthwards with flames streaming from it. Both occupants of the Beau saw the big flash as the doomed Heinkel hit the ground. Disappointingly for the crew of the Beau, that was the last seen of the other Heinkel as neither Ground Control nor Ross on the AI were able to locate it after its companion had been brought down.

In all that night, the enemy had sent over approximately 250 bombers, but at least 10 of the raiders had been destroyed by the RAF night fighting squadrons. 29 Squadron's share had been two: one to Bob and the other, a Ju 88, to another pilot of the unit.

Bob's Heinkel had come to grief near Richmond and the next day Bob was invited to visit the site of the crash. However, he had seen enough of such things. The severed leg which had been uncovered while searching through the remains of the aircraft shot down earlier by his CO still lingered in his mind. However, he asked those who did go to bring back souvenirs for Ross and himself. They returned with an Iron Cross decoration* taken from the dead pilot and two German inflatable life-saving jackets. These were less bulky and restrictive than the RAF version due to the latter having an additional kapok filling. Bob was to wear this enemy 'Mae West' for the rest of his war.

A couple of days later, almost as their final fling at Britain before turning their dreams of conquest upon Russia, the Luftwaffe mounted one of their biggest night raids of the war. In *Scramble*, there is a reference to over 500 enemy aircraft being involved and to a report that 33 of these were shot down (4 to the AA guns). However it was not a good night for the Braham/Ross combination as the AI in their aircraft became unserviceable. For once others in 29 Squadron stole the limelight with two or three enemy destroyed.

By then, the crews of the Luftwaffe night bombers would have been quite relieved to be transferred to the new Russian front. Their losses were becoming serious. In one way their former night successes over Britain were acting against them. The fires which they had created in the big English towns could all too clearly be seen by the British night fighter crews and the sight of these had further inflamed the hearts of the crews of the ever growing numbers of RAF night fighter squadrons. These crews now found that they had in their hands means of revenge. Not only were their Beaufighters vastly superior to the Blenheims and Defiants which they were replacing but they had learnt that their AI sets were no longer the annoying, often unserviceable, adjuncts which they had once seemed to be.

Moving 29 Squadron into the front line of battle did wonders for the unit's morale. Prior to the move, the aircrews had had little to show for all their endeavours and many self-inflicted losses which they had sustained. Moreover, other

---

* To the RAF's credit, this was returned to Germany for the dead man's next of kin.

night fighter squadrons had achieved much better results and the Press was already showering adulation on John 'Cat's-eyes' Cunningham for his many victories at night.

May 1941 must have been a glorious month for F/O J.R.D. Braham DFC. He had shot down an enemy plane. He had found a nice home for his lovely young bride quite close to West Malling. It was part of a large house with its own cherry orchard. What could be lovelier, war or no war, than to be newly married to a gorgeous twenty-year-old wife, 'lovelier than a young Elizabeth Taylor', among the cherry blossoms of Kent in springtime?

The squadron used the relatively quiet period which accompanied Germany's onslaught against their erstwhile Russian ally to build up its strength. In any event the short summer nights would have reduced their activities.

Bob, and others who took the trouble to do so, used part of this quiet period to get to know personally some of the Ground Controllers upon whose skill so much of their success depended. Even voices came to be recognized over the airwaves and it was not too unusual for a controller, once being advised that the aircrew above had obtained an AI contact, to sign off his or her role in the chase with such words as 'O.K. Go get him, Bob.' It all helped to build up an efficient *three*-man team: The Ground Controller, the airborne radar operator at his AI set and the pilot with his eyes on his ring sight and his finger on the firing button.

Meanwhile the squadron's losses were being replaced and this time by crews which had been more thoroughly trained in the difficult art of night fighting. Experienced crews who had scored victories at night were being sent as instructors to the Operational Training Units where they passed on to each new batch of 'Sprogs' the lessons which had been absorbed by them during the period when much had to be learnt the hard way: by trial and error tactics and, sadly, by fatal accidents to others.

Bob, having served a year as a Flying Officer, was duly promoted to F/Lt. Long before this, he had been acting as deputy to the Commander of B Flight. Guy Gibson, with the acting rank of S/Ldr, continued to lead A Flight but Charles Widdows had handed over his command of 29 Squadron to Wing Commander Colbeck-Welch DFC. However, Charles remained at West Malling as Station Commander and continued to operate from time to time, usually in his 'private' Hurricane as and when his many desk duties allowed.

Although Bob Braham continued to operate with Sgt Ross throughout that summer of 1941, after June the number of enemy aircraft over Britain became fewer and fewer. Sadly, the squadron continued to lose about one crew a month due to accidents such as the difficulties of landing at night or the failure of an engine in flight.

The Beau could be landed with one engine inoperative, but it was not easy to do so. Also by then Bob Braham had become one of the few pilots at West Malling who had been thoroughly trained by the RAF during the leisurely pre-war years. The new intake did not have this advantage. Their training had had to be rushed through and was far less thorough. In all probability the Braham/Ross combination destroyed another enemy raider on the night of 23 June 1941. The difficulty which Bob Braham experienced in being able positively to claim this enemy aircraft as 'Destroyed' was due to the fact that he had to pursue the enemy out of the squadron's normal Sector Control area into the adjacent Hunsden Sector Control. As a result he was not, at the time of attack, in radio/voice communication with any Ground Control station. Bob, therefore, did not know precisely where he was when, at the end of the long chase, he opened fire on what he describes as an 'E/A' (enemy aircraft) in his Log Book but which in *Scramble* he designates a 'Heinkel': i.e. an He 111.

Whatever enemy aircraft it was, Ross, by skilful use of the AI, had directed Bob to his favourite position of 200 yards astern and slightly below the enemy aircraft. The raider was hit many times and sparks flew off it. It descended rapidly with smoke pouring from it. The contest had begun at 10,000–11,000 feet but Bob wisely ceased to follow the Heinkel below 5,000 feet. He felt obliged to break off the chase as he did not know where he was and was out of touch with any ground radio station. Not being familiar with the area beneath, he had a genuine fear that if he went lower, he might become snared by one of the many balloon barrages which were a prominent feature of wartime Britain. RAF pilots all had a great dread of balloon barrages. To be shot down in combat by the enemy seemed to be almost an acceptable 'part of the game' but to meet one's end by being ensnared in a home balloon barrage seemed to be ten times worse.

Although observers on the ground saw a plane on fire crash in approximately the area over which Bob had been operating, no positive claim for the destruction of any enemy bomber was made by Bob. This was due, in part, to there being other night fighters in the area and that one of these had claimed a 'kill'.

Postwar research has shown that two enemy bombers did not return to their bases that night. Since only the one positive claim was made, the likelihood is that Bob almost certainly destroyed the other one. If this was so, then at war's end, Bob Braham would have had 30 confirmed victories in all. Moreover, 20 of these would have been scored at night. In Appendix C (Bob Braham's list of combats with the enemy compiled in his own hand-writing), Bob does not even mention this engagement although clearly he had set an enemy aircraft on fire and it was last seen plunging downwards to almost certain destruction. The claims of Bob Braham were almost painfully honest.

8

Further Successes for Bob and Guy

Guy Gibson damaged a Dornier in April and Bob Braham probably destroyed a Heinkel in June. In determination, there was nothing between the two. When the enemy resorted to lower levels, thereby partially defeating the effectiveness of the Mark IV AI, both Bob and Guy experimented with ways to counter this tactic. In this, they were aided by a new chain of low-level ground radar stations.

Sadly, throughout this period, the squadron lost a Beaufighter in most months due to the problems which faced all night flying pilots in 1941. The losses were not generally due to enemy return fire although this was reported during several abortive chases; F/Lt Humphreys was nearly shot down by it. The July success for F/Lt Braham is significant because it was the first success which he enjoyed with his replacement radar operator, after the Canadian Ross had been posted away. The new radar operator was Sticks Gregory, the ex-drummer of Debroy Sommers dance band. Sticks had been trained as an observer/navigator. It was to his advantage over ex-air gunner radar operators that it was probably easier for a navigator to become a skilled AI operator than for an air gunner. In the first place there was a higher educational requirement. It was also an advantage that a navigator, by his very trade, was accustomed to giving his pilot directions. 'Alter course to . . .' was part and parcel of their usefulness in the air. After July 1941, the only confirmed victories in the air for 29 Squadron for quite some time were scored by Bob Braham: one in September and two in October.

After the big raid on London on 11 May, when the City was set on fire and over 1,000 civilians killed, the number of enemy targets to find and chase continued to decrease.

29 Squadron was active during October when 147 sorties were flown but, apart from Bob's successes, there were only a few claims for Probables and Damaged, Guy Gibson alone chalking up half a dozen of these. Other squadron crews did, occasionally, get contacts but then found it devilishly difficult to maintain them in the darkness. Enemy pilots now jinked this way and that, especially when suspecting that they were being followed.

It is interesting to compare the personalities of Bob and Guy. Those who knew them both have attested that they were never friends. For one thing their roles in 29 Squadron kept them apart, Guy being the senior flight commander and deputy CO. However, socially at least, their wives must have got on well. Joan Braham has advised that Guy became godfather to their son Michael.

Even with Beaufighters, Mark IV AI and much improved Ground Control, the operational successes of the squadron during the whole of 1941 were limited. In all, the squadron flew 1,062 operations yet destroyed only 12 enemy aircraft. It is also revealing that two pilots, namely Bob Braham and Guy Gibson, accounted for 9 of these 12. When it is considered that these two were men of exceptional skill and keenness and were well versed in the difficulties and dangers of night flying, it is all too clear that the chances of success for the others were slight.

For a while the two aces seemed to be competing in a neck and neck race. Bob's success on 13 March was followed the next night by Guy's first kill. During May, Guy scored first with a confirmed victim on the 3rd but Bob caught up five days later. Bob, of course, had the benefit of the time spent earlier with the squadron on Blenheims. Bob's second success in 1941 was his third overall.

Neither of the two renowned pilots scored in June but each downed another enemy aircraft on the night of 6 July. Even on those nights when neither scored a success, they both continued to pursue the hunt relentlessly. Neither was the type ever to give up. 29 Squadron was fortunate indeed to have at the same time two pilots whose accomplishments have become part of the folk history of the Royal Air Force.

In considering their different rôles in the squadron, the different circumstances which had brought them to 29 Squadron and their different personalities, it should always be borne in mind that Guy Gibson was a regular career-minded pre-war officer whereas Bob was on a five year Short Service commission. It also has to be remembered that when F/Lt Gibson, soon to become S/Ldr Gibson, was posted to 29 Squadron, it was his official 'rest' period. Guy Gibson and his charming young wife, Eva, a former ENSA girl from Penarth, set up home nearby. As the senior Flight Commander, i.e. No. 2 in the Squadron, Guy also had duties other than flying. By nature he seems to have been a reserved man. His school record at St Edwards, Oxford (where both Douglas Bader DSO & Bar, DFC & Bar and Adrian Warburton DSO & Bar, DFC & 2 Bars plus an American DFC had also been) was just a plain average. He neither excelled at games as Bader had done nor been an odd-ball loner as was Warburton.

In 29 Squadron, S/Ldr Gibson spent little time with the ground crews. He was apt to drive his car up to an aircraft for a flight and, upon return, depart swiftly for the de-briefing and then off home. Braham by contrast lived in camp, always had time for a friendly chat with the ground crews, had been with the squadron for years and was known to everyone in it.

Although Guy Gibson liked a good party, he was not one who took every opportunity to indulge in the often crazy horseplay that was a feature of every RAF mess in wartime. Men at parties with wives are generally less wild than those without! Later, of course, Bob Braham also acquired a wife but, as will be seen later, he was generally against having her close to the squadron.

Several 29 Squadron groundcrew have pointed out that Bob Braham and Guy Gibson adopted different attitudes towards those who serviced their aircraft. John Brownbridge, for example, describes Bob (and Sticks also) as 'God's gift to groundstaff. Always a bonus for the groundcrew after a kill' and goes on to add 'he was a far cry from his opposite number . . . Guy Gibson. . . .'

Bob Braham, on the other hand, had by 1941 became very much *the* 29 Squadron man. It was not just that he was in the process of establishing himself as the unit's top fighter pilot but also that he became almost their one and only *permanent* pilot. By the time that he did eventually leave the squadron, he had been there for over three years and had served under no fewer than six different squadron commanders! It is little wonder therefore that, when in November 1941 there was a major high level conference at HQ Fighter Command at Stanmore to discuss AI radar tactics and appropriate training methods for night fighting crews, 29 Squadron was represented not by its CO, nor its senior flight commander but by F/Lt Braham DFC along with Sticks Gregory, then still a flight-sergeant. The other night fighting squadrons were represented by their respective wing commanders, including the much heralded John 'Cat's-eyes' Cunningham. Yet it was a very high powered conference with the 'father' of radar Robert Watson Watt present. Sir Henry Tizard, the scientist, who did so very much to promote the intelligent use of airborne radar during the war, was also there. Air commodores, group captains and HQ wing commanders were there in numbers.

This conference covered a wide range of subjects, all associated with how to get the best use out of AI and it may well have resulted in the posting, soon after, of both Guy Gibson and Bob Braham to help in the all important training of future crews. And who would know more about it than those two, especially Bob? The complete details of the successes scored by Bob Braham during 1941 are as follow:

13 March This has already been described. This was the Dornier which strangely continued to fly on after first being attacked while Norman Ross struggled to reload and to get the cannons again to fire. This action took place near Wells. The enemy, that night, was bombing Liverpool heavily.

8 May Again flying with Sgt Ross. This was the Heinkel 111 which crashed near Richmond and from which, rescued from the remains, was obtained the German type 'Mae West' which Bob Braham was to wear for the rest of his war.

23 June Although this is only claimed as a 'Probable', it would seem highly likely that it was a 'kill'. A Heinkel 111, flying so slowly that Bob, in order to get himself into an ideal position, had to lower both undercarriage and some flap, was chased for 5 minutes. Eventually Bob got himself within 200 yards and was able to give the enemy a good burst of fire. The plane then caught fire, sparks flew off it and it went into a shallow dive with smoke coming from the fuselage. This was the occasion when Bob Braham had, during the chase, strayed out of range of his own Control sector. Consequently, he did not know exactly where he was, and, of greater concern to him, nor did he know if balloon barrages were below him. Accordingly he broke off the chase when at 5,000 ft. Although the Observer Corps did note an explosion and fire in the air in the vicinity, no positive claim was made or confirmed.

6 July Sgt Ross had been replaced by Sticks Gregory (Ross having 'retired' from the scene with a DFM). This Ju 88 was quite brilliantly picked up on AI by Sticks as, when first sighted visually at about 6,000 ft, it passed across Bob's track almost at right angles. It took six quick corrections from Sticks to enable it to be followed by AI. Although Bob opened fire from astern at only 200 yards, this proved to be quite a contest with the rear gunner of the Ju 88 returning fire with accuracy. Bob had to skid his Beau out of the way. The Ju 88, although hit, was far from finished. Bob's second burst of fire had to be made from an acute angle. The amount of deflection he used was well aimed as the Junkers' starboard engine started to smoke heavily. However, the rear gunner again returned fire which passed close. A third burst from Bob seemed to do the trick. Return fire from the Ju 88 ceased, more sparks flew off the bomber and Sticks was able to see it crash into the sea (near the Thames Estuary) in flames. In all 172 rounds of cannon ammunition had been fired – a mixture of ball, HE and incendiary and over 700 rounds of .303, both armour-piercing and incendiary.

12 September At 9,000 ft Sticks Gregory obtained an AI contact and, due to his prompt actions, eventually led Bob Braham to the enemy which was detected visually at about 400 yd but 200 ft below. Sticks had 'ordered' an immediate throttle back and Bob had only managed to keep behind the enemy, which was flying at only about 140 mph, by lowering the aircraft's wheels and carrying out S turns. Again this night combat turned out to be quite a lengthy battle, largely due to the Beau having only one cannon operating correctly. Two fired off only a single round and another jammed after 10 rounds. This left Bob with mainly only his six machine-guns. The rear gunner of the Heinkel 111 fired back and, although smoke could be seen to be coming from the enemy bomber, Bob momentarily lost all contact due to the avoiding action being taken. However, the over-keen He 111 rear gunner again opened up at the Beaufighter and this enabled Bob to relocate his quarry visually. With only machine-guns still working, Bob fired a long burst. Bob had had to dive his Beaufighter down to get the aircraft correctly aligned and thus had overshot his foe. The Heinkel went down nearly vertically and although it passed through cloud before hitting the sea – an event which prevented Bob and Sticks from seeing its final destruction – the crash was observed by coastguards. In all nearly 1,700 rounds of .303 had been poured into the Heinkel.

This successful kill shows how difficult it was for a night fighter when shooting down an enemy aircraft above the clouds to obtain positive confirmation of the destruction of the plane.

The failure of the Beau's cannons also shows how important it was for those responsible for inserting the ammunition rounds into the drums to get it 100 per cent right. The cannon failures in this case were attributed to misfeeds but the report mentions that the stoppages could have been corrected in the air by the operator if he had known how to do this in the dark innards of the Beau. Doubtless this was yet another lesson to be learnt the hard way: by experience. Every attack made the next one a mite more liable to be successful.

28 September The near impossibility of obtaining confirmation of a 'kill' is shown by this attack in filthy weather. Although Sticks was able to direct Bob to within 150 yd of the enemy aircraft, and although Bob opened fire at this short range with all ten guns working perfectly and although his hits were seen, the enemy was immediately able to dive into the clouds. All that Bob could do was to fire further bursts into the clouds acting upon Sticks's directions. As the contest was taking place at 10,500 ft and only a few miles from the Belgian coast, there was no hope of any British observer being able to confirm a kill. This attack also emphasizes the difficulty of night fighting. Due possibly to the wet weather, the radio of the Beau started to crackle and fade. With a cloud base of only about 300 ft in rain, it took all of Bob's skill and experience to be able to land back safely. The Ground Controller who led the Beau towards the Heinkel was S/Ldr Mawhood. He was one of the Controllers whom Bob had got to know personally and whom he regarded highly. For an attack under these poor conditions at some distance from the UK, it was more than ever necessary to have *three* skilled persons on the top line: pilot, radar operator and Ground Controller. Kills were essentially team efforts.

19 October This was the same combination of Braham, Gregory and Mawhood. Again it required almost razor quick work by Sticks to direct Bob into the best firing position. The enemy was a Dornier bomber and it was half in cloud when first sighted. It required only a short burst from cannons and machine-guns to destroy it. Bits flew off it and the tail seemed to break away. No return fire was received or noted and the bomber dived vertically down to certain destruction. This was the second Dornier to break up when hit by the Beau's awesome fire power. Heinkels and especially Junkers 88s appear to have been more protected and stoutly constructed. The Dornier's twin tails may have made it more vulnerable. Quite remarkably, only 8 or 9 rounds of cannon fire per gun and about 25 rounds of .303 per gun had been expended.

24 October As was the case of the two previously mentioned attacks, this enemy aircraft was again first tracked by the Foreness Ground Control station. It was shadowed and tracked for about 30 minutes before Bob and Sticks had it within visual sight. The enemy was then identified as a Heinkel 111 and attacked from almost point-blank range: 50–75 yd being mentioned. Visibility must have been extremely poor. After a 3-second burst, the enemy's starboard engine caught fire. This was followed by explosions in the fuselage and the Heinkel dived straight down. It could be seen, burning, on the surface of the sea, off the coast near Lowestoft.

Guy Gibson's contributions to 29 Squadron during 1941 were also considerable. In February, operating as usual with his skilled RO, Sgt 'Jimmy' James, he twice fired upon a flare-dropping aircraft in the Grimsby area, without being able to claim any result. On 14 March, the same team shot down a Heinkel 111 off Skegness. The aircraft broke up with bits hitting the Beau's wing, yet another occupational hazard. In April, they held an aircraft 'in sight' on AI for 15 minutes before it managed to escape by taking avoiding actions. A few days later, they had a long engagement with a Dornier at 10,000 ft. Both aircraft fired several bursts and, although hits were observed by S/Ldr Gibson, he could only claim it as 'Damaged'. In May, the same pair claimed their second success. But, since the AI played no part, it was really a success for Gibson and the Biggin Hill Controller who had vectored Guy to the enemy. The Observer Corps were able to confirm the kill. They saw the bomber crashing into the sea near Shoreham, Sussex. Later that night, Guy chased another enemy aircraft which at 600 ft crashed into high ground without a shot being fired. No claim was made, although the chasing crew seem to have been wholly responsible.

During a night patrol on 10 May, Gibson and Sgt 'Jimmy' James had a number of Heinkel contacts. They were experiencing some cannon trouble and only managed to fire at one of these with no visible result. Three more AI contacts were picked up on another night in June and two more on 5 July. On that occasion the AI was faulty. However, on the 7th, all went well and they destroyed a Heinkel 111 near Sheerness. The pair took part in inconclusive chases during September when, for the first time for about a year, one of the enemy aircraft was identified as a Ju 87 Stuka. This highly manoeuvrable single-engined dive bomber was always able to avoid any night fighter if aware that it was being pursued. Bob once tried to follow one down as it dived away but, since the Stuka could dive almost vertically using dive brakes at a relatively slow controlled speed, the Beau soon overshot. During Bob's dive, he reached a speed of approximately 400 mph. This damaged the Beau's structure and Bob nearly ended up in the sea when barely able to pull out at such a high speed.

Guy Gibson did manage to get in some shots at other Ju 87s which were raiding Dover during October and he claimed two as 'Damaged'. In his autobiography *Enemy Coast Ahead*, he mentions that a watcher on the cliffs saw one go into the sea but even this was not regarded as sufficient evidence for official confirmation of a 'kill'. The RAF was always most strict about the confirmation of night victories. Guy chased four more enemy the following night but got no visual sightings. As he had another three contacts three nights later, he had a busy but frustrating week. On another occasion Guy was shot up when about to land and his radar operator, who was Sgt Bell on that occasion, was wounded. Being shot up by enemy intruders was another ever-present threat to night fighter crews.

Before 1941 ended, Guy Gibson was posted to join No. 51 OTU as that training unit's Chief Flying Instructor. During his period with 29 Squadron, he had shot down three, probably destroyed a Ju 87 Stuka, caused another enemy aircraft to crash to destruction, been credited with three more Damaged and had chased several others. Guy and Bob had done much to raise the morale of the squadron; a unit which when Guy had joined it had seemed to Charles Widdows to be 'going nowhere'.

The year 1941 had been a memorable one for Bob Braham. He had been promoted, appointed deputy Flight Commander, and had shot down exactly one-half of the enemy aircraft credited to the squadron. He had met and married Joan, had been singled out to represent 29 Squadron at high-level HQ meetings and had had his annual assessment as a pilot upgraded to 'Exceptional', the highest possible assessment. Moreover he had been awarded a bar to his DFC. Already he was being regarded as one of the outstanding night fighter pilots of the war. And night fighting, with the Battle of Britain long over, was now Fighter Command's principal defence problem. John Cunningham and Bob Braham were showing that it was one that could be solved: difficult but nevertheless possible.

But the year was not all happiness for F/Lt Bob Braham. During August his mother became seriously ill. Joan, who had come to live near Bob at West Malling, had been a VAD nurse and it was agreed that she should go to help Josephine, Bob's sister, to look after Mrs Braham at Duxford where his father had the Rectory. Bob had a great love for his mother who had suffered from a heart complaint for some time. When pneumonia set in, the end was near. Bob managed to arrange a few flights to the Duxford RAF station in between operational trips but sadly his mother died on the 13th. Bob was able to fly to Duxford for the funeral.

Joan's departure to live away from West Malling quite suited Bob in one way. Much as he loved his wife, Bob did not want her to be close at hand. The job was always dangerous, and sadly, Beaufighter crews were still being lost due to landing and other accidents. Sticks Gregory, for example, before becoming Bob Braham's regular radar operator, had earlier had to bale out at night when one Beau experienced engine failure and a few weeks later he had also survived a Beau crash landing. Bob was dedicated to operations and he considered that his first duty, while the war was on, was to his Service and squadron.

By 1941, Bob Braham had become an enthusiastic destroyer of the hated enemy. By coincidence, on 13 December, the night when unbeknown to him, his mother was dying, Bob and a group of hearty others had gone to Maidstone for a night out. As usual, they tumbled into their battered old cars for what was usually a rather mad and hectic drive home. In all there were five in a tiny Austin 7: three officers and two girls. Bob was in the back. The car ran into another vehicle (all too easy in the blackout with only heavily masked lights allowed). All were injured to some extent and Bob had to have a nasty gash over one eye stitched. Only one person was seriously hurt and, tragically, this girl died on her way to hospital. It must have thrown a damper on the unit and especially on those most concerned. Death in the air was half expected, but death on the ground was not.

The year 1941 also introduced several changes of enemy tactics. Once the enemy bombers began to realize that they could be tracked down at night, their tactics changed. On their last big final fling in May when as many as 33 had been destroyed by fighters and guns, they became increasingly adroit at taking avoiding actions. They also no longer came over at their 10–15,000 ft levels, where AI range was 2–3 miles. Dropping mines in the Thames Estuary from very low levels became a frequent enemy operation and, at that height, the AI Mark IV was all but useless. Mention has also been made of the use of Ju 87 dive bombers on good moonlight nights when targets such as Dover harbour could be seen clearly.

Another innovation, this time one of the RAF's making, took place during 1941. This was the use of night fighter squadrons in daylight. This would be ordered when the weather at home stations was considered to be too poor for normal daylight operations.

Only a night fighter equipped with AI could reasonably hope to intercept the enemy invaders in bad flying weather. Bob Braham flew a few of these day operations. They cannot have been welcomed because, due to the poor visibility, they meant they would have to terminate with a dicey landing back at base with clouds almost on the deck. The Beau's AI could help to a degree, and in Bob's case he had the benefit of having had a Beam Flying Course. However, any attempt to land in weather so bad that the Hurricanes and Spitfires had to be grounded was fraught with danger. An idea of the difficulties that the 1941 night fighters had to face daily can be gauged from the fact that, during the whole of the year, apart from the successes of F/Lt Braham and S/Ldr Gibson, the *only* other successes for 29 Squadron were those scored by one of the unit's COs, Charles Widdows (and he was badly shot up, wounded in the leg and lost his radar operator during a later flight); by P/O Lovell, and by P/O Grout, who was killed later in the year in a Beaufighter accident.

Bob Braham appears to have taken no official leave during 1941 but he did manage a few days off at Duxford during his mother's illness, death and funeral. He was also detached away from the 'front line' for two weeks in November/ December when he and Sticks, who by then had rightly been awarded the DFM, were sent to Ayr, Scotland to assist in the training of 141 Squadron. This night fighter unit had just been converted from the single-engined easy-to-fly Defiants to Beaufighters and its pilots needed all the help they could get. It is significant that this took place soon after both Bob and Sticks had attended the high-level Fighter Command HQ conference. It is regarded as a clear indication that already HQ had their eyes on Bob Braham. However, at the time neither Fighter Command, and certainly not Bob Braham, a recently promoted F/Lt, had any idea that within a year this young determined pilot, in the uniform of the youngest wing commander to command an operational unit in the RAF, would become the Commanding Officer of that same 141 Squadron: and would be leading it into new waters and lasting glory.

Before beginning another chapter and taking the Bob Braham story beyond 1941, it seems appropriate to sketch very briefly the astonishing and unique career of another quite different type of RAF night-fighting pilot of the same era . . .

This was F/Lt Richard Playne Stevens who during 1941 became the top-scoring night fighter pilot of the RAF although he never had the opportunity to use either an appropriate aircraft or airborne radar! Stevens was an older pilot than most, having been born in 1909. He had served in the Palestine Police Force in 1932 and had been a civil airline pilot before the war, flying newspapers and mail from Croydon to Paris daily. He joined the RAF in 1939 at the age of 30.

Operating with 151 Squadron, and flying only single-engined Hurricanes – a type which was never seriously considered as a first-rate night fighter – Stevens managed, during 1941, to shoot down no fewer than 14 enemy aircraft plus one shared, as well as being credited with two Probables and one Damaged. How he accomplished this amazing feat is a story which appears to be largely untold. He is known to have been guided towards his victims by Ground Control and to have been aided by some of our searchlights: not that our searchlights illuminated a great number of enemy raiders. After being awarded the DSO and DFC & Bar, he was posted to 253 Squadron in November but lost his life on the night of 15/16 December when attempting an intruder raid upon an enemy bomber base, Gilze-Rijen, in Holland. As far as is known, no other Hurricane pilot employed in the role as a night fighter scored anything remotely close to his number of victories; and the very fact that all the emphasis during 1941, when Stevens was scoring so heavily, was being placed by Fighter Command upon the use of AI in twin-engined Blenheims and Beaufighters indicates that Fighter Command regarded him as a one-off brilliant maverick who was achieving results in a manner that others would be most unlikely to match.

It is believed, but not known for certain, that Stevens's wife and children were killed in an air raid on Manchester: a good reason for hunting night raiders so ardently!

Generally throughout the war, with the exception of the publicity accorded to John 'Cat's-eyes' Cunningham, the feats of the RAF's top scoring night fighter pilots were not publicized to the extent of those of daytime fighter pilots. Another example of this is that the many accomplishments of Wing Commander Branse Burbridge, DSO & bar, DFC & bar, and his radar operator, Bill Skelton, who likewise received the DSO & Bar and DFC & Bar, remain virtually unknown to most whether in the RAF at the time or not. Yet the evidence is that this duo shot down more enemy aircraft at night (21 destroyed, 2 Probables, 1 Damaged plus 3 V1 flying bombs) than either Bob Braham or John Cunningham!

Moreover, it is known that both these individuals survived the war. Their reluctance to tell their story may well be due to both having religious convictions. Branse, for example, was even a lay-preacher during the war and was apt, as a fellow member of 85 Squadron has pointed out, to preach sermons about Jesus Christ on Sunday before going out the next, or possibly even the same, night to make another successful 'kill'. Although both individuals have been tracked down in recent years – and both now bear the title of Reverend – neither is willing to co-operate in having his war-time exploits described in print.

9
A Not Uneventful Rest Period

The policy of the RAF throughout the war was to give the operational pilots and other aircrew members regular rest periods. After a given number of operational trips, or a given number of operational hours, a posting to either an HQ appointment or, more usually, to an Operational Training Unit (OTU) would be promulgated. At the OTU, the pilot or other aircrew member would become an instructor. It was a good system as it meant that those who would soon be going to the squadrons for operations would be instructed by those who had recently been taking an active part. It also ensured that all aircrew were given a much needed rest. A tired pilot was the very last person to be allowed to make a judgement about his own state of fatigue. An OTU was the last stage of the training of a new aircrew intake. Pilots would by then have had to have made the grade both at an initial EFTS and at a subsequent Advanced Flying Training School.

Bob Braham had been with 29 Squadron even before the first shots of the Second World War were fired. Few pilots had flown for so long without receiving a posting to a supposedly less dangerous area away from the aerial 'front line'. Two factors had been responsible for this. In the first place, Bob was a keen, efficient and useful member of the squadron. Both he and his various Commanding Officers had persistently fought against his being 'rested' in a backwater. Also, the various Commands laid down different criteria regarding when operational pilots should be forcibly rested. The criteria were based largely upon the casualty rates suffered on operations. Fighter pilots, especially during the Battle of Britain, needed rest more frequently than did (say) pilots of Coastal Command on Atlantic patrols where the losses from the enemy were fewer. Night fighter pilots, while operating over the UK, were seldom lost due to enemy action; therefore they were expected to continue to operate for long periods before being sent off as instructors or to other relatively safer flying duties. The fact that heavy losses were being continuously incurred during normal night training and night operations seems not to have been taken fully into account, if at all. Rest periods appear to have been based solely on the chances of a pilot surviving against an enemy.

Also, by having friends in high places, some pilots seemed able to avoid being posted away as instructors. Guy Gibson may well have been one of these. His growing reputation in Bomber Command may have enabled him to be 'rested' while operating with Fighter Command.

It may have been that Bob Braham, the top scorer of his squadron, was aided in his efforts to avoid a rest by his various COs. No leader gives up his best man without a struggle. However, neither Guy nor Bob could continue to operate indefinitely. The axe fell first on Guy. On Christmas Eve 1941, he was posted to No. 51 OTU, based at Cranfield, Beds., one of the Command's two night fighting OTUs. There he took up the mantle of Chief Flying Instructor.

Bob's turn was soon to follow.

Before parting from 29 Squadron, F/Lt Braham in his then favourite aircraft, Beaufighter X7550, became involved in a temporary exchange of personnel with a pilot of the Rolls-Royce Merlin-engined Beaufighters of 255 Squadron. This was also a night fighting unit based at Coltishall. 29 Squadron's Beaus, like most others, were powered by Bristol Hercules engines.

While at Coltishall in January 1942, Bob obtained permission to fly to Desford, which was near Leicester where his wife was now living, in order to spend a 48-hour period with her. At that time she was about eight months pregnant with their first child. Bob took with him another pilot and

Guy Gibson's radar operator, Jimmy James. Their role was simply to get the aircraft back to Coltishall. Bob didn't make any study of the route nor did he ask James, who was a navigator, to do so. As a result, he could not find the airfield at Desford and had to land at another to ask where he was and how to find Desford. Always almost painfully honest about his own shortcomings, Bob, never one to hide behind others, got out himself to ask the embarrassing questions before proceeding on his way. Sadly, on its return to Coltishall in the hands of the other pilot, the aircraft crashed and was largely wrecked. Neither the pilot P/O Davison nor Sgt James was injured but Bob was left to mourn the temporary loss of an aircraft with which he had enjoyed so much success and to which he had become attached.

Jimmy James has given a good account of this story if only to emphasize the difference in character between Bob Braham and Guy Gibson. It explains, in part, why the two were never close friends. Guy Gibson and Bob Braham were two quite different personalities. Jimmy maintains that if Guy had been flying to an airfield not well known to him, he would in the first place have mentally briefed himself about where it was and how best to get himself there. Guy would also have briefed his radar operator and seen to it that he had the right maps and navigational implements. Also, in the most unlikely event of still getting lost and having to land to find out where they were, Guy, always a correct officer in the air (he never called his long-established radar operator Sgt Jimmy James by his Christian or nickname), would have ordered the radar operator to get out and find where they had landed. Jimmy adds that Bob and Sticks were so pally in the air that, if Bob had asked Sticks to get out and find out where they were, a likely reply would have been: 'Not b—— likely Bob, you got us lost, *you* find out!' Jimmy, although full of admiration for Guy, his piloting skill, his devotion to duty, his intelligence and his unlimited courage, always had to call him 'Sir' in the air, as well as on the ground. Their relationship was stonily formal and correct in the best Service tradition.

In assessing the two great pilots, Jimmy James makes the point that, although Guy Gibson was also 'young in years', he was old for those years. On the other hand Bob behaved at times more like an overgrown schoolboy. He was, for much of the time, a quite private person but a mischievous grin was always likely to break out. Guy, of course, as a Flight Commander (and one who probably had been briefed by Group to help to get the squadron he was going to into better shape), had responsibilities that Bob was yet to acquire. Also Guy, living out of Mess with his young wife Eva, did not always take part in the various, often quite crazy, pranks that the operational pilots were apt to enjoy when off duty in the Mess or when letting off steam in the local pubs. Guy, as befits a pre-war Regular officer, took his responsibilities seriously and, although he also liked a good party, he behaved more circumspectly when in the Officers' Mess, as his senior position required.

Jimmy James (his real name was Richard) and Sticks, however, became good friends. They shared a billet together in what Richard describes as a 'monk's cell' and despite the differences in their ages and backgrounds became good room-mates. Doubtless they shared their operational experiences as the squadron's two most successful radar operators and learned one from the other. Happily, they were both recommended for commissions at the same time, attended the same Board and, in January 1942, were commissioned as P/Os on the same day.

It is interesting that the successful teams of Gibson/James and Braham/Gregory were both composed of crew members where the radar operators were quite a bit older than their pilots. The same also applied to the renowned night-fighting team of Wing Commander Cunningham and Jimmy Rawnsley. Could it have been that it was easier for an older man, in the normally inferior position of radar operator, to be able to take over during a chase and give firm directions to a younger pilot? Until put in the air with an AI set to operate, most crew members would have been used to *receiving* orders from, rather than giving them to, their pilots. It must have been exceptionally difficult for a young radar operator, who had formerly been an air gunner, to find himself telling an older pilot with a higher rank and status than his own to 'turn this way: slow down, *slow down* more, hold it there', etc. What was wanted was a brisk 'Turn port *now*!', not a tentative 'I've got a blip on our port side, Sir.'

The long-delayed posting blow fell on 28 January 1942, when F/Lt J.R.D. Braham, soon to be followed by P/O Gregory, was posted to No. 51 OTU. It was a memorable period for Sticks as he had been commissioned only six days previously and, shortly before that, had been awarded the DFM. Other events were also happening to Bob Braham. In February, his devoted wife Joan gave birth to their first son Michael and, just before leaving 29 Squadron, Bob had been awarded a bar to his DFC.

Bob had, as usual, fought against being posted away, but Group was adamant that he needed a rest: also that 51 OTU needed all the experience that Sticks and he could best provide.

After some wild farewell parties, Bob departed to Cranfield and later came to collect Sticks in a small communications Lysander. It is interesting to note that all RAF airfields had somehow acquired some kind of non-operational transport plane. Quite a few of these had arrived at airfields after the chaos which attended the fall of France in 1940 when many official records were destroyed and when any plane which could fly was flown back to almost anywhere in Britain. Some RAF stations had obtained Ansons or Oxfords which were especially useful as they could carry many passengers. Fuel and pilots to fly these planes, which often did not officially exist, were always at hand. The Anson and the Lysander were easy to fly so experienced pilots simply got in them and flew them. The Oxford was not so easy but many pilots had been trained on this type when converting to twin-engined aircraft. Even small training Tiger Moths and Magisters somehow found themselves at operational airfields. If HQ knew about such unofficial acquisitions, they kept quiet about them.

At Cranfield, where both Bob and Sticks were assigned to join No. 3 Squadron of the Training Unit, the principal type of aircraft used was still the obsolescent Blenheim night fighter.

The posting turned out to be a lucky one for Bob because the chief AI instructor of Bob's Training Wing was a F/Lt Harry Jacobs and it didn't take Bob and Harry long to appreciate that both were on top of their respective jobs. 'Jacko', as all called Jacobs, soon became a close friend of Bob's and the friendship was to last a lifetime. Jacko and Bob also became a formidable night fighter team.

Few determined pilots relished OTUs. Not every pilot likes instructing and some of the best pilots never made good instructors. Bob seems to have taken it all in his stride while also being on the lookout for a more active role in the war. One such opportunity arose when he and Sticks had an interesting two weeks posting to Tangmere, Sussex. There, they were attached to 219 Squadron, another night fighting unit, in order to evaluate a new Mark V AI set. This set included a second cathode ray tube alongside the pilot. The theory was that the pilot himself could then do his own final stalking, if he so wished, after the radar operator had first directed him towards a 'blip'.

Theory and practice do not always match. In the opinion of both Bob and Sticks, the Mark V was *not* a help. The pilot found that the continual shifting of focus from flight instruments to radar scope was distracting rather than helpful. Each task demanded undivided attention by an expert. Trying to cope with both meant that neither was receiving the attention it merited. Other experts, such as John Cunningham, independently came to the same conclusion about Mark V AI. A well-established team working in harmony, with the radar operator concentrating upon the AI and the pilot upon his flying while following the instructions coming to him via his earphones, brought forth the best results.

On the night of 13 March, while at Tangmere, Bob had two narrow escapes. First an engine of a Beaufighter abruptly cut out on him, necessitating a difficult emergency landing.

Then, after taking off again, this time an engine caught fire. However, by then the pilot who had been experiencing difficulty in making the grade at his EFTS had become an adroit Beaufighter pilot. Again Bob landed back without further damage.

On another occasion, when flying a Dominie (a military version of a pre-war twin-engined commercial biplane) from Ibsley in Hampshire back to Cranfield, Bob became so ill at the controls that he temporarily passed out. Sticks was dozing in the back but luckily Jacko was up front and fully alert. Bob came round to find Jacko holding the controls of the aircraft with one hand and gently slapping Bob's face with the other. It transpired that Bob had caught German measles. With his great hatred for the Germans, to be told that he was thus afflicted was adding insult to injury! However, once resuscitated by Jacko, Bob managed to complete the flight without further incident.

It was typical of Bob Braham's hatred of the enemy that one weekend in June he and Sticks decided to pay a visit to their old unit, 29 Squadron, which was still operating out of West Malling. The CO, Ted Colbeck-Welch, readily agreed to their taking part in a night operation. Bob's excuse for the visit was that 29 Squadron's Beaus had recently been provided with the very latest Mark VII AI and he wanted to see for himself how well it would work. His theory was that Sticks and he could then pass this information to their pupils. However, he had not advised No. 51 OTU about the visit.

In a Beau fitted with the new Mark VII AI, Bob and Sticks had an uneventful sortie on the Saturday. On the Sunday, however, the enemy came over in large numbers to bomb Canterbury and the squadron had its hands full. As a visitor, Bob had to make do with a Beau fitted with the older Mark IV AI. However, in spite of not being guided towards an enemy by the Ground Controllers, who were fully occupied in directing many other aircraft, Sticks picked up a contact on his AI and they pursued it at speed as it hurried away from the Kent coast towards Germany after having dropped its bombs. The chase had begun at 10,000 ft and been continued in a shallow dive at over 300 mph. Bob eventually caught up with an enemy aircraft and by the time he could open fire, it was about 15 miles east of Sandwich and slightly below him. Both aircraft were by then fairly close to the water but still descending. Although not certain of the exact identification, Sticks and Bob thought that the enemy plane was probably a Dornier 217. Bob's burst of accurate fire resulted in the enemy diving into the sea where it exploded and burnt for a while. It was Bob Braham's eighth victim destroyed, but a unique first kill while on 'Operational Rest'!

As the weather back at base was worsening fast with fog gathering, Bob was directed to try to land at Manston on the Kent coast, instead of returning to West Malling. At Manston the weather was also rapidly closing in but Bob just managed to get the Beau down before the fog finally rolled in from the sea. It was very much 'touch and go'. Unfortunately, the Beau landed much too far up the runway and overshot on to rough ground, crashing into some wire and small buildings. The plane was not too badly damaged but accident procedures and the fog meant that Bob and Sticks were not able to get back to Cranfield until quite late the next day. Here they were summoned to appear before the CO. Quite naturally the two miscreants were rebuked for absenting themselves and visiting another unit without prior permission. However, when Bob told the CO of their success, the atmosphere became warmer. In the end the CO was left trying to work out whether the 'kill' should officially be credited to No. 51 OTU, which had supplied the crew, or to 29 Squadron, which had provided the aircraft!

As Bob relates in *Scramble*, a whale of a party developed that evening in the Mess. A vast goblet was filled with champagne and Bob and Sticks were invited to consume it all. Bob recalls finding himself locked in the loo feeling frightfully ill. Jacko climbed in through the window to rescue him and put him to bed. Sticks was in no better shape. At OTUs kills were extremely rare and the event must have been a much-welcomed morale booster for the eager pupils.

Bob's unofficial activities did not attract adverse comment from HQ and, later that month, he was promoted to the rank of Acting Squadron Leader and made the CO of No. 3 Squadron of the Training Unit. Sensing that other instructors shared his opinion that instructing was a necessary but boring job when compared to operations, and now in a position of authority, Bob instituted a nightly operational patrol flown by the instructors. In their obsolescent Blenheims, there was little chance of downing any Germans, who by then were well aware of RAF night fighters and had adopted a number of new and effective counter-measures. However, it made a welcome change for both instructing pilots and radar operators. As might be expected, Bob himself took part in some of these operational flights, either with Sticks or his new 'find' Jacko.

A normal rest period at an OTU was six months and, as the end of his stretch drew near, Bob was constantly agitating to get back to 'the real thing'. His pleas did not go unanswered. On 24 July 1942, a few days short of his six months with No. 51 OTU, Bob and Sticks were both posted back to 29 Squadron, still at West Malling. Nothing could have pleased Bob more and, to put the icing on the cake, he was put in charge of A Flight with his acting rank of Squadron Leader confirmed.

Bob had not relished being an instructor but, while with No. 51 OTU, he had added another enemy kill to his mounting total. He had personally been able to report that Mark V AI was not a practical improvement. He had become a father for the first time. He had managed to keep Sticks with him throughout. He had again been promoted and he had teamed up with the efficient Jacko. His rest period had not been wasted – Bob Braham was returning to his old much loved unit as a flight commander, and in Kent. This meant that if the Luftwaffe were again to send over large formations of night bombers he would be well placed to deal with them.

Bob Braham, well rested, was raring to go.

10
Back with 29 Squadron

It would not be out of place here to add a word or two about Joan. It is germane to this tale that right from the start Joan seems to have understood that, for the duration of the war, she, her marriage and even the children which she was to bear her John would take second place to her husband's role as an RAF pilot and leader. Thanks to Joan's exemplary acceptance of this at times hard-to-bear fact, Bob Braham was able to devote his considerable energies to the task uppermost in his mind: destroying as many enemy aircraft as was humanly possible. Yet Bob was not a bloodthirsty man who revelled in the art of killing others. As he once confessed to his Intelligence Officer, he had a sneaking regard for the nameless and often brave airmen whom he was killing. He recognized that they also had wives or sweethearts, and mothers too. However, Bob had been trained before the war as a pilot in a fighting Air Force and he saw it as his professional duty to destroy as many of the enemy as possible. Fortunately, he was never asked to go out at night to bomb some unrecognizable target in the centre of an alien town. His operations were all against those who were bent upon destroying the country and institutions which he had been brought up to respect.

Like most who had roles to play in the war, Bob Braham drew much strength from the broadcasts of Winston Churchill and, in other ways, was a willing 'victim' of the effective wartime propaganda that was so skilfully presented to the British people. He had soon developed a genuine and profound hatred of the enemy and had seethed at the bombing of Coventry in November 1940. He regarded himself as being among the privileged few who had it within their power to shoot down the perpetrators of such wanton destruction.

Joan's part in all this was not inconsiderable, though even in correspondence she undervalues her contribution. In her own words: 'I was always a very separate part of John's life and during the war was aware that I came a distant second to the RAF. I accepted that fact and was really rather proud of it . . . John didn't have to worry constantly about my reactions. When he got away to spend time with me, and later with my sons, he came into another world and could relax . . . we kind of rediscovered each other every time and I always felt that I'd sent him back "cleaned", as it were, inside and out.' Joan Braham clearly had many more assets than simply good looks.

In truth, although not one in a thousand would admit it, many young pilots during the war were at times in need of 'a shoulder to cry on, a bosom to lie on'. Underneath all the surface bravado, bonhomie and lighthearted gaiety of a wartime flying Mess, there were undercurrents of fear, with the pilots' nerves stretched as taut as violin strings. Every pilot needed the likes of Joan Braham and, if in other cases the moral standards of the age slipped a bit, much credit must go to the 'generous' girls of Britain for the part that they played in comforting the boys in light blue. The alternatives – letting off steam in wild pranks, almost suicidal 'beat ups' of airfields (in defiance of orders) and the crazy drives back to camp with inebriated pilots driving poorly maintained ancient cars, must have accounted for a great number of serious or fatal, and quite unnecessary, accidents. Bob himself, while relieved to have found in Joan a wife who understandingly accepted his decisions that, for the most part, she should live with her parents and *not* close to camp, was not thereafter immune from some of the wild alternatives.

Irrespective of where he was living, a pilot during the heat of war found the normalities of life difficult to retain. Life, love and danger were inexorably intermixed. Danger at times was deliberately courted – almost as if it were an addictive drug. Bob Braham's natural attributes fortunately kept him saner than most. He had an inbred ability to strike up close relationships with other efficient crewmen. In the heat of battle, a man with a 'buddy' is much better off than a man alone with his thoughts. Bob and Sticks made a good pair. So did Bob and Jacko. Later Bob and his Intelligence Officer Buster Reynolds became close associates. Each could sustain the other in such alliances.

No two pilots had the same built-in mental strengths. Sooner or later all would begin to display signs of 'the twitch'. The tragedy was that the pilot himself was one of the last to realize it, and often, when it finally occurred even to him that he was not 'quite the man he used to be', he would deliberately choose to ignore the symptoms, doing all he could to appear totally unaffected, totally unafraid. The worst stigma for aircrew of the RAF in wartime was to be grounded for LMF (Lack of Moral Fibre), which most people interpreted as a pseudonym for cowardice. To avoid being grounded for LMF, many a pilot whose resources had been stretched far beyond his natural limits, carried on regardless; often with fatal results to themselves and all who flew with them. It was very rare for a pilot to report that he had had enough and ask to be grounded; those that did usually found the medical officers understanding and helpful.

Returning to 29 Squadron as a squadron leader and flight commander, a slightly more mature Bob Braham appears. Throughout his career, right back to his schooldays, one of Bob Braham's outstanding characteristics was that he always steadily improved at whatever task lay before him. He always took his duties seriously. In positions of command he was conscious of the value of building up good morale among those under him. His first such responsibility had been at No. 51 OTU where his initiation of the instructors' nightly patrol was a great morale booster to his Training Flight. As a flight commander, he was determined to be a popular one, and to lead from the front and by example. His reputation in the squadron itself almost guaranteed him popularity and his 'escape' from No. 51 OTU to spend a weekend with the unit can only have enhanced the already high esteem with which all in 29 Squadron regarded him.

The squadron itself had changed. When Bob had left it six months before, only Guy Gibson and he seemed to have truly mastered the difficult art of night fighting with Mark IV AI-equipped Beaufighters. Now, thanks in part to the much better training that pilots received at the OTUs, kills were more frequent and were spread more evenly around the squadron.

The night fighting arm of Fighter Command had also grown in structure. Even the Press had become enamoured with at least one notable exponent of the art. John Cunningham, unquestionably the most able of the early night fighting experts, had caught the attention of the media who dubbed him 'Cat's-Eyes' Cunningham. He loathed his nickname, but even more embarrassingly, the Press also began to attribute his exceptional score of enemy aircraft shot down at night to the imaginary belief that John Cunningham ate lots of carrots in order to improve his night vision! Soon, the whole country was being urged to eat carrots so as to be able to move about more freely in the black-out! The truth was that AI was still top secret and even if the Press had known of its existence, they would not have been allowed to write about it. They had to think of something and somehow the absurd carrot story emerged. Moreover, at the time food rationing was severe and carrots were plentiful!

Many new faces greeted Bob on his return to 29 Squadron as only a few of the old aircrew remained. But many of the new faces were not entirely unknown as quite a few had been instructed by Bob and Sticks at the OTU. Historically, as Bob himself points out in his autobiography, *Scramble*, the war news at that time – July 1942 – was almost all bad. The Germans had penetrated 1,000 miles into Russia and were fast approaching the all-important oil fields of the Caucasus. They had also reached the suburbs of Moscow and Leningrad. In Egypt Rommel had swept the 8th Army in the desert so far back that he was now poised menacingly within 60 miles of the big British naval and military base at Alexandria. To cap it all, the Japanese were overrunning the Pacific and were within bombing range of Australia, and the German U-boats were winning the Battle of the Atlantic.

Only in the air were the Allies making progress. The big build-up of Bomber Command had begun and whenever the weather permitted, a huge force of mainly four-engined bombers would fly nightly far over Germany, making a mockery of Goering's futile boast that no enemy aircraft would ever drop a bomb on the German Reich. The American 8th Air Force was also rapidly expanding its base in Britain and their deadly massive daylight raids upon other German targets were causing much damage. As well as the growing number of night fighter squadrons equipped with excellent aircraft, the latest AI sets and well trained crews, Fighter Command was daily sending waves of Spitfires over France and the Low Countries in order to lure the Luftwaffe into the air. The air superiority which had been won over Britain was being gradually extended over the Continent. Even gallant little Malta, that much bombed and besieged island, had regained air superiority over its territory.

The Russians were suffering under the full weight of the German armies and in an effort to help Russia, the Allied Air Forces were enticing the Luftwaffe to look westward towards Britain and the Low Countries. The Luftwaffe was also tied down in the Middle East where the RAF had been largely responsible for stopping Rommel before he could reach the Nile. At sea, Admiral Doenitz's U-boats still held sway in the Atlantic and were creating appalling damage but even here Allied planes, now fitted with the more effective airborne ASV (Air to Surface Vessel) radar, were beginning to mount a serious challenge to the killer U-boats and deadly wolfpacks. Nowhere, except in the air, had the tide yet turned in the Allies' favour but some signs of recovery were at last within sight.

Morale in 29 Squadron was good. Ted Colbeck-Welsh, who had also shot down an enemy aircraft during Bob and Stick's brief visit to the squadron in June, had been replaced by the equally popular W/Cdr R. Cleland. The squadron was also blessed with the charismatic Station Commander 'Pop' Wheeler; having fought as a First World War pilot, winning the MC and DFC, he had also been an active night fighting pilot earlier in this war. Another change which enhanced 29 Squadron's efficiency was that all the Beaus were now equipped with the Mark VII AI which picked up the enemy at a greater range and was more effective at lower altitudes than the earlier version.

Throughout the war, improvements to airborne radar were constantly introduced although they were not always an immediate blessing. The newer, more sophisticated models were apt to suffer numerous teething problems. Also, each new development required even the experienced radar operators to go back to 'square 1', and start all over again. Within days of Bob's arrival, S/Ldr Richards (a squadron 'guest') had shot down a Heinkel 111, while P/O Handley was credited with a Probable on the same night. Two nights later P/O Heybroek had damaged another. The Canadian pilot P/O Pepper, with his radar operator P/O Toone, shot down a Ju 88 on 8 August. Pepper and Toone were soon to establish a name for themselves as a successful night fighting team. It was almost inevitable that, as their reputation grew, they should become known as 'Pepper and Salt'. Pepper was in Bob's flight but it wasn't long before Bob, flying again with Sticks, demonstrated that this young pair were not going to steal all the thunder.

On 9 August Bob Braham shot down his ninth confirmed victim and nearly got another. The victim was a Dornier 217. Bob closed to within 300 yards, having been skilfully guided there by Sticks, and a short burst of fire from all ten guns fired from his favourite position of slightly below the raider was sufficient. Bits flew off the Dornier which dived vertically into the sea with the port engine and fuselage on fire. Almost at once Control directed Bob and Sticks towards another aircraft which they were able to identify as another Dornier 217. However, before Bob was able to manoeuvre their

Beau into a firing position, a searchlight illuminated both enemy and pursuing aircraft. Bob was momentarily blinded and the lucky Dornier crew was able to dive safely away.

It is typical of Bob's own modesty, and his interest in others of his flight, that his personal Log Book devotes four whole lines to Pepper's success on 8 August but only two lines to his own kill on the following night. For this latter he merely writes, in his usually very neat print: 'PATROL, 1 DORNIER 217 destroyed 40 miles ENE FORENESS. 1 long burst. No return fire.' Regarding Pepper's success on the 8th he wrote: 'PATROL. CHASED SOUTH WHERE P/O PEPPER WAS PATROLLING. HE GOT IT. BLOODY GOOD SHOW ON HIS PART. I LANDED AT MANSTON ON ACCOUNT OF BAD WEATHER.'

This last sentence is a reminder that night fighting always had other dangers than those of aerial combat. Night flying and bad weather are a dangerous mix. Interestingly, the combat report of Bob's attack refers to 'P/O Gregory DFC & Bar.' This cannot be right. If Sticks had by then been decorated twice, as was probably correct, the designation should have been 'DFC, DFM'. Bob is correctly described as 'DFC & Bar'. Before the month of August was out both Braham and Pepper were to score further successes.

Pepper and Toone destroyed a large German raider, believed to be a four-engined Heinkel 177, on the night of the 20th. On the 24th, S/Ldr Braham, not to be outdone, took part in an action which possibly destroyed a Ju 88. This happened while Sticks was enjoying some leave (which respite Bob seems to have forgone) and sensibly Bob sent for Jacko, still at No. 51 OTU, to replace him. Having collected Jacko, Bob then personally 'delivered' Sticks by Beaufighter to an airfield near his home in the north of England. (It was also during one of the few periods when Bob had made arrangements for Joan to be living close at hand in East Malling, although his main duties meant he could not have seen much of her. In addition, during August, he flew to RAF Duxford to spend a night there on no fewer than five occasions. His father was the RAF Chaplain there so obviously there was some kind of family matter requiring Bob's close and constant attention. For these flights Bob used a station Magister light aircraft.)

The details of Bob's attacks on 24 August are interesting for a number of reasons. Mention has already been made of the error in ascribing a DFC & Bar to Sticks in the official combat report. Worse still is the squadron's official Operations Record Book (Form 541). For the month of August 1942, this makes no mention of F/Lt Jacobs operating with S/Ldr Braham, which he did on at least two occasions, but persists with the incorrect information that P/O Gregory continued to operate as Braham's radar operator. For example, it says that Sticks, who was on leave, flew with Bob twice on 23 August, whereas in fact Bob made three flights that day, all with Jacko! It also omits to mention that the next day Bob and Jacko had an encounter with a Ju 88, which is confirmed by both the combat report and also Bob's own signed log-book. It records instead an uneventful flight for Bob and Sticks! As at least one other experienced researcher can confirm, the *official* records of what took place in the RAF during the war are not always correct. In contrast, a pilot's personal log-book, which had to be signed each month by the squadron commander, is almost inevitably correct as far as it goes. A pilot knows who he flies with!

The confusion is not really too surprising as squadrons during the war had better things to do than record for posterity, or for RAF records, the events as they were happening. Generally, a squadron's record is *most* correct when least is happening and *least* correct when most is happening. Malta was an example. It was bombed so often and the action was so constant that few bothered to record the daily catastrophes and, in the knowledge that what records were kept were likely to be destroyed, it was practical to avoid this chore.

Much was happening around Britain during that August period when both Pepper and Braham were scoring successes. On 19 August an Allied force, consisting mainly of Canadian ground troops, made a daring but unsuccessful raid on Dieppe. The ground gained was a good deal less than had been hoped but the lessons learnt were invaluable for the gigantic D-Day invasion of Europe nearly two years later. The attack also lured the Luftwaffe into many costly engagements.

The encounter of 24 August was Jacko's first with Bob. They chased a Ju 88 and most probably shot it down into the sea as bullet strikes on it were noticed. However, the final shots of the contest took place at such low level over the sea that Bob had to break off the attack at an estimated 50 ft. Some 'erratic' return fire was received but it inflicted no damage. The interesting point is that the improved radar enabled the chase to be continued at very low levels.

It was not only the aircraft's radar that was being constantly improved but also the Ground Control system. Here another new chain of radar stations had been established. These were designated CHL (Chain Home Low). Soon they would be further enhanced by yet another chain, the CHEL (Chain Home Extra Low). These developments had come about because the German Air Force, never slow to learn from experience, had realized that too many of their high-flying bombers were simply not coming back. With their hands full in Russia and the Middle East, the number of German bombers available to raid Britain was greatly reduced from the levels of the winter of 1940. Now only a few dozen would attempt to attack at night: a paltry number compared with the ever-growing numbers available to Bomber Command, now launching raids of hundreds, occasionally thousands, of bombers.

The Germans were known to have had some kind of radar from the first days of the war. Consequently they too were aware that the type of radar available at that stage of the war was unlikely to be able to detect low-flying aircraft. It behoved the British 'boffins' to prove the German scientists wrong and to keep at least one step ahead of the enemy in the radar war.

It was also noticeable that, by 1942, enemy raiders flew faster and were constantly weaving and taking avoiding action, even against an invisible enemy. Our bombers were doing likewise. Losses of up to 20 per cent were being experienced at night and no force could sustain such losses without, at least, a change of tactics. It was because Bob had to break off his attack on 24 August at 50 ft that neither he nor Jacko saw the enemy actually hit the sea. As Fighter Command required definite confirmation from its crews, this Ju 88 could only be listed as a 'Damaged' but few aircraft built could expect to survive after being hit by the awesome firepower of the Beaufighter's four 20mm cannon and six machine-guns.

Bob and Jacko saw more action four nights later. The enemy had adopted a tactic of sending over bombers at both dusk and dawn; possibly they hoped to find a period of inactivity when the day fighters of the RAF had packed in and the night fighters had not yet got into their stride? Fighter Command countered this by instituting Beaufighter dusk and dawn standing patrols. Bob and Jacko were on one of the former during the evening of 28 August, flying in Bob's new favourite Beau, V 8284. Soon after dark, Ground Control directed them towards an enemy aircraft. With the Mark VII AI, Jacko was able to pick up the enemy at 2½ miles even though it was flying at wave-top height. It was identified as a Ju 88 at a height of about 150 ft. With the Junkers still below them, Bob opened fire at a range of only 200 yards. The results were brief but spectacular. The Ju 88 was hit several times. A large explosion was seen in the centre of the fuselage and the enemy dived steeply into the sea, leaving a big splash and a momentary glow under the water.

The destruction was witnessed not just by Jacko and Bob, but also by an American 'passenger' standing behind Bob. Lt Kelly, a USAAF ground radar officer, had come along for the ride in order to see how the British used their AI. No doubt he was impressed!

The victory was a triumph for one of the new CHL radar stations; a triumph for the new Mark VII AI; a triumph for F/Lt Jacobs; a triumph for Bob (whose tenth success it was) and for the Controller, F/Lt Hill, who only the day before had gone to West Malling to discuss with Bob and other aircrew how best to tackle the growing number of low-flying enemy raiders. The successful crew had taken off at 8 pm and were back on the ground again by 10 pm. But their night's work was not finished. After a rest and a cat-nap in armchairs in the crew room, Bob and Jacko took off again for the following morning's dawn patrol. Kelly was again invited to join them. Although he had been ecstatic with excitement in the air during the dusk success, this time he declined: not unnaturally, given that he had been celebrating the success at the bar!

For a second time that night, the CHL (or CHEL) ground radar found Bob and Jacko a customer, another low-flying Ju 88 raider. Again Jacko had obtained a blip at 2½ miles and had skilfully brought Bob into a good firing position. Although Jacko had flown with Bob far less often than Sticks, the two had quickly struck up the same kind of rapport that made an efficient team. This attack was almost identical to the one of only a few hours previously. The Ju 88 was again hugging the waves. Bob had to descend to much the same level and again opened fire at about 150 ft from a position just above the enemy. This time, however, Bob was not so lucky. Instead of exploding and diving into the sea, the Ju 88, although hit by at least two strikes, remained flying and promptly took violent evasive action. A dogfight then ensued only a few feet above the Channel. In the course of this, the Ju 88 managed to pass underneath the Beau and from this advantageous position the fire from its rear gun position hit Bob's plane with an ominous rattle. The port engine of the Beau immediately burst into flames. Bob, however, was equal to the emergency. He switched off the engine and operated the fire extinguisher which doused the flames. He also called Jacko via the intercom to see if he had been hit as a number of strikes had clearly been heard. Jacko was OK but the damage to the Beau was sufficient to cause Bob to break off the engagement straightaway and head for home. Whether the enemy aircraft streaked for home or, like the earlier one, plunged into the sea, is unknown. Neither Bob nor Jacko gave it another thought.

Their problem was to try to nurse their wounded craft back to a friendly airfield.

Bob's log-book shows that, as with his previous flight, there was a passenger on board. He is not named and the combat report makes no mention of him, nor do the squadron records admit his presence. Perhaps he was a ground crewman who unofficially had 'come along for the ride'. If so, he was getting more than he was expecting! For whatever reason (and the presence of an extra man on board seems quite likely), Bob Braham was experiencing great difficulty in keeping his Beau in the air on the one remaining good engine. It was also possible that other hits had damaged the Beau, adversely affecting its performance. He had several times in the past overcome this problem without too much ado but this time he seems to have had grave doubts as to whether or not he was able to keep the aircraft in the air. The low height may have been another reason for the difficulties which now faced him.

Bob Braham's first thought was to get his aircraft away from the nearby French coast as fast as he could. Dawn would soon break and he had no wish to be detected in his damaged condition by enemy day fighters. The smell of burning on board also added to his anxiety. The good engine was operating at full throttle simply to keep the Beau in the air and an aircraft engine at full throttle is unlikely to last too long, this maximum output being normally reserved solely for take-off. The CHEL (or CHL – *Scramble* refers to CHEL but the combat report refers to CHL) rose to the occasion and gave Bob a course to steer to the nearest home airfield – a small grass strip at Friston on top of Beachy Head.

Fearing that they would have to ditch in the Channel, as would have been the case immediately if the good engine had faltered even temporarily, Bob told Jacko to tighten his harness. If there was an unofficial third person on board, almost certainly he would have had no safety equipment and certainly no harness to tighten. The third man in a Beau was strictly a 'standing only passenger' with no official seat or status. In the crisis Bob seems to have forgotten him.

Between them, Jacko and the Ground Controller encouraged Bob not to abandon the Beau and eventually the friendly coast came within view. But even with the aircraft now slightly lighter due to the fuel consumed, Bob did not think that he could gain the required height to climb directly to the airfield on top of Beachy Head. Instead, he crossed the coast at a lower level and laboriously nursed his Beau gently upwards over an area where the gradient was less steep. It was by then almost broad daylight and Bob must have been exhausted after his busy night with two demanding flights.

Although Bob managed to climb up to the level of Friston airfield without incident, he had still not gained sufficient height for a normal circuit. He decided to land at once without even lowering the aircraft's wheels. Touching down as carefully as he could, he managed to control the aircraft as it slid to a halt on its belly. It was just as well that he had cut short the circuit for, as the aircraft slithered to a halt, the good engine, which had been running at full power for so long, decided that enough was enough. It seized and caught fire. The airfield had already alerted the emergency services and almost before the Beau had come to a halt, the fire tender, ambulance and station doctor were alongside. However, Jacko beat them to it. He had jumped out of the plane as it slewed to a halt and was already applying the portable fire extinguisher to the blazing engine. As for the unofficial third person on board, how he got out and how he returned to West Malling are not recorded. Some things are better left unrecorded!

On examining the crashed Beau, it was discovered that the Ju 88 had riddled it with accurate fire and that one bullet had passed through Bob's seat but without injuring him. As neither Jacko nor Bob had seen the Junkers disappear into the waves, and because it was by then so close to its home friendly territory, the best that could be claimed was a 'Damaged'. If it was shot down, then surely the Luftwaffe had lost an ace pilot – one who had outwitted Bob Braham. (What did the German pilot claim? He could not have been blamed for claiming a victory.)

Bob could not help but admire the German pilot who, flying a plane designed as a bomber, had out-manoeuvred his Beaufighter and who had all but shot him down owing to his skilful execution of steep turns beneath him at near zero feet. In such a manoeuvre, one wing tip of the Ju 88 must have been within inches of the water; all this at dawn, too.

After a hearty breakfast, Bob and Jacko were flown back to West Malling by the squadron commander W/Cdr Cleland who had personally flown to Friston in the station's Oxford to collect his ace pilot and the highly skilled F/Lt Jacobs.

The next day was a day off for both Jacko and Bob. The normal drill for night fighting crews was to be at readiness for two consecutive nights and then have two whole days off. This admirable schedule meant that a crew that had been 'at the sharp end' for two consecutive nights, when they might have to operate twice each night, could on their first day off get themselves involved in any nonsense, such as a wild party, and still have the following day to sleep in late so as to be in good shape for their next spell of night duty. On 29 August Bob and Jacko had arranged to pick up Joan in Jacko's car for a welcome night out. It worried Bob a lot that Joan might find out how close to a ditching he had come, and with some reluctance, he decided that he must tell her himself briefly what had happened. For one thing his non-appearance on the morning of the 29th meant that she must have realized, doubtless with mounting anxiety, that something unscheduled must have happened to him on his second night flight of the 28th. Not for the first time, Bob regretted that he had insisted that Joan should remain with her parents at Leicester, where she would have remained in blissful ignorance of that eventful night.

The day after Bob and Jacko had so nearly come to grief, there was another reminder of the ever-present dangers and difficulties that night fighters faced. S/Ldr Parker, the squadron's other flight commander, crashed on take-off. Happily, however, on this occasion 'Sir Isaac' didn't claim a personal victim as both crewmen escaped injury, although the

Beau was badly damaged. 'Sir Isaac Newton' (usually abbreviated to 'Sir Isaac'), was supposed to have discovered gravity and hence, whenever an aircraft behaved more like a brick than a flying machine, 'Sir Isaac' was given the blame. Sadly, throughout the war, 'Sir Isaac' claimed hundreds, if not thousands, of victims. Both sides suffered cruelly as hastily trained airmen were asked to fly the new and ever more powerful aircraft that had been rushed into production and were assembled by inexperienced girls. These aircraft were increasingly given bigger and bigger loads, often far beyond their original capabilities, on ever more demanding tasks.

Even experienced pilots such as S/Ldr Parker could find themselves unable to cope in certain circumstances. The history of almost every type of aircraft used in the Second World War on either side followed the same course of 'development': more fuel for greater range, followed by more guns or bombs for increased effectiveness and, if it was still able to fly, then more fuel and more guns and/or bombs were added. A type designed to fly safely at (say) 25,000 lb maximum weight would soon be operating at 27,000 lb; then 28,000 and in the end at over 30,000 lb. Also, the aircraft's original clean aerodynamic lines would, bit by bit, be eroded by the addition of new devices. Some idea of the dangers inherent in this process can be obtained by following the career of the German Heinkel 111 bomber. During 1944, this pre-1939 bomber was modified to carry a V1 pilotless plane – the so-called 'Doodle-bug' – after the original launching sites across the Channel had been overrun. This massive weapon was loaded *under one wing* and thereby unbalanced the aircraft as well as overloading it. The pilots were then expected to fly over the North Sea at only 50 ft in order to approach Britain without being picked up by radar. The experiment was stopped after seventy-seven Heinkels and their crews were lost on such sorties. Yet only sixteen of them were claimed by the defending fighters sent to intercept them. Sixteen for the RAF: sixty-one for 'Sir Isaac'?

After the activities of August 1942, September proved to be

a placid month for the squadron. No score of any kind was claimed. Probably, after the flurry of activity generated by the Dieppe raid, over which the greatest dog-fights of the whole war took place, the Luftwaffe was licking its wounds. Certainly, custom for 29 Squadron was slack. Also, of course, only about 35 per cent of the Luftwaffe was engaged on their Western defences. Most were still in Russia, with a growing number also in the Mediterranean. However, 29 Squadron did take part in one event, the repercussions of which continue to this day. By using night fighter squadrons in almost any weather conditions, in daylight on those days when the meteorologists predicted that the weather would be too bad for the Spitfires to operate, the concept of the all-weather fighter plane was thus born and within a decade had been universally adopted by air forces the world over. With bombs soon to be added, the all-weather fighter-bomber was created.

From Bob Braham's point of view, September 1942 provided only two events worthy of note. Sticks Gregory returned from leave, thus allowing Jacko to return to his OTU responsibilities as Chief AI instructor much the wiser for his personal experiences with 29 Squadron. Soon these would be officially recognized and, for the valuable contributions which he had made towards the successes of the nights of 24 and 28 August, he would soon be awarded a well-deserved DFC. Doubtless his outstanding work as a chief ground radar instructor at No. 51 OTU was also taken into consideration. The other event of note – scarcely one that he would have relished – was that Bob appeared on a BBC radio programme to give a talk, heavily restricted by security, on the work of the RAF night fighters. Often such talks were deliberately intended to be listened to by the enemy and such information as they gave was therefore deliberately liable to mislead.

Early in October Jacko's DFC was announced at the same time as Bob's award of the more prestigious DSO. As the holder of the DSO, DFC & Bar, S/Ldr Braham was now unquestionably one of the fighter aces of the RAF. In general pilots disliked the term 'ace' but it was a term that the public had seized upon with relish and the successful aircrews were stuck with it regardless of their personal feelings. At that time, of course, the Allies' successes were mainly in the air and the public needed this kind of propaganda boost. In October 1942 there was still little else in the war to shout about although within a month or two the tide would have turned almost everywhere. The citation of S/Ldr Braham's award mentioned the ten enemy aircraft which he had definitely destroyed. It also mentioned how he had managed to bring home a badly damaged aircraft and land it 'at a small emergency landing ground', but without naming Friston. It also described Bob's leadership of his flight 'with courage and absolute determination' – an apt description of Bob's aggressive attitude towards his hated enemies.

The promulgation of these awards, and the official decision of the town of Maidstone (which lay close to West Malling) to present the squadron with a silver cup subscribed by the people of the town, gave 29 Squadron personnel plenty of excuses to hold exuberant parties both in their Messes and in the local pubs. After one such lunchtime session, which had included much drinking in pubs after the legal closing time (then 2 pm), Bob, driving in a rather inebriated state, ran into a traffic island. The local police, although normally remarkably tolerant to the wilder excesses of aircrews, found themselves obliged to take action against this damage to public property. In due course, Bob found himself hauled up before a local court where he was fined the sum of £5, then about a week's salary for a flight lieutenant. At that time drinking and driving was not heavily frowned upon and there was never any question of a miscreant losing his licence for such an offence.

By now 29 Squadron had collected quite a fine array of silver trophies. Initially, they had acquired a cup on which details of every confirmed 'kill' were engraved. After the arrival of the Beaufighters, the inadequacies of such a small trophy soon became obvious and a much larger one was purchased. Now the Maidstone cup could also be proudly displayed. It all helped to create, and fortify, good squadron morale.

October 1942 can, in retrospect, be seen as the zenith of Hitler's successes. Thereafter, especially after the twin defeats that his armies suffered at Stalingrad and Alamein, the once all-conquering German fighting machine was increasingly on the defensive. Thereafter it was driven inexorably back towards the confines of the German (and Italian) homelands. Only at sea, in October 1942, did the Germans continue to score successes. The U-boats were still decimating the Allied convoys in the Atlantic and elsewhere, and the monthly total of Allied tonnage sunk in November 1942 – over three-quarters of a million tons – was never exceeded. Also at sea, the Japanese were still advancing ever further southwards and had reached almost to the backdoor of Australia where outposts such as Port Darwin were seriously threatened. Likewise the Japanese armies had overrun Malaya and Burma, and around Chittagong were knocking on the Eastern gate of British India.

However, in the air the Allies were more than holding their own, with both RAF and USA Air Forces growing day by day more dominant. Moreover, it was apparent to shrewd observers that the Luftwaffe, even by the summer of 1942, was already stretched beyond its limits. Due to Hitler's lack of foresight, fostered by his belief that Britain would not continue to fight after the defeat of France in 1940, the German production of military aircraft had not been greatly stepped up. Losses suffered by the Luftwaffe during the German drive across Belgium, the Netherlands and France, and the heavy losses, about 1,800, incurred during the Battle of Britain, had not been fully replaced, even before the unprovoked assault upon the USSR.

With the subsequent entry of the USA into the war in December 1941, the imbalance in aircraft production would soon become heavily weighted in the Allies' favour. Britain and the USA would soon be producing more than two aircraft for every one made in Germany and Italy. Moreover, the quality of the Italian aircraft was always suspect. Russian production would also reach enormous proportions although, again, the quality was probably inferior. Yet air superiority would, in the end, largely control the outcome of the war.

Although the Luftwaffe shot down Russian aircraft in their thousands, it was never without some cost to themselves, albeit a disproportionately low one. Also, at all times but especially during the Russian winters, the German equivalent of 'Sir Isaac' was steadily at work. Another factor militated against the German air forces. After their successes on land in 1940, they did not attempt to design and mass-produce long-range four-engined bombers capable of reaching and destroying the Russian armament factories which had been taken back to the Ural mountains and beyond. Thus, Russian tanks and aircraft continued to be manufactured in vast numbers even though the Russian front line continued to be pressed further eastwards. As a result, when the German war machine was stopped on the River Volga at Stalingrad, the Wehrmacht found itself outnumbered and out-gunned both in the air and on the ground.

Some idea of the scale of the air war over Russia can be gauged from the numbers of Stormovik aircraft produced. This light Russian day bomber – not too unlike the Fairey Battle – was the modern type most produced by any nation in the Second World War. The numbers manufactured exceeded 36,000 but by war's end barely a handful remained. Yet the Stormovik's large cannon was capable of destroying most German tanks.

The far-reaching decision of the Allied leaders, so ably led by Churchill and his friend President Roosevelt, that Germany must be defeated before Japan, exacerbated the problems piling up for the Luftwaffe. By summer 1942 they were having to fight on four distinct fronts (some might say on five): the Russian Front, which alone covered well over a thousand miles; the Middle East Front, where Rommel needed an Air Force to match that of the Allies if he was to take Egypt; the Home Front, defending Germany against the growing attacks of Bomber Command and the US Air Forces; and lastly the 'Western Front', where a force was needed in France to counter the Fighter Command daylight sweeps and also to defend the U-boats in their bases along the French Atlantic coast.

The fifth front was Malta – and to subdue this island fortress, a whole Luftwaffe air army (Luftflotte) had been moved to airfields in Sicily. This tiny outpost was proving to be more than just a thorn prick. Hitler's decision to reduce the island to rubble by bombing had backfired. Although the Luftwaffe had at least two bombers attacking Malta for every one that was available to Rommel in Africa, Malta not only refused to yield but in May 1942 the RAF on the island inflicted a defeat on the large German Air Army stationed in Sicily for the purpose of wiping it off the map. In all, the Germans lost more than 1,000 aircraft over Malta. On top of all this America's entry into the war resulted in the Germans being faced with massive daylight, as well as night time, bombing raids. The USAAF's 'Mighty Eighth' fleet of four-engined bombers was growing in size daily. In the Middle East too, the USAAF's Ninth Air Force was also proving an invaluable aid to the Allied Desert Armies.

Although at the start of October 1942, the war on land and at sea was yet to turn in the Allies' favour, it continued to go well for Bob Braham and the pilots of 29 Squadron's A Flight. On the 17th, F/Lt Esplin and his radar operator Palmer, shot a Ju 88 into the sea. Two days later, Bob was sent off in daylight on one of those days when the weather conditions prevented the day fighters from operating. Flying again with Sticks, he was put on the trail of an enemy aircraft by his friend, the efficient controller David Mawhood. They were by then able to recognize one another's voices over the airwaves. Bob soon caught sight of the enemy, which he recognized as a Dornier 217. However, before he could open fire effectively, the enemy aircraft, which must have sighted him almost simultaneously, ducked into the clouds below.

Sticks had not been idle during the chase. He had already

detected the enemy plane on his Mark VII AI set and when Bob shouted, 'Its up to you now, Sticks', the chase was continued in the clouds by non-visual electronic means. Working in unison, Sticks, with his eyes glued to the set, directed Bob into a position just below and a few hundred feet behind the still invisible enemy. By then the speeds of the two aircraft had harmonized. Bob, although still 'blind' in the clouds, pulled up the nose and fired a burst, more in hope than real anticipation of success. Nothing happened except that the Beau was rocked in the slipstream of the unseen enemy. This was always another hazard to overcome. Whenever really close to, and immediately behind, an enemy, and at the exact moment when a good burst of fire could be best aimed, the slipstream of the plane being stalked was apt to cause the attacker's aircraft to buck about, reducing the chances of accurate aim. Even a big aircraft such as the Beau could be thrown about by slipstream much like a rider of a bucking bronco at a rodeo. This was one reason why successful night fighters like Bob and John Cunningham both preferred a position immediately behind the enemy but a few feet below. Being below also reduced the chances of the enemy first seeing the night fighter. He who shot first at close range was liable to win.

In this case, undeterred by the enveloping clouds which still masked both aircraft from each other, Bob and Sticks tried again. This time, after all ten guns had once more spewed forth their deadly hail at the unseen target, Bob distinctly saw flashes and sparks ahead. From past experience he knew this meant that the enemy had been hit. Clearly Bob must have been absolutely certain that the blip on Sticks's screen represented an enemy aircraft. He was one pilot who took every care to ensure that he did not fire upon friendly aircraft.

As if in confirmation of the strikes which Bob had seen, the 'blip' on Sticks's two radar scopes abruptly disappeared. The blip also disappeared from the radar screen of the Ground Controller. Although these signs indicated that Bob and Sticks had destroyed yet another raider, they did not constitute positive proof that the enemy had dived into the sea below and the official ruling was that Bob and Sticks could only claim a 'Damaged', not even a 'Probable'.

It is interesting that Bob was able to recognize the voice of S/Ldr Dave Mawhood. Just as aircrew visited ground radar centres to see at first hand the problems that the controllers faced, so Ground Controllers visited the squadrons; moreover, key personnel from both the squadron and Ground Control had jointly attended night fighting conferences at Group HQ. It all ensured that the vital cooperation between ground and air was strengthened and maintained.

Rather unfairly, while the successful aircrews received gallantry medals, the controllers were scarcely ever honoured. Attempts were also made in the squadron to understand better the problems which the home AA gunners had to overcome. Sadly, this form of 'togetherness' didn't always work out as planned. During October, for instance, on the very day when an officer from the local AA gun site was at West Malling giving a talk about his unit, a Beaufighter of 29 Squadron was shot down by our own guns and both crewmen were killed. Later that month three more Beaus were fired upon by friendly gunners but luckily none was hit.

In one important matter, the night fighters stationed at West Malling were more fortunate than some. Their airfield was only a few miles away from the RAF aerodrome at Manston where one of the longest and widest runways in Britain had been purposely built to serve as a massive emergency runway for all types of plane in distress or caught out by bad weather conditions. It was equipped with every known approach and landing aid including FIDO (Fog Investigation and Dispersal Operation). This literally set fire to the edges of the runway to guide the pilots down. The heat also helped to disperse the fog. Bomber Command crews, often badly shot up, headed for Manston when in difficulties. Later large numbers of USAAF planes also headed for it (and two similar airfields further north) when in dire straits.

As well as having its enormously long and extremely wide

'all-weather' runway, Manston was superbly equipped with crash tenders, medical aid and ambulances. On many occasions crews of 29 Squadron, especially when operating during adverse weather conditions by day or night, sought refuge from the elements and thankfully headed for Manston. Aircraft which had been shot up and which had no flaps and/or brakes, and also perhaps, were operating on only one good engine, would head for its broad, welcoming, well-lit runway. Ideally all RAF airfields should have been so built and equipped but the facilities at Manston must have cost at least ten times more to provide than normally was the case. The huge runway is today still in use as an international civil airport, capable of handling large, modern jet aircraft.

Frustrated as Bob may have been by his inability to be able to claim more than a 'Damaged' as a result of the chase in the clouds on 19 October, compensation came only a week later. This time it was S/Ldr Guest of Watling Ground Control who played the opening role. Again it was a daylight operation carried out in weather conditions when 'even the birds were walking'. The likelihood of any enemy activity on such a day seemed remote and consequently Bob had given Sticks the day off. When the unexpected call for an immediate scramble came, Bob Braham had had to grab the only radar operator readily at hand. This was Sgt Heywood, a newcomer to the squadron. Bob's thorough self-training and preparations here paid a dividend. He had himself flown on a few occasions as an AI operator in order to understand the difficulties that radar operators faced. As a result, although Sgt Heywood had scarcely seen a Mark VII AI set before, Bob was able to help him whenever the indications shown on the cathode ray tubes required further interpretation.

His guidance paid off. When the blip appeared on Sgt Heywood's screens in approximately the right place, the novice radar operator confidently called out, 'I've got contact', and thereafter continued to give Bob the directions he needed. A visual identification in the murk was obtained at only 300 yards and although the enemy jinked desperately, with the rear gunner firing wildly, Bob was able to close up and fire a long burst at a Ju 88 which, after being hit several times, dived hard to starboard and plummeted straight into the sea from about 5,000 ft. In spite of the rain and poor visibility both Bob and the now excited Heywood were able to observe the large oil patch which the aircraft had left as it dived to its death about 10 miles south of Beachy Head.

Sgt Heywood's natural elation at his first success was definitely *not* shared by Sticks. P/O Gregory, now the proud bearer of the ribbons of both the DFC and DFM, was *not* amused. For days Bob had to put up with his grumbles at having been left behind, thereby missing out on S/Ldr Braham's officially confirmed eleventh victory.

However, Sticks did not have to wait long before once again enjoying the sweet taste of success. Only five days later Braham and Gregory, this time operating in their more usual role of night fighters, were to score once again. During a night patrol, while being directed by P/O Mason from Foreness Ground Control station towards an enemy intruder, the AI set, not for the first time, decided to go 'on the blink'. Bob immediately asked for another aircraft from the squadron to be scrambled in his place. While awaiting the replacement, he continued, optimistically, to patrol as directed. He had by then lost his original contact. However, when another enemy aircraft was detected by Ground Control, Bob and Sticks went to investigate. Sticks was having great difficulty in getting any kind of intelligence from his AI set and the enemy had passed over the Beau before Sticks managed to pick it up. Despite the problems, Sticks eventually managed to direct Bob into an attacking position. At a range of only about 150–200 yd, Bob was positively able to identify the aircraft ahead of him as a Dornier 217. Keeping station about 50 ft below his quarry, Bob was able to pull up and dispatch the bomber with two short bursts of fire. Dorniers always seemed to go down in flames more easily than the more advanced Ju 88 bombers. In this case, the enemy's port engine broke away in pieces and the aircraft was later seen to explode. It was S/Ldr Braham's twelfth victory. Although the Dornier did not appear to have spotted the chasing Beau – judging by the absence of return fire in spite of the close proximity of the attacker – it was none the less jinking and twisting throughout its flight. This constant evasive action indicated that, by October 1942, the Luftwaffe bomber crews had become very concerned at the risks they ran of being detected and shot at by RAF night fighters. Bomber Command aircraft used the same tactic over Germany at night. Although Bob Braham had, during the latter part of October, shot at and hit no fewer than three enemy aircraft, destroying two of them for sure, this considerable feat was not the number one talking point of the members of A Flight, 29 Squadron. The combination known as 'Pepper and Salt', had done even better. F/O G. Pepper and P/O J.H. Toone had managed to destroy three enemy aircraft, all three of them on the night of 31 October. For quite some time this was a record in the Command.

It all took place on the same night when Bob and Sticks were having problems with their AI set. Pepper and Salt carried out two patrols that night, not in itself an unusual event. During the first of these, they were vectored towards an aircraft which they identified as a Dornier 217. A brief engagement followed during which the enemy's starboard engine caught fire. By then Pepper had overshot his target (an all too common occurrence with over-keen crews). However, they were able to get around again into a good firing position, guided by the sight of the flaming Dornier. They gave it one more burst whereupon they had the satisfaction of observing the aircraft drop, still burning, into the sea.

As the Germans seemed determined to mount night attacks upon the cathedral city of Canterbury, it was not too long before Pepper and Salt were airborne for their second sortie that night. Again they were vectored towards a contact. Again they took up the chase, homing in on the target by skilful use of AI. The intruder was identified as a Dornier 217 and once again they opened fire and shot it down, but this aircraft crashed on land and blew up with a terrific flash, probably caused by its bombs exploding on impact.

Bob and Sticks meanwhile, champing to get airborne again, were forced to wait while the radar mechanics worked to rectify the defect in their aircraft's AI Mark VII set. Pepper and Salt completed their memorable evening's work when they were once more directed towards a Do 217. This, too, like the one which Bob and Sticks had chased and caught, was continuously jinking violently. Two more bursts of fire from the Beau's multiple guns were enough to send this Dornier diving steeply downwards into the sea.

By the time Bob and Sticks were given a fully serviceable aircraft it was, as Bob had written in his pilot's log-book, 'a bit too late for anything', although they did get airborne. The raiders had by then departed but minus four Dornier 217s accounted for by 29 Squadron. Before ending the tales of success for 29 Squadron that October 1942, it is worth noting, for the benefit of those who pursue squadron records in the Public Record Office at Kew, that Form 541 of the Operations Record Book of 29 Squadron for 26 October 1942 – the day that Bob scored his eleventh confirmed victory – fails to make any mention of this feat. It even fails to record that Bob and Sticks operated that night. One has to search out the actual Form F540 – the Intelligence and Combat report – produced by 11 Group, to obtain the official details of this kill. HQ had time enough to record the details of victories and ample staff to accomplish this. The busy squadrons, by contrast, regarded the keeping of records as annoying 'bumph'.

October 1942 was not, however, all sweetness and joy for the squadron. As usual, at least one Beau had come to grief when attempting to land in bad weather and, as well as having had several aircraft shot at by friendly gunners, others had had to be diverted to strange airfields when the weather at base had closed in. This was always an anxious period for a tired crew at the end of a flight with the fuel gauges dangerously low.

The weather during November 1942 was, as might have been expected, even worse than in October for flying and many of the crews suffered when attempting to land back at base. The winter months in Britain were those when 'Sir Isaac' chalked up many of his victims. During November Pepper and Salt survived an emergency landing on one engine after the other had seized up in flight. On that occasion, they safely landed on Manston's long wide runway. Strangely, it was on a fine sunny November day that this team's luck finally ran out. For some unknown reason, this likeable young pair, during a routine daylight practice, came to grief, with their Beau diving vertically into the ground near Rochester. Such was the impact, there was no hope of either man surviving.

This event cast a dark shadow over the squadron and their funeral was attended by all available personnel. During their relatively short period with 29 Squadron – the first fighting unit that either had joined – they had shot down six enemy aircraft and damaged another. F/O Pepper well deserved the DFC & Bar which he had been awarded. The saddest moment for Bob Braham came when, as flight commander, he had to break the news to Pepper's young wife. This was always a ghastly and harrowing task. In this case it was made even more poignant as Bob and Joan had made friends with the charming young couple during the brief months when all four had been at West Malling together.

November 1942 was a bad month for 29 Squadron. They scored no successes but lost several aircraft to 'Sir Isaac'. One young pilot, Sgt Ryan, crashed twice but on each occasion was able to walk away unhurt. Generally this was the pattern as the Beaufighter was an aircraft of exceptional strength.

The Beaufighter had both good and bad features. It had at all times to be treated with some respect in the air. If a pilot tried to do too much with it, the Beau could bite back. While it was exceptionally rugged, its revolutionary sleeve-valve engines initially gave trouble. However, their power was impressive and, as the war progressed, not only was this upgraded but engine reliability improved. It was also an advantage that they were air-cooled units, unlike the Rolls-

Royce Merlin engines which depended upon a glycol coolant and which were in trouble if that supply was ruptured or otherwise ran out. The Beaufighter was manoeuvrable and had, for that time, a good range for a fighter aircraft but in both these respects the Beau was soon outstripped by the remarkable 'Wooden Wonder': the De Havilland Mosquito. The Beau's greatest asset, apart from its structural strength, was its unrivalled firepower. When a Beau opened up with all ten guns, any aircraft in its direct line of fire stood little chance of surviving.

In stark contrast to the grim occasion of the funeral of young Pepper and P/O Toone, only a few days later, Bob found himself taking tea with King George VI at Buckingham Palace. The royal family had decided that, with American airmen already pouring into the country in ever increasing numbers, many of them flying themselves across the Atlantic in their planes, it would be appropriate to invite a number of American airmen to Buckingham Palace on Thanksgiving Day, this being one of America's most prestigious holidays, which was always held in late November.

To help cement the growing friendship between the airmen of the RAF and their counterparts in the United States Air Forces (the USA had at that time both an American Army Air Corps (USAAC) and also a similar Navy one), Their Majesties had also invited a number of leading RAF pilots. Bob was one such representative of Fighter Command.

With all the royal family present, along with such VIPs as Prime Minister Winston Churchill, the occasion was at first rather a formal and overwhelming affair for the likes of Bob Braham but along with the tea, laid out on a vast array of tressle tables, stronger drinks could also be found. Informality then took over! As Bob recorded in *Scramble*, 'Everything was done to make guests feel at home.'

Bob got into the spirit of the occasion by going back to the flat of an American colonel of the USAAF with whom he had been chatting. There he was, as he puts it, 'introduced to Bourbon'. One can imagine that several such friendships were truly cemented by this kindly gesture of the royal family, reinforced by the plentiful supplies of Bourbon and other powerful drinks which the Americans always seemed to have in plenty.

December seems to have been no more successful than November. Doubtless the poor flying weather affected both sides and, as a result, 'customers' for the RAF night fighters were few and far between. The overstretched Luftwaffe did not have the bombers to spare for risky ventures over Britain. Their prime consideration by the end of 1942 was the defence of their homeland from the massive night raids carried out by Bomber Command, and the increasing threat posed by the USAAF's large daylight bombing fleets. The enemy also had to keep fighters in airfields just across the Channel to counter the number of day fighter sweeps that Fighter Command was carrying out in an attempt to lure the Luftwaffe into battle. The Allies' air front line was steadily being pushed back deeper and deeper into Europe in preparation for the day when Allied ground and naval forces would commence the gigantic task of landing troops for the recapture of Europe.

By early 1943 the Germans were also having to divert aircraft to the Mediterranean where the Axis successes of the summer of 1942 had fallen into a sharp decline. After defeating the British Eighth Army in June 1942 and capturing the port of Tobruk, Rommel and his Afrika Korps, along with his Italian troops, had been badly routed in the battles at Alam Halfa and Alamein and had failed to complete the conquest of Egypt. By November they were in headlong flight. They had to retreat for over 1,000 miles, giving up Benghazi and concentrating what remained of their armies at and around Tripoli. Throughout this rout, the Allied planes dominated the skies, capturing Axis airfield after airfield. Rommel's demands for aircraft to counter the Allied air superiority were incessant. A similar situation had developed in Russia but on an even larger scale. The vast German armies surrounding Stalingrad had been encircled and crushed. For the first time in German history, a German field marshal had surrendered and then gone over to the enemy, so furious was he about Hitler's absurd orders that there should be no orderly retreat.

The German field commanders on all Russian fronts were emitting desperate pleas for more and more planes with which to stem the Red Army's advances. On top of all these victories for the Allies, Anglo-American forces had in November 1942 effected a surprise landing in French North Africa around Algiers. Although the French hardly relished this invasion of their (neutral) part of Africa, they had soon perforce come to accept it. A giant pincer movement then began. With the Eighth Army driving westwards towards Tripoli and the new invaders advancing eastwards along the north shores of Algeria into Tunisia, the German–Italian armies in North Africa were being compressed into a redoubt. Again Rommel's demands for more planes were being received at Marshal Goering's Luftwaffe HQ.

In all these battlefields in Europe and Africa, the Allies were in command in the air. Malta had also inflicted a defeat upon the Luftwaffe. It was a pattern which was being repeated in the skies over both Tunisia and Tripolitania. Herman Goering, the overweight and boastful head of the Luftwaffe, had once publicly announced 'that no Allied plane would ever penetrate the defences of the German Reich'. Yet by 1943 up to one thousand heavy bombers, mainly four-engined types, were doing so by night and similar numbers of American forces would soon be doing likewise by day.

It is little wonder therefore that, in these circumstances, relatively few German bombers were available for night raids on Britain, whose night fighting defences had been raised to an effective standard. The few German raids on Britain would henceforth be mainly carried out by swift fighter bombers, usually Fw 190s, on hit-and-run sneak raids against towns close to the English Channel. S/Ldr J.R.D. Braham's period of service with 29 Squadron was now drawing to an end and, with it, the brief period when his loyal wife would have the delight of creating a home near him during the war.

During December 1942 Bob Braham was summoned to 11 Group HQ for an interview with the AOC. He had qualms about the meeting. Had some of his wilder exploits in local pubs come to the AOC's attention? Would his motoring offence be under discussion? Bob himself knew that some of his antics as a flight commander hardly fitted in with the established procedures of the RAF. All this was at a time when some disciplinarian at HQ had issued the edict that NCO aircrew were *at all times* to address their officers as 'Sir', even when in the air as part of a two-man crew! Bob had not the slightest intention of reinforcing this nor did he make any move to see that others did so. It was an edict that was widely ignored and was soon rescinded. S/Ldr Braham had been 'Bob' to the likes of Sticks long before his radar operator had been commissioned, and this informality was copied by many others. The outspoken aircrews from Australia, Canada and elsewhere paid scant respect to such 'stuffy' British rules and it would only have generated friction within the squadron to try to enforce such an edict. As soon as the tide turned and the first signs of an eventual Allied victory could be perceived, some Command HQs, especially those which were staffed by elderly pre-war trained Regular RAF officers, made attempts to restore what they considered was 'proper pre-war discipline'. But by then the operative end of the RAF was almost entirely in the hands of air crews who had never been to Cranwell College and who had come to do things in their own practical ways.

Bob knew that he had done well. He must also have been aware of the loyalty and respect that he had gained from all in the Squadron but he had, in the words of the popular post-war song, done it 'My way' and not the established way.

The A Flight Commander of 29 Squadron knew only one way of leading and learning. He led by example and he learned by experience. Faced with a new task, he first tried it out himself. If it didn't come right first time, he tried it again. He was no theorist but rather a person who clearly thought much about what might go, or had gone, awry and was prepared to learn from his own and others' mistakes. He was always a steady improver.

Air Vice-Marshal Saunders, AOC 11 Group, Fighter Command, saw Bob at once. Bob need not have worried. The AOC was quick to inform S/Ldr Braham that he would be promoted immediately to the acting rank of wing commander and that he would, almost at once, be posted to take command of 141 Squadron, another night fighting Beaufighter unit based at Ford, between Bognor Regis and Littlehampton in Sussex.

A new chapter in Bob Braham's life was about to open up and he soon learned that, as the day fighter ace W/Cdr Paddy Finucane had by then been killed, he was, at 22, the youngest wing commander in the RAF to command an operational squadron. Wing Commander J.R.D. Braham DSO, DFC & Bar returned from 11 Group HQ to West Malling to tidy up his affairs in an even more purposeful state of mind – not that anyone in 29 Squadron could imagine that anything more purposeful than Bob as a flight commander was humanly possible.

11
Squadron Commander

Wing Commander J.R.D. Braham had been given a responsible task. As the CO of a twin-engined squadron he was responsible for the welfare, performance and behaviour of hundreds of men and women. As the war progressed, aircraft became more and more sophisticated and the number of specialists required to keep them operational steadily increased; also, as the size of the RAF grew and grew again (by 1943 its numbers exceeded a million), more and more paperwork seemed to be required in order to hold its many strands together. Bob Braham would have been the first to admit that he knew little (and cared less) about the vast piles of what he termed 'bumph' which flowed unceasingly into his office IN trays. He had never been a student at the RAF Officers College at Cranwell. He was not a Regular RAF officer, but a make-shift Short Service commissioned one. Also, ever since day one of the war, he had been too busy flying aircraft to bother overmuch about the finer points of administration. He was no avid reader of the King's Rules and Regulations, as applied to His Majesty's Royal Air Force. He may never have even seen them.

As if all this were not enough to daunt Bob Braham, the position to which he had been appointed carried with it special challenges and responsibilities. During their talk the AOC of 11 Group had advised Bob that 141 Squadron was 'in the doldrums'. Bob Braham was, in effect, being sent to sort out and inspire a unit that had lost its way. Whenever a squadron in wartime hit a bad patch, it was usually due to a combination

121

of two factors: lack of success in the air and indifferent leadership on the ground. 141 Squadron was no exception.

The squadron had had a rough time for most of the war. During the air battles of 1940, it had been one of the few unlucky fighter squadrons to have been equipped with the Bolton & Paul Defiant fighter aircraft. This single-engined two-seater fighter, with a rear seat occupied by an air gunner in a turret, had proved to be no match for the German Me 109s. On one occasion, in an engagement against this formidable opponent, the squadron had lost six Defiants in the space of only half an hour.

Soon thereafter, all Defiants were withdrawn from their designed role of day fighters and used instead as night fighters. However, initially without even AI on board and with inadequate range, the aircraft again had not met with success. At this period almost anything that could fly was being tried out as a night fighter, largely because the RAF lacked a plane suitable for the task. Blenheims, Hurricanes, Defiants and the much mauled and inadequate Battles had hastily been adapted and used at night in attempts to counter the bombers which nightly raided Britain during the winter of 1940.

As might be recalled, during 1941 Bob Braham had by coincidence been temporarily assigned to 141 Squadron up at Ayr, in Scotland to assist in the conversion of that unit's aircrews from Defiants to Beaufighters. But even with Beaus, which they operated from Ford airfield in Sussex, 141 Squadron had still not been very successful at stalking and shooting down enemy aircraft at night. Moreover, the fact that many of its senior officers were living off station with their wives had not helped the squadron to develop a sense of pride or cohesion. Consequently the leaders were seldom around to inspire confidence and restore morale. On top of which, as with all other such units, 141 Squadron was not immune from the accidents and losses that night flying, bad flying weather and the ever-present 'Sir Isaac' were liable to inflict.

Even at Ford, luck had seemed to be running against 141 Squadron. The airfield lay close to the English Channel and had been the target for several German Fw 190 hit-and-run raids. Airmen had been killed and living quarters demolished to such an extent that many crews were now billeted out in nearby Bognor Regis.

11 Group had paved the way for the arrival of W/Cdr Braham. They had removed the CO, one of the flight commanders and the adjutant in advance of his arrival. While this 'cleaned the slate' for him, it also meant that he would not have the experience and benefit of other senior officers to guide him in his new role, one for which his previous RAF experience left him very unprepared. It was a daunting challenge.

Possibly because he had been advised that the living-out of senior officers was thought to be one cause of 141 Squadron's low spirits, Bob decided immediately, but with great personal reluctance, that he would not allow Joan to look for a home for herself and their son close to Ford. However, as the surprise posting to 141 Squadron had come about during the last week in December, he decided that he and Joan would remain near West Malling a little longer to enjoy a rare Christmas break together. It was at about this time that Joan broke the news that she was pregnant again. Perhaps this made him even more determined to pack her off to her parents in Leicester.

Bob had always reckoned that when the time came for him to join the ranks of those aircrews reported as 'missing' or 'killed in action' (as most rational aircrew, deep in their hearts, had come to accept as inevitable), it would be much better for Joan to be already settled with her parents. Perhaps, too, the harrowing experience of having personally to inform Mrs Pepper about her husband's death had left its mark.

Several encouragements helped Bob to undertake the big challenge ahead of him with some optimism as well as his habitual determination. The AOC had advised Bob: 'If there is anything you need to get the squadron into good shape, simply ask for it.' Another bonus materialized when Bob took himself down to Ford on an inspection visit before taking command. There he met F/Lt 'Dickie' Sparrowe, the new adjutant who had only recently arrived. Dickie and Bob hit it off at once. For the next year or so, Bob was able to lean with confidence upon the administrative experience of his able and older principal 'office' assistant. A good squadron adjutant, like a good squadron medical officer, or intelligence officer, was worth his weight in gold. In Dickie Sparrowe, Bob had found a man whom he could trust implicitly to 'run the shop' while he got on with the squadron's operational demands, as he was determined to do. At Ford, 141 Squadron shared the airfield with two experimental units. One was the RAF's Fighter Interception Units (FIU), which tried out Fighter Command's latest ideas on airborne radar and other tactics. The other was the Royal Naval Air Fighting Development Unit (NAFDU), which carried out not too dissimilar work for the Fleet Air Arm (FAA). Bob was soon to get to know, and use, both establishments; especially the FIU.

Before he departed from 29 Squadron, Bob was presented with a beautifully made model of a Bristol Beaufighter, suitably identified with the number V 8284, his former favourite personal plane which he had crashed at Friston. The model was made for him by his devoted groundcrew, using metal taken from one of that aircraft's written-off propellers salvaged from Friston. It was displayed and mounted on parts of a piston ring taken from one of the crashed Beau's Hercules engines. It is believed still to be in Joan Braham's possession.

The departure of Bob Braham from 29 Squadron, the unit for which he worked so effectively, on and off, for almost four years, was officially recorded in the Squadron's Operational Record Book on 24 December 1942 in these words: 'W/C Braham, who was posted yesterday to Ford, flew back today and spent some time in the Mess. Everyone will be extremely sorry to see him go as he was a great figure in 29.' This was a tangible mark of respect and affection for the man who had helped so much to make it one of the most renowned squadrons in the Command. Obviously, his departure was a good excuse for quite a few beery parties in the Mess and at the local hostelries. Sticks

Gregory was also posted to 141 Squadron so as to remain with Bob and help him to get that unit into good fighting trim. This, of course, called for more cheerful parties. Sticks, like Bob, was a popular figure, renowned in the squadron, in Group HQ and in Fighter Command.

One of the few key officers of 141 Squadron who had stayed on at Ford was the Intelligence Officer, F/Lt 'Buster' Reynolds. Before the war Buster had been a solicitor. Bob soon came to rely on Buster much as he did on Dickie Sparrowe. The three of them were to form a dedicated team which saw to it that 141 Squadron would climb out of the doldrums.

From the outset, W/C J.R.D. Braham DSO, DFC & Bar was determined not just to bring 141 Squadron up to scratch but to forge it into as good a unit as any in Fighter Command. In Buster, his IO or 'Spy', he found a worthy ally. The two were to remain friends for the rest of Bob's life. I had the pleasure of meeting Buster Reynolds during late 1990. By then, he was well over 80 years old but his memory of the events of the war remained as clear as a bell. Buster regards Bob Braham as one of the truly great personalities of the Second World War, a man whom he will never forget, nor regret knowing. Another key member of 141 Squadron at that time was the squadron's doctor. Medical Officer James Dougall was an Irishman with all that race's individualism and personal traits. He was known affectionately as 'The Mad Irishman', and Bob and he were to share many zany situations together. It would seem that Dougall's outlandish sense of fun held some sort of fascination for the new, very young CO. All in all, squadron morale was soon to be raised.

The very presence of such a distinguished and highly decorated pilot as Bob Braham must in itself have been a boost for all personnel of the squadron.

The new wing commander made an immediate good impression. First he called all the aircrew together and informed them in no uncertain terms that, within a short period of time, he intended, with their help, to make 141 Squadron into one of the finest night fighter squadrons in the Command. This was music to their ears as many of the intake who had been brought in to replace the older hands were keen youngsters experiencing their first taste of squadron life; also it would be their first crack at the enemy after long weary months of discipline and training. Bob then assembled the groundcrews and gave them a similar talk. Here again, the effect was immediate. Don Aris, the armourer whose patient research has done so much to make this book possible, commented that although he had worked under a number of COs during his two years in the RAF, this was the first time that one of them had specifically addressed the groundcrews, or had personally appealed for their help in making their squadron a notable one. Bob's style of leadership always seems to have been of the 'Fall in and follow me' type, and he combined this with an open display of courage, energy, aggression and enthusiasm which soon spread to most around him. If Bob's enthusiasm did *not* strike a responsive chord in a few men he lost little time in getting rid of them. Like other very positive men, Bob Braham was never one to suffer fools gladly. Bob's other great quality as a leader was that he never treated men of inferior rank as inferior human beings.

During the early part of January, Joan and their young son stayed on for a short time near West Malling as Bob found that he had to make occasional visits there to tidy up his affairs. On one such visit, during an otherwise blissful couple of days with a husband whom Joan would in future see only rarely, 29 Squadron was scrambled to meet an incoming night raid. Although Bob Braham had officially ended all ties with his old unit, his determination to get at the enemy was so great that he immediately offered his services to 29 Squadron's new commanding officer, W/Cdr Wight-Boycott. Joan was normally a wonderfully tolerant and understanding wife. She had even raised no protest at being advised to go back to her parents, but this was too much. For once she was really mad at her husband. Fortunately, Bob's offer was turned down by the new 29 Squadron CO, and later

Taunton School, where young John Braham was a boarder for two years before he passed his School Certificate examination. (Don Aris)

The Bristol Blenheim Mark IV. An obsolescent bomber by 1941, it was used as a night fighter in 1940/1 in the absence of anything better but it lacked speed and fire-power. Although AI was fitted to some, the device was in its infancy. The extra gun pack (four .303) can be seen beneath the fuselage. (Imperial War Museum CH 2898)

The Heinkel 111 bomber was used by the Germans throughout the war. Bob Braham shot down five, and probably six, of these, and damaged another. (Imperial War Museum HU 1186)

Bob Braham wearing the Luftwaffe 'Mae West' salvaged from an He 111 which he had shot down. (Imperial War Museum CH 13625)

The Hawker Hurricane, the type in which F/Lt Richard Stevens shot down fourteen enemy aircraft (plus one shared), although the Hurricane was never a first rate night fighter nor was it equipped with airborne radar. For his amazing feats, Stevens had been awarded a DSO and DFC and bar by 1941. Sadly, he was killed soon afterwards. (Imperial War Museum CH 1501)

W/Cdr Guy Gibson VC, DSO and bar, DFC and bar. Although far better known as a Bomber Command ace and the pilot who led the raid on the German dams, Guy was also successful as a night fighter pilot in 29 Squadron, flying with his talented AI/observer 'Jimmy' James. (Imperial War Museum CH 13618)

29 Squadron, 1942. W/Cdr Colbeck-Welsh, the CO, is in the centre (seated) with Guy Gibson on his right and Bob Braham on his left. 'Jimmy' James is behind Guy and 'Sticks' Gregory is behind Colbeck-Welsh. (R.H. 'Jimmy' James)

Guy Gibson and 'Jimmy' James hamming it up for the camera as Guy says farewell to his AI/observer and 29 Squadron. (R.H. 'Jimmy' James)

Richard 'Jimmy' James, Guy Gibson's skilled radar operator. Together, they shot down four enemy aircraft and damaged several others. 'Jimmy' James and 'Sticks' Gregory became good friends, and both were commissioned on the same day. (R.H. 'Jimmy' James)

Dornier 215 bomber. Some of these aircraft were later modified to serve as night fighters. They were very similar to the Do 217s, five of which Bob Braham destroyed. (Imperial War Museum HU 2709)

G/Capt. John 'Cat's-eyes' Cunningham, DSO and bar, DFC and bar. In partnership with his observer Jimmy Rawnsey, John was the RAF's much acclaimed first night fighter ace. With radar still secret, his successes were attributed to the enhanced night vision he acquired from eating carrots! (Imperial War Museum CH 13614)

F/Lt Jimmy Rawnsey DSO, DFC, DFM and bar, John Cunningham's brilliant AI observer. (Imperial War Museum CH 13639)

A Beaufighter night fighter with the AI aerials prominent, transmitting from the nose, receiving on the wings. (Imperial War Museum CH 15213)

W/Cdr Braham salutes at the Battle of Britain special service. Joan is behind him. (Joan Braham)

Bob and 'Jacko', probably photographed on the day they were decorated by King George VI at Buckingham Palace in 1942. Jacko was then awarded the DFC and Bob the DSO. (Joan Braham)

F/Lt Jacko Jacobs photographs Bob and Joan outside Buckingham Palace. (Joan Braham)

An artistic photograph of a night fighter Beau. Judging by the number of victory emblems, it might have been flown by Bob Braham or John Cunningham. (Imperial War Museum CH 15214)

The nose of an Me 110 night fighter adorned with the cumbersome aerials needed for the German airborne radar. This far-from-deadly day fighter became a formidable night fighter for the Luftwaffe. Bob destroyed six of these aircraft, all over enemy territory at night. (Imperial War Museum CL 3299)

An Me 110 under attack at night, with debris flying from it. Camera guns had limited usefulness at night. (Norman Franks)

The fast and versatile Ju 88 bomber made an excellent night fighter. Later, even more aerials were added, some of them in the tail. In skilled hands, the Ju 88 was a match for the Beaufighter. Although they were difficult to destroy, Bob Braham is credited with having shot down four and damaged another four. (Imperial War Museum HU 2735)

141 Squadron at RAF Wittering, July 1943. Third from the left in the middle row is F/O Parrott who flew with LeBoutte. Fifth from the right is Harry White and to his right is R/O Mike Allen. In the front row, Sticks is third from the left and Charles Winn is fifth from the left; next is Station Commander G/Capt. Legg, with Bob on his left, then S/Ldr Davis, LeBoutte (wearing glasses), Adjutant Sparrowe and extreme right the 'Mad Doc', F/O Dougall. (Don Aris)

F/Lt Lucien Leboutte, the enthusiastic and elderly Belgian who served as a junior officer in the RAF. Between 1942 and 1944 he flew with 141 Squadron as a night fighter pilot, completing more than fifty operational sorties. Two years later he was appointed Chief of Staff of the Belgian Air Force, with the rank of Major-General (Air Marshal). (Musée Royal de Armée Bruxelles, via M. Evrard)

The nose of a night fighting Mosquito. The four machine-guns have been replaced with a dome containing the Serrate and other electronic devices. It was in just such an aircraft that W/Cdr Branse Burbridge, with his skilful R/O Bill Skelton, shot down twenty-one enemy aircraft at night later in the war. Both men were awarded the DSO and bar, and DFC and bar. The Mosquito's speed and range were both superior to the Beaufighter's, and this highly manoeuvrable aircraft became the Allies' most successful night fighter of the war. the ports of the four deadly 20 mm cannon are clearly shown. (Imperial War Museum ATP 12184F)

Left to right: Air Commodore David Atcherley, W/Cdr Wykeham-Barnes, an Intelligence Officer, and the pugnacious Air Vice-Marshal Basil Embry. By war's end Basil Embry had been awarded the DSO and three bars in addition to the DFC. As W/Cdr Smith he flew on operations, notably on the night of D-Day, 6 June 1944. (Imperial War Museum CL 2739)

Bob Braham and Sticks Gregory in front of the day fighter Mosquito in which they went on Ranger operations, looking for targets of opportunity. (Imperial War Museum CH 13175)

Bob and Sticks, both wearing salvaged German life-jackets, standing under the nose of a Mosquito of the mark in which Bob, often with Sticks, shot down nine enemy aircraft during daylight Ranger patrols. This successful pair were awarded between them four DSOs, five DFCs and a DFM. (Imperial War Museum CH 13174)

Members of 141 Squadron ground crew. Without their skills on the ground, little could have been accomplished in the air. These Canadians were ground radar specialists. (Norman Franks)

The Luftwaffe fighter ace Robert Spreckels, who shot down Bob in 1944. He is pictured in the cockpit of an Fw 190. (Norman Franks)

The Focke-Wulf 190 was probably Germany's best fighter aircraft of the war, and some 19,000 were built. Bob shot down two of them. (Norman Franks)

W/Cdr Bob Braham. With two rosette bars each for his DSO and DFC, it is easy to see why these ribbons seemed to be 'riveted' to his tunic! (Joan Braham)

At their reunion near Hamburg in 1961 Bob was at last able to buy Robert Spreckels the long-promised Scotch. Their wives seem to be enjoying the celebrations as much as the pilots. (Joan Braham)

A 141 Squadron reunion in London after the war. Left to right: F/Lt Jacobs, F/Lt Marriott, 'Doc' Dougall (jacket undone), unknown, Sticks Gregory, Adjutant Dickie Sparrowe, Bob Braham, Lt-General Lucien LeBoutte, F/Lt Freddie Newton, S/Ldr Harry White and F/Lt Michael Allen. (This last pair proved to be almost as successful as Bob and Sticks.) In front: W/Cdr Kelsey, W/Cdr Winn and W/Cdr Davies, all successful and decorated pilots. Don Aris has calculated that between them, the men in this picture had been awarded no fewer than thirty-one gallantry and other RAF awards. (Harry White via Don Aris)

Bob was honest enough to admit that he realized that he was being both selfish and unfair to his devoted wife.

It turned out to be a memorable night for W/C Wight-Boycott. Before the night was over, he could claim to have shot down four enemy aircraft, one more than the record achieved by the Pepper and Toone combination. But overall, it was not such a good night for 141 Squadron as one of their aircraft was shot down by friendly fire: probably by another night fighter or possibly by the AA gunners. Luckily, the crew had been able to bail out without injury. This duo, with F/Lt Cook up front and Sgt Warner at the AI set in the rear, had earlier achieved the rare experience of having disposed of an enemy bomber without even firing a shot. (Guy Gibson and Jimmy James had experienced a similar victory.) This unusual event had taken place a week or so before Bob had been posted in as CO. A Dornier 217 had been detected and a chase had ensued, with both aircraft twisting and turning at extremely low altitudes. The combat came to an abrupt ending when the Dornier flew slap into the Bognor Regis gasometer, only a few miles from the squadron's Ford base.

W/Cdr Braham commenced his operational career with 141 Squadron with an uneventful dusk patrol, flying as usual with Sticks Gregory in the Beau's rear seat. This sortie took place on 27 December but it was not until about a month later that he was able to increase his own score and raise the squadron's morale with another successful sortie. This victory took place on 20 January 1943.

Bob Braham's thirteenth victim was another Dornier 217. By then, Bob, always most punctilious about identifying an aircraft before opening fire, must have known as well as anyone in the RAF what a Dornier bomber looked like at night, since he had attacked so many of them.

Both aircraft seem to have caught a glimpse of the other simultaneously and a night dog-fight, with both aircraft firing bursts, followed. The pilot of the Dornier was throwing his plane about violently in attempts to evade the attacker. Throughout the contest both aircraft were flying in excess of

200 mph. This Dornier seems to have been sturdier than some previous ones; perhaps increased protective armour had been fitted after so many previous losses over Britain? It was only after a chase and attack which had lasted for over 15 minutes that Bob, who by then had fired several long bursts into the enemy, had the satisfaction of seeing the Do 217, now at 15,000 ft, plunge earthwards in a death dive with smoke pouring from it. It appeared to be crashing on land but at the last few seconds, it missed the cliffs and plunged into the sea, leaving behind a tell-tale swirl of water. In all Bob had fired 335 rounds of cannon shells and over 500 rounds of .303 ammunition. Throughout the contest both Bob and Sticks had observed countless strikes on the Dornier but the Beau had not once been hit by the return fire.

Bob Braham, ever one to blame himself for alleged inefficiencies, explains his relatively ineffective shooting on the fact that, when called upon unexpectedly to scramble for the sortie, he had been drinking in a pub and was not as clear-eyed or as clear-headed as he might otherwise have been. The long contest speaks well for Sticks's ability to maintain contact on the AI set. An enemy at night, twisting and turning desperatly to avoid destruction, poses a host of problems for a radar operator with his eyes glued to his tiny cathode ray tubes. On his set the blips were only a few millimetres wide and the screens would have been cluttered up by myriad flickering green lines. The record books of night fighter squadrons are full of references to instances when a crew has been vectored by Ground Control to an enemy and picked it up on the plane's AI set, only to lose contact during the last few vital moments of the chase.

After their success, Bob and Sticks tried to find another customer although by then the Beau was almost out of ammunition and during the battle with the Dornier two of the four cannon had jammed.

There is another significant detail about the events of the night of 20 January 1943. From the Squadron's Operations Record Book, it can be seen that Bob and Sticks had taken part in four sorties on the previous night and at least one on the night previous to that, the 18th. Perhaps this explains why Bob was relaxing in a pub when called upon to supply another aircraft on the 20th. Bob's own personal log-book indicates that he had flown three sorties on the 18th, not just the one. However, when recording night patrols/sorties, there is always some confusion. On many nights the crews would have taken off on (say) the 18th but landed back on the 19th. Even a flight which departed at 0015 hrs on the 19th might have been recorded as having taken place on the night of the 18th. Whichever version is the more correct, the evidence is clear that W/Cdr Braham was NOT one of those COs (and they did exist), who sat in their office coping with mounds of paperwork and leaving the dangers of operational flying to others. In Bob's case, as the squadron records show, he flew dangerous missions at least as often as any other pilot of his squadron while still managing to keep his head above water in the office. As his flights were taking up most of the nights, he could not possibly have got anything like a normal amount of sleep.

It can easily be imagined how much all this was helping to build up the squadron's morale and confidence. Bob's victory of 20 January would also have added to the unit's restoration process. Moreover, it had come at a very opportune time. Only the night before, F/Sgt Guthries and his radar operator, Sgt Wellington, had had the misfortune to have an engine cut dead. It was about midnight and Bob, himself just airborne, had overheard the emergency call from the crew. After that there was only an ominous silence. The squadron's worst fears were confirmed the next day when Wellington's body was washed ashore. This was the kind of drawn-out loss which naturally depressed a unit. After the initial emergency call, there was a period when hope remained, but it ended with confirmation that another two good men had been lost due to a mechanical failure. This loss had come soon after F/Lt Cook's aircraft had fallen to our own defences. A confirmed kill by the CO was the best of all tonics to such events and it was the squadron's only victory in that month.

By clearing out many aircrews from his new squadron and replacing them with new crews straight from the OTU, Bob Braham had set himself a problem. However, he now set about solving the difficulties caused by having so many novice crews in his squadron. The squadron still had to take its fair share of operational sorties yet had too few experienced crews to do so. The new pilots, most of whom had only flown Blenheims while at OTU, were still being converted to the more powerful Beaus. With 'Sir Isaac' always hovering in the background, this could not be rushed. It all took time. The handful of experienced crews were called upon both to instruct and to operate, and they were fast becoming exhausted. Bob Braham himself seemed to be inexhaustible but the other older hands who had to carry out operations as well as conversion training were made of more normal clay!

During February Fw 190s twice strafed the airfield within one week. These events naturally interrupted the training and other schedules. This was another cross to bear for the few hard-working experienced crews at Ford.

Bob remembered the parting words of the 11 Group AOC: 'If you want anything, just ask.' Consequently he asked for an interview with Air Vice-Marshal Saunders. Up to this moment there is scant evidence that W/Cdr Braham was a long-term thinker. His forte seems to have been acting swiftly – almost impulsively at times. Now, with increased responsibilities, a new side of Bob Braham emerges. The proposition which he put to his AOC was that he should be allowed to withdraw his squadron from the front line temporarily and take it elsewhere so that he could lick it into shape without having to fulfil heavy operational commitments every night. He pointed out that his experienced crews would soon be worn out or due a rest period; also that he was reluctant to expose his novice crews to the dangers of night operations until he was satisfied that they could cope. Not unless he could take the squadron to some quieter backwater would he be able to train them up to the high standard required. He reckoned that unless his pilots could fly the Beaus with almost subconscious ease and the radar operators could operate the AI sets accurately and work in complete harmony with their pilots, they would be unlikely to come out on top when engaged in combat with the enemy at night; they were unlikely even to find the enemy at night.

This proposition came at a time when the Command's day fighters were suffering considerable losses during their sweeps over enemy-held territory; this was due, in part, to sending out 'new boys' who were falling to the guns of the enemy's experienced fighter pilots. These new boys were, sadly, often put in the most exposed places in the obsolescent types of day formations which were still being used.

Bob Braham's request could not have been an easy one. He knew that he was exceptionally young to have been placed in charge of a squadron. By nature, he was as aggressively minded as any pilot in the RAF, yet he was prepared to admit, after only a couple of months in command, that he wanted to withdraw his squadron from the front line of action. It took great courage to admit this. One wonders if he was influenced by Buster and Dickie?

The AOC was as good as his word. After some discussion, it was agreed that 141 and 604 Squadrons should exchange places and aircraft. Both were Beaufighter squadrons of Fighter Command but their roles were very different. 604 Squadron was a dayfighter unit based at Predannack in Cornwall, close to Land's End, and its role at that time was to assist Coastal Command in a number of ways. The Battle of the Atlantic had reached its climax and could go either way. Coastal Command patrols over the Bay of Biscay, using long-range aircraft with enhanced sophisticated radar, were causing concern to Admiral Doenitz and his U-boat commanders. A new element had also entered the long drawn out Battle of the Atlantic. Some squadrons of Coastal Command were being fitted with the two million candle-power Leigh Light and after first being guided towards a U-boat by a much improved version of their airborne ASV radar, were turning night into day, leaving the U-boats nowhere to hide.

To counter the growing threat to their U-boats from Coastal Command's day attackers, the Germans had already moved long-range fighters, principally Ju 88s, to airfields on the French Atlantic coast. These were flown against the Sunderlands and other Coastal Command aircraft which were successfully attacking U-boats as they moved to and from their bases in the Bay of Biscay. Coastal Command countered this move by positioning several Beaufighter and Mosquito squadrons at airfields around Cornwall. These patrolled over the Bay on the lookout for the enemy's Ju 88s and twin-engined Messerschmitt fighters which threatened the big Coastal planes now hunting down U-boats with growing success.

At Predannack 141 Squadron would share the airfield facilities with 248 Squadron, a Coastal Command unit equipped with day fighting Beaus. In Cornwall 141 Squadron would primarily concentrate upon building up and perfecting their night fighting techniques, working in conjunction with the local Ground Control stations but using their own aircraft as 'targets'. However, 141 Squadron also found itself being used for a number of daylight operational purposes. It was all good operational experience for the new aircrews.

141 Squadron was soon taking part in the numerous Air Sea Rescue searches that took place whenever Coastal Command aircraft failed to return. On these flights there was sometimes, officially, a third crewman whose role was simply to search for any wreckage or survivors. The squadron pilots, including Bob himself, also made attempts to intercept the daily German Ju 88 meteorological flights. These aircraft were sent out each morning towards Ireland and were tracked by Ground Control radar with such regularity that they came to be dubbed the 'daily milk run'. However, they were difficult to intercept as they were operating beyond the area which could be swept continuously by the local Ground Control radar sets. Yet they constituted a real threat to the Allies as, apart from supplying the Germans with weather data, they also kept an eye open for potential shipping targets for their U-boats.

141 Squadron's move to Predannack was not popular among

the crews. Many of them had been in training for a year or more since first being accepted in their respective Air Forces (some were members of the Royal New Zealand Air Force, the Royal Canadian Air Force and the Royal Australian Air Force) and all were fanatically keen to get at the enemy. To be removed so soon from active night operations in order to undertake operations in what was considered a backwater and endure even more training irked them more than a little.

But by mid-March W/Cdr Braham was satisfied that his squadron was fit to resume an active role. As Predannack was in 10 Group, Fighter Command, Bob Braham had to start afresh to establish good relations with the hierarchy of a new Group HQ. The AOC was absent when Bob took himself to Bath, the site of 10 Group HQ, with his request to resume full-time operations. Instead, W/Cdr Braham was seen by the Deputy AOC, none other than Air Commodore Basil Embry. This officer was one of the most renowned RAF pilots of the entire war and his reputation went before him like a bow wave. Perhaps Bob knew that Basil Embry would be in charge and had deliberately chosen this moment to visit Group HQ. It seems likely, as the two men had much in common and immediately hit it off. If it were possible for anyone to be more determined to defeat Hitler than Bob Braham, then Basil Embry was that person. Stories about him are legion and by the war's end he had been awarded no fewer than *four* DSOs as well as other gallantry medals. When taken prisoner early in the war, he had escaped by strangling one of his guards. As a result there was a price on his head in Germany and an edict which said that never again should he fly over enemy territory: an edict which he got round by flying under a fictitious rank and name! Braham and Embry were to see a lot of each other before the war ended. Both had piercing eyes. Both had an implacable hatred of Nazi Germany; both were fuelled by near inexhaustible energy, and both were inclined to make their own rules.

Bob Braham's proposition was that 141 Squadron should carry out Ranger operations over enemy-held territory within range of Predannack, and that it should also assist Coastal Command patrols over the Bay of Biscay. (A Ranger is an opportunistic operation: a flight simply looking for any likely target to attack.)

All this must have been music to Embry's ears. He readily agreed, his only proviso being that 141's night fighter training should not suffer. Bob assured him it would not.

Since some parts of AI, in all its forms, were still regarded as secret, it was agreed that, when operating over enemy territory, 141 Squadron's Beaus would first have to be stripped of all evidence of this device to prevent it falling into enemy hands. On those nights when the moonlight made identification of ground features possible, the aircraft of 141 Squadron engaged on Ranger operations would simply proceed over north-west France at low level and shoot up enemy targets of opportunity, such as airfields, trains, lorries, and railway stations. The U-boat bases on the French coast were dependent on supplies being brought in by surface transport. Bob's plan was to disrupt that essential link. Railway lines gleam brightly in the moonlight, making them all too obvious to the attackers.

Navigation would be a new problem. On normal night fighting sorties over the UK, the Beaus were under the constant surveillance of friendly Ground Control stations which were always on hand to supply any navigational aid and directions required by the pilots. However, on Ranger sorties over France the aircraft would be beyond the radar range of the UK controllers. The radar operators would now have to act as navigators as well. By 1943, they had become in effect highly trained radar interpreters and were being used for little else, and although some had previously been navigators others had been simply air gunners. It became essential, therefore, to give all of them refresher courses in the art of night navigation over the sea and land. Meanwhile, the squadron waited with mounting excitement for the first good moonlight night.

As might be expected, W/Cdr Braham, with Sgt Blackburn as his navigator, carried out the first of these Ranger operations. By then, Bob and his Intelligence Officer, Buster Reynolds, had become firm friends. This was important as the success of these missions would largely depend on the selection of the most appropriate targets and Buster was in a position to advise on this. With Bob's full encouragement, Buster came along as the third man on the trip, standing behind his CO throughout. This kind of action further fortified the unit's fighting morale. 'If an old man like him, who had not the slightest obligation to risk his neck, or ever leave his office, was prepared to go low flying over enemy territory at night, then others. . . .'

Bob Braham successfully found himself a primary 'target', and attacked an eastbound train in a dive from 1,500 to 500 ft, scoring hits on the engine and leading carriages. The train halted with clouds of smoke and steam pouring from the engine. The train included a flak truck, but despite its fairly accurate fire it failed to score any hits upon the Beau. The date was 20 March 1943. Although this was the squadron's first official Ranger, Bob himself had flown a trial flight of the area around the north-western French coast a week earlier.

Other crews also operated Rangers that same night. Among them was F/O Le Boutte, a quite remarkable Belgian pilot who was considerably older than most operational pilots. Le Boutte had been a senior officer in the Belgian Air Force when his country had been swiftly overrun in 1940. He had been taken prisoner and it took him a year or more to escape and get to England where he was welcomed into the RAF and given a relatively junior rank. F/O Le Boutte was determined to avenge himself upon the Germans who had overrun his homeland and imprisoned him. Apart from his age, flying was made more difficult for him because of his poor eyesight. Unusually for the time, he was allowed to operate wearing glasses but even then some of his landings and ground manoeuvres kept the ground crews on their toes when Le Boutte returned from a flight and parked his Beau at night.

According to Sticks, a number of doubts about such an old and poorly sighted person being allowed to fly on operations were forwarded to the Belgian Air Force authorities in Britain but the answer always came back: 'Le Boutte must continue to fly.' This continued even when he was due a normal operational rest period. As a result, this brave Belgian was not rested operationally for the best part of two years with 141 Squadron. Meanwhile, despite his physical limitations, Le Boutte had acquired a reputation second to none as a train and transport 'buster'. He revelled in it.

Much later in the war, when the Allies were firmly entrenched in Europe, the squadron had moved up to a base in Belgium. Le Boutte was still operating with them as a result of the 'Le Boutte must continue to fly' signals. At the new base, Le Boutte, by then an RAF flight lieutenant, disappeared briefly only to reappear in the uniform of a high-ranking Belgian officer! It transpired, according to Sticks, that he had been sufficiently senior in the BAF that when the signals inquiring about the advisability of his continuing to fly were received, he himself had been able to send back the stock answer 'Le Boutte must continue to fly'. It is fitting that such a gallant pilot should, after the war, have been appointed Chief of the Belgian Air Force with a rank equivalent to that of Air Chief Marshal. His example must have been another morale booster to the others in 141 Squadron: 'If the "Major" [as he was affectionately known] can do it, then so can I.' Le Boutte's wonderful fighting spirit against those who had desecrated his country was matched throughout the Allied Air Forces by numerous brave Frenchmen, Poles, Norwegians, Czechs, Dutchmen and others. None fought with greater determination than those who had managed to escape their conquered homelands and reach the shores of Britain, often after the most hair-raising experiences.

The Braham brand of aggression seems to have rubbed off on many in 141 Squadron, but one squadron leader who didn't match up to Bob's high standards was swiftly posted elsewhere. It was never easy for men older and more senior than the youthful squadron commander, especially those Regular officers who had been trained at Cranwell before the war, to become junior to the likes of W/Cdr J.R.D. Braham. It was not helped by the fact that Bob almost delighted in *not* paying overmuch attention to the Regular and correct way to run a squadron from the confines of a CO's office. Some senior officers could adjust, and accept, his brand of leadership. Others found it all too much to swallow. Resentment tinged with envy was all too common among these older and nominally senior officers. At the time of his appointment as CO, Bob Braham was only a newly promoted flight lieutenant, but with the rank of Acting Wing Commander!

To Bob's delight the replacement for the posted squadron leader was an old friend, Charles Winn. They had first met in 29 Squadron years before and had become firm friends.

In April 1943 an incident took place which clearly demonstrates Bob's aggressive spirit and brand of leadership. It became known that a large merchant ship carrying crucial supplies for the enemy, probably iron ore, was heading from neutral Spain for a French port; it was protected by several destroyers and flak ships. A plan was made for Coastal Command aircraft to attack it with bombs and torpedoes. The Beaufighters of 248 Squadron at Predannack would serve as fighter escorts to the bombers and would also be used to strafe the decks of the escorting ships immediately before the torpedo aircraft attacked at low level. Bob Braham obtained permission for three of his Beaufighters to join in the attack as further fighter protection and strafers.

Much of the plan went awry. The Beaus of 248 and 141 Squadrons never joined up with the torpedo-carrying Hampdens and Wellingtons. As a result, the unescorted attackers scored no hits and at least one was shot down. Bob Braham and his three Beaus also failed to meet up with the five Beaus from 248 Squadron. Bob was, of course, personally leading his small flight and in spite of the failure to link up for a joint attack, W/Cdr Braham pressed on.

The mission, even as planned, was one which was fraught with danger, yet Dougall, the 'Mad Irishman', had decided to accompany Bob as an extra man in his cockpit! In fact it was Dougall who first spotted the smoke of the enemy convoy. By then the bombers and torpedo planes had already made their unsuccessful attacks. This did not deter Bob. He ordered his three Beaus into the attack even though the larger force of five Beaus of 248, with whom Bob was in radio communication, refused to support him in this. Perhaps with some justification, their leader advised Bob that he didn't think it was worth the risk as none of the Beaufighters carried bombs.

In all, the big merchantman was protected by four German destroyers and two torpedo boats, all armed to the teeth with AA guns. The hail of fire which greeted Bob and the other two Beaus as they dived to attack with all guns blazing was truly murderous. By some near miracle, Bob and one other pilot survived although both aircraft were hit. The third Beau was not so fortunate and crashed into the sea with one engine on fire.

Although Bob inflicted some damage on the torpedo boat which he had attacked and at which he had fired over 500 rounds of 20 mm cannon shells causing a large fire aft, the wisdom of attacking such a heavily armed vessel, without attacking the cargo ship, the object of the exercise, must be questionable. Was the loss of one Beaufighter and its crew (and it could well have been more than one) a fair return for the damage inflicted upon the enemy torpedo boat?

The lack of action by the five Beaus of 248 Squadron which circled around during this fierce engagement was definitely *not* appreciated by Bob Braham, nor by others of 141 Squadron. If all eight had attacked simultaneously, the casualties on both sides might well have been more. Perhaps even the vital cargo ship might have been set on fire? Bob was even less pleased when he learned that this very important strike mission had been led by one of 248 Squadron's senior NCO pilots and not by the unit's CO. It is believed that the NCO pilot was soon thereafter posted elsewhere. In *Scramble*, Bob mentions that the CO of 248 was also posted away but a subsequent research in the operational records does not accord with this.

It is also possible that W/Cdr Braham was hauled over the coals for his almost reckless bravery as, some three months before this engagement, Fighter Command had sensibly decreed that the very few successful night fighter pilots should *not* be put at risk unnecessarily on any kind of operation other than night fighting. The instruction is dated 23 January 1943 and reads: 'The AOC has referred to Fighter Command Instruction No. 7/1943 dealing with Ranger Operations and the reasons for the restrictions imposed on Squadron Commanders and the best AI crews. Experience has shown that one good AI crew is capable of bringing down more enemy aircraft at night than the accumulated efforts of a considerable number of mediocre crews. Whenever there is a heavy attack upon the country (at night), it had been found that it is the Cunninghams, Brahams, Peppers and, more recently the Wight-Boycotts who account for the lion's share of enemy casualties.'

On two accounts, therefore, both as one of the 'good AI crews' and as a squadron commander, W/Cdr J.R.D. Braham should not have risked his neck on this dangerous shipping operation, nor should he have embarked on any of the relatively low-casualty Ranger operations. To go ship-busting in the face of such heavily armed escorts was practically an act of open defiance of this particular instruction. Bob could, of course, counter that if one of his superiors such as Basil Embry continued to risk his neck against orders, then why should he not do likewise?

A diversion for Bob came when he was told to go to the Bristol Aircraft and Aero Engine factory in that city and give the workers a pep talk about their fine Beaufighter aircraft and the Bristol engines with which it was powered. Never one to relish the spotlight of publicity, Bob, after a few introductory words, turned to Sticks beside him and ask him to take over. Unprepared, Sticks gave Bob the kind of glare which could have killed, but thereafter did a splendid job and soon had the canteen occupants roaring with laughter at his jokes, many of which were made at Bob's expense. The photograph which shows the pair dressed in their best blue was probably taken at this event.

'Doc' Dougall also relates an amusing account of how Bob and he, during a similar publicity exercise, pulled off a boyish prank. They decided to change roles and while the 'Mad Irishman' shot a terrific line about all the aircraft he had shot down, Bob aired his knowledge of gynaecology! The Mad Irishman seems to have brought out the mischievous side of Bob Braham, whose schoolboy nature was never far from the surface. On another occasion the two of them, with Dickie Sparrowe in tow, were on their way to a village dance which they feared might be rather dull. Consequently, when they espied a horse in a field, Bob and Dougall decided that it would liven things up a bit if they were to arrive at the dance astride the beast. Somehow they succeeded in catching and mounting the poor animal and, with Dickie leading it by a rope, they duly arrived on the dance floor!

The aggressive side of Bob's flamboyant nature took over on one occasion, nearly causing him to carry out a most unworthy action. After two of his Beaus had been shot down on operational patrols over the Bay of Biscay, Bob began to suspect that allegedly neutral Spanish fishing boats had helped in their destruction by reporting their positions to the Ju 88 aircraft responsible for their loss. Quite how this could have been done requires a lot of understanding. Nevertheless Bob, in company with another Beaufighter of his squadron, deliberately set out to wreak revenge on any neutral Spanish fishing boat they might encounter. In due course, the hunters came across a small fleet of them and Bob promptly dived to attack. At low level, when he was about to press the firing button, he caught sight of a small child sunbathing on the prow of the vessel. As the child waved to him the aggression in Bob's soul faded and he hastily pulled away and ordered the other Beau not to attack. The whole episode was a shameful one as, in the first place, Bob had resorted to deception, having for once kept his intentions secret from others in his squadron. Also he was in direct defiance of the Group order that in no circumstances were neutral fishing boats to be attacked. Clearly, if Bob had pressed home his attack, all involved would have been sworn to secrecy. Yet it is typical of Bob's personal honesty that he relates all this in *Scramble*; otherwise it would never have become known.

Bob Braham's aggressive attitude did, however, find a legitimate outlet during a routine patrol over the Bay of Biscay when he sighted a U-boat on the surface. This he blasted with cannon and machine-gun fire during two low-level attacks (again defying Fighter Command's instructions to confine his activities to night fighting). He had the satisfaction of seeing his 20mm cannon shells rupturing one of the enemy's exterior fuel tanks. The oil slick it left behind indicated that the U-boat would probably have to return to port for repairs and refuelling. U-boats were so soundly constructed that the chances of even 20 mm cannon shells inflicting serious damage were slim in the extreme but it seems quite likely that the hail of fire from the Beau might have killed or wounded those of the crew who were exposed in the conning-tower or who were manning the U-boat's own Oerlikon anti-aircraft guns. On another Bay of Biscay patrol Bob came across three motor torpedo E-boats. These were also strafed and hit and would almost certainly have had to return to base for repairs and to disembark casualties.

During a period when Sticks was not available, Bob and the New Zealander Sgt Blackburn developed a good rapport and became an effective team. One of Bob's greatest virtues was his ability to work effectively with almost any radar operator. His hail-fellow-well-met attitude towards those of lesser rank and status must have made it easier for his various radar operators to get on good terms with their ace pilot and squadron commander. Sgt Blackburn proved to be adept with the AI set and was also a good navigator. Bob flew with him on a number of Ranger sorties and was sufficiently impressed to recommend him for a DFM. Sadly, tragedy intervened.

One of the squadron's more senior pilots was an undisciplined Australian who on one occasion incurred the wrath of both Bob and the station commander at Predannack by carrying out a hair-raising beat-up of the airfield at low level. It was so dangerous that Bob had experienced difficulty in persuading the station commander not to instigate court martial proceedings against the Aussie. It was eventually left to Bob to deal with his pilot in his own way. Bob's rather lenient punishment was to give the Australian a severe tongue-lashing. It was not easy for Bob to deal with this miscreant too harshly as he himself had, on an earlier occasion, also beaten up the airfield in one of his more high-spirited moods. The difference was that Bob's beat-up, although daring and low, had been carried out with such sureness and skill that one of the other crewman on board has confirmed that not for a moment did it seem to him to be dangerous.

Despite having been severely warned by his squadron commander never to be so wild and foolish again, on a day when Bob was absent at a Group Conference, the Australian again beat up the airfield; not once but repeatedly, each time getting lower and lower. As seemed inevitable to the watching crowd who had been drawn by the noise, the Beau eventually hit an obstruction with a wing tip and crashed into an aircraft maintenance area where it disintegrated. It could easily have killed a score of airmen in the area but only the two crewmen on board were killed. The radar operator was the able Sgt Blackburn.

Faced with the unenviable and agonizing task of breaking the news to Sgt Blackburn's young widow, Bob attempted to soften the blow by telling her that her late husband had just been recommended for a DFM. The young woman, who already had an inkling of the unnecessary nature of her husband's death, replied bitterly, 'What good will that do him now?'

It was another harrowing scene that probably lingered in Bob's mind long afterwards. It certainly appears in detail in *Scramble*. Buster Reynolds, who came to know Bob perhaps better than any other RAF officer, said that he never saw him more angry. The fact that the incident had taken place behind his back, and that the pilot had been specifically warned made it all the more infuriating. Bob may also have felt twinges of conscience because, having pleaded to be allowed to deal personally with the Australian's first wild beat-up, perhaps he had been too lenient. Perhaps he also felt a sense of shame because he too, before being burdened with the responsibility of commanding a squadron, had committed a similar offence. Years earlier, he had daringly flown low over Blackburn to impress a former girl friend. That the undisciplined Australian had killed the brilliant Sgt Blackburn, whom Bob personally knew and admired, compounded the tragedy.

Only a few days after Bob's attack on the German torpedo boat in the Bay, he was summoned, together with the Intelligence Officer Buster Reynolds, to Fighter Command HQ at Stanmore near Northolt airfield. They flew there in one of the Squadron's Beaus. At Stanmore they met a number of senior officers and some of the leading scientists of the day, including men who were producing more and more electronic and radar devices for the RAF to use against the enemy. Robert Watson-Watt, the father of radar, and the brilliant Sir Henry Tizard, chief government scientific advisor, were the principal innovators in this field but behind them was a growing empire of 'boffins' who had helped develop a number of important military electronic weapons. Many of these 'boffins' were based at the TRE at Malvern.

Even in the squadrons, there were now quite large numbers of official 'Special Signals' personnel. As 'Barny' Barnard, then an AC I Fitter 11E, amusingly relates, with their glasses and scruffy appearance, these characters drove the disciplinarian warrant officers round the bend. However, they were not all like that, as photographs show. All too obviously these specialists, who were largely Canadian, knew little about RAF discipline, and may not have marched a step in their lives, yet as radar specialists they were invaluable. Nor, given the mystery surrounding them and their top secret work, could they even be too closely questioned. Bob would soon get to know these specialists as the object of this particular meeting at Fighter Command HQ was to inform him that 141 Squadron had been selected for a completely new night fighting task.

By April 1943 the massive scale of Bomber Command's night raids on Germany, with as many as a thousand aircraft being sent out on a few occasions, had roused the Luftwaffe to take determined and successful counter-measures. The Germans had by then developed an effective radar-operated warning system and were using this to aid their night fighters. The system was composed of two networks of radar stations situated between the UK and the German cities; the inner network was called the Würzburg control system while the outer radar chain was known as Freya. Together with the Himmelbett systems of guns and searchlights around their north-west coast, the radar system formed an effective defensive system comparable to that which the RAF had established to protect the UK.

The British probably had a small headstart with radar when the war began but the Germans had caught up fast. Also, like the British, they had modified some of their day fighters and faster bombers to act as night fighters. These were also fitted with efficient airborne radar sets, known as Lichtensteins. Thus equipped to counter the RAF's massive bombing raids at night, the enemy had built up a sizeable force of Ju 88 and Me 110 night fighters which were shooting down the RAF's Halifaxes, Stirlings, Lancasters and Wellingtons in increasing numbers. They were even starting to use their best and latest day fighters, the Me 109Fs and Fw 190s, at night, on freelance or 'Wild Sow' operations, although these aircraft lacked the latest radar devices and the range required for the job. To make their larger night fighters even more deadly, the Germans also developed an upwards-firing gun. This weapon, which they called *Schrage Musik* ('Slanting Music') was a 20mm cannon which fired upwards at an angle of 70 degrees. This proved to be deadly against our night bombers which had no guns positioned to fire at an aircraft flying almost directly beneath them. On some nights fifty or more RAF heavy bombers were lost, each with a crew of about six men.

The backroom boffins in the UK were continuously working on this kind of problem and liaison between the scientists and the RAF throughout the war was excellent. Men like Professor Jones and Sir Henry Tizard spent their time working out what the enemy scientists were doing and then devising counter-measures. For example, the frequencies of the radars used by enemy night fighters had been correctly ascertained by various means. The RAF countered this by sending over night fighters equipped with a device that enabled them to home in on to the radar transmissions of the German night fighters. The device produced by our scientists could not yet indicate the range between the two night fighters, only the direction of the enemy planes. It was at this stage of development when Bob Braham, whose enthusiasm and drive had by then become almost legendary in Fighter Command, was selected to try out this new device with 141 Squadron.

In one way, 141 Squadron was the natural choice. Having been pulled out of the front line at Bob's request to sharpen up its techniques in Cornwall, and due to Bob's subsequent idea of allowing his crews to go on Ranger operations over France at night, the crews of 141 had been obliged to learn, or relearn, the difficult art of night navigation. Other night fighting units had no reason to do this as they still relied on Ground Control to direct them to their targets and then get them home again. On future flights over Germany searching for night-fighters to attack, 141 Squadron crews would be far beyond the range at which they could be picked up on home radar ground stations.

Self-navigation was a vital requirement for this new tactic. The new device on board, yet another technique for the crews to master, was code-named Serrate because for some technical reason the edges of this particular radar screen appeared ragged, or serrated. As Serrate could only detect the direction of the enemy, it was also necessary for the Beaufighters to use some form of AI. The idea was that the initial contact would be made by Serrate but as the Beau homed in on the enemy night fighter, it would then come within AI range and the chase could continue, guided by the Beau's AI set in the normal manner.

However, the AI requirement posed a problem. Until the decision was taken to experiment with Serrate, the policy had been that no RAF aircraft fitted with AI should cross into enemy-held territory. The frequency and details of our airborne radar were still regarded as a secret which the enemy should not learn. Curiously, BOTH sides considered their radar devices to be secret although by 1943 both sides knew practically everything that there was to know about the other! A compromise was reached. The night fighters of 141 Squadron armed with Serrate would be allowed to carry on board the earlier Mark IV AI, but not the more advanced and more effective Mark VII, nor the subsequent versions about to be introduced.

W/Cdr Braham's 141 Squadron was detailed to leave Predannack and move to Wittering, nearer the North Sea, at the end of the month. Here, once all their new Mark VI Beaufighters had been equipped with Serrate and the Mark IV AI, they would begin practising for their future role. Their orders were to fly over those parts of Germany which came within their limited range, mixing with the RAF's Main Force bombers; once they had detected the Lichtenstein radar transmissions emitted by a German night fighter they were to home in on these until the enemy also appeared on their AI screens; finally they were to close to within visual range and destroy the enemy night fighters which were causing such heavy losses to Bomber Command. This was, incidentally, only one of the measures the RAF was taking to curb their heavy losses in a situation which was becoming critical. Losses of fifty or more bombers at a time HAD to be stopped somehow.

Night navigation over blacked-out enemy territory was never easy. Bomber Command had found that, even with experienced navigators who had been carefully trained to concentrate solely on that one task, accuracy could not be assured. Accordingly, it was decided that in addition to everything else on board, the 141 Squadron Beaus engaged upon Serrate operations would also be equipped with the latest parabolic electronic navigational aid, code-named 'Gee', which was another semi-secret device. It all added up to a daunting task but HQ Fighter command knew their man. If anyone could make this cocktail of devices a success, then surely it had to be Bob Braham, aided by his faithful and efficient radar operator, Sticks Gregory. History had shown that if just one crew could make a sophisticated system work, then in due course others would eventually learn to do likewise. As with the much simpler form of radar-controlled night fighting over Britain, only a few combinations of pilots and radar operators had really mastered the ability to track down and destroy enemy aircraft. So it would be with Serrate.

The radar operator's seat in the back of the Beau was now hemmed in with an array of electronic gadgets. Clearly the RO was going to be very busy on future operations with 141 Squadron. Clearly also the German night fighters would no longer enjoy such easy pickings. In attempts to make life difficult for them, a whole array of counter-tactics were being deployed by 1942/43. Mosquito Intruders were sent to circle around the known German airfields at night in order to attack them as they took off and returned. Elaborate 'spoof' raids were carried out alongside the real Main Force bomber stream to lure the enemy night fighters towards the wrong areas. 'Window' was dropped in vast quantities; these foil strips cluttered up the Würzburg screens of the ground radar stations and rendered them less intelligible. Aircraft sent over Germany with radar-jamming devices further complicated their radar system. RAF planes flying with the main bomber force would begin carrying German-speaking radio operators who would issue phoney R/T instructions to the crews of their night fighters. A whole host of subterfuge and counter-measures were being employed, or were in the pipeline, at the time when Bob Braham and 141 Squadron under his highly motivated personal leadership entered the fray.

Could Fighter Command reduce the heavy losses of Bomber Command? Would Serrate work? Only time and Bob Braham could tell, but clearly it was never going to be easy.

12
Bomber Support

It took several weeks of preparation before Bob Braham and 141 Squadron could initiate any new stratagem. For most people the task of learning the new tactics would have been challenge enough, but not for Bob. As Buster and others have confirmed, Bob would sometimes feel so frustrated at his relative inactivity that he would, on the spur of the moment, hail some unfortunate fellow – often Buster himself – into his office for a few rounds of fisticuffs! Provided with boxing gloves, the unfortunate victim would become the outlet for the CO's surplus aggression. But it was not done to hurt: Bob was much bigger than most, including Buster, and it was simply his way of letting off steam. Sometimes he would engage others in wrestling bouts. The last few days of April 1943 saw Bob visiting both Group and Fighter Command HQs to discuss the new tactics, and it was during one of these absences that Sgt Blackburn had been so unnecessarily killed. The day after this tragedy, the groundcrews of 141 Squadron left Predannack for Wittering in Lincolnshire. The aircrews followed later, flying up in their Beaus. A rear party, flown up in Handley Page Harrows, completed the move.

Wittering was a pleasant pre-war RAF station with solidly constructed hangars, brickbuilt quarters and a well drained landing area. This was a welcome change for RAF personnel who had come to expect Nissan huts, hastily prepared airfields and very basic hangars, all temporary buildings set down in what invariably became a sea of mud and often miles from anywhere in a bleak and desolate countryside.

141 Squadron was also equipped with new Mark VI NF Beaufighters. Both Gee and Serrate were then added, the latter at Defford. At one point a couple of aircraft were also fitted with bomb racks but this idea was soon dropped. During May a few normal night operations were carried out against enemy raiders over Britain but the crews spent much of the month making themselves familiar with their new aircraft and equipment. Each aircraft had to be flown to wherever the latest gadget or device was to be added. Once the aircraft were modified, the aircrews then had to spend as much time as possible in getting acquainted with the latest 'toys' that the boffins had devised for them. Flying training was largely carried out at Drem in Scotland. Serrate was top secret and in the remoteness of Drem there seemed little chance of the enemy getting even an inkling of what was about to threaten their night fighter crews.

For the first time, an aircraft was fitted with a device which would enable the crew at night to pick up, and home in on, the radar transmissions sent out by an enemy aircraft. Yet such was the pace of development on both sides that, within a year or so, this would become the pattern for most aerial night warfare with counter-counter electronic devices being added to aircraft to such an extent that some began to resemble Christmas trees, so overloaded were they with external aerials mounted on top, in front, on the sides and even protruding from the rear. Every additional aerial increased drag, reduced performance and was apt to ice up in cloud, further reducing performance.

Apart from being extremely busy in the air on training details and in organizing the many changes, Bob himself was in constant demand at various HQs for conferences as new problems arose and novel tactics had to be worked out. He also had the additional anxiety that Joan was about to bear him a second child: another fine son. Consequently he also managed to squeeze in a few brief visits to Desford, the RAF airfield closest to Leicester where Joan now lived with her parents.

A few Ranger operations carried out by 141 Squadron took

the crews over Germany for the first time and doubtless constituted good navigational practice for the crews involved.

At several of the conferences at HQs, Bob took his old friend S/Ldr Charles Winn with him. Buster Reynolds and Sticks Gregory also often attended. W/Cdr Braham had, by then, built around him a close-knit team of friends and experts. Dickie Sparrowe, his adjutant, was another who belonged to this elite group. By then Bob had rid the squadron of anyone that he felt fell short of his exceptionally high standards. His team could now cope efficiently whether Bob himself was there or not. Dickie was often left 'in charge of the shop' while the others were away. Bob as usual does not seem to have taken any leave although he must have been overdue large amounts.

For the forthcoming operations over Germany, the limited range of the Beaufighters meant that they needed to be based at an airfield as close as possible to the German frontier. The Beaufighter had never had a vast range and the Mark VI, thus modified with all the additional equipment, seems to have had even less endurance than the earlier basic night fighter versions. As a result, crews briefed to go on future Serrate operations would first need to fly to airfields such as Ford in Sussex, Bradwell Bay in Essex, West Malling in Kent or, most frequently, to Coltishall near Norwich. A few armourers, refuellers and radar/radio specialists would be sent to these airfields (which varied according to the targets Bomber Command intended to attack) where they might stay for a few days on detachment in order to be on the spot to deal with last minute adjustments or to fix technical faults not encountered by more normally equipped aircraft.

On 14 June, some six weeks after 141 Squadron had moved away from Predannack, W/Cdr J.R.D. Braham DSO, DFC and Bar, leading as ever from the front, carried out the first Serrate operation. True to form, he also shot down an enemy night fighter, an Me 110. It was his fourteenth confirmed victory in the air. It is not clear to what extent the Serrate device contributed to this success. The chances are that it did so and in *Scramble* Bob implies as much, but such was the secrecy surrounding the whole project that there is not the slightest hint of its even being on board either in the official squadron records or in those at Group HQ. No mention of the device appears anywhere for many months.

Bob was not the only pilot of his squadron to operate that night on Serrate sorties. Others also participated in this new form of aerial warfare but Bob was the only one to be successful. He was patrolling at about 10,000 ft in an area where it was known that the Germans had a number of night fighter airfields which would probably be active that night. Sticks was with him (who else?) and was somehow able to report to Bob that their aircraft was being *followed* by an enemy night fighter. The most likely explanation is that, although the Serrate transmissions were designed to be emitted forwards, a smaller, but largely unplanned, stream of electronic pulses was also emitted rearwards. It is possible, but most unlikely, that Sticks had visually sighted an enemy aircraft behind them – unlikely because his many duties required that he would have to spend most of the trip with his face glued to the visor of one 'magic box' or another; also unlikely because with the sky full of RAF bombers he would not have been able to identify visually a following aircraft as unfriendly unless warned of its presence by the Serrate 'black box' on board. In the bright moonlight, Bob responded quickly. He swiftly turned his aircraft through 360 degrees so that he was now following the enemy. A dog-fight ensued, with Bob handling the big Beau almost as if it were a Spitfire. Before long he was able to get the enemy aircraft, which he identified as an Me 110, into a position from which he was able to apply some excellent deflection shooting from a lethal range of only 200 yards. The long burst from all ten guns was decisive. A hail of incendiary and semi armour-piercing bullets and shells raked the enemy from cockpit to tail.

The Me 110, never a type to take heavy punishment well, caught fire and dived almost vertically downwards, crashing north of Staveren, Holland. Bob had used about 300 rounds of cannon fire and over 500 .303 bullets. No return fire was observed. A German night fighter, accustomed to picking off the relatively slow and vulnerable four-engined heavy bombers of the RAF with comparative ease, had met its match. It was an historic event as it had occurred over enemy territory. Henceforth the Ju 88s and Me 110s, which formed the bulk of the Luftwaffe's radar-equipped night fighter force, would have to face a new deadly menace. From that moment onwards, the life of their crews would become increasingly uncomfortable. They already faced intruder Mosquitoes which waited around their bases to pick them off when taking off or landing; now they faced a threat in the upper air. By coincidence, the next day, a second bar to his DFC was awarded to W/Cdr Braham, although the previous night's victory had nothing to do with this very rare honour.*

An idea of the time lapse between deed and a normal gallantry award can be gained from the fact that Bob's latest citation refers to his having destroyed only eleven enemy aircraft. Even before taking off on the Serrate operation, Bob had officially destroyed thirteen for certain. In other respects the citation sums up Bob's efforts and personality well. Part of it reads: 'This officer is a fearless and determined leader whose qualities have inspired the Squadron he commands . . . . his most recent achievements include an attack on a U-boat and on a motor torpedo boat which was set on fire. His fine fighting spirit and keenness have set a praiseworthy example.' Why the citation should mention the attacks on the U-boat and the torpedo boat, events which happened well after his thirteenth confirmed victory, and yet refers to only eleven

---

* All awards had to observe a chain of recommendations before being announced. Even with the so-called 'Immediate Awards', it still took a number of days before confirmation could be announced. 'Immediate Awards' were not always popular, as the general belief was that they were only given in circumstances where the prospect of the recipient remaining alive for long enough to recieve a normal award was regarded as slight!

victories cannot be satisfactorily explained, except to comment that during the war the Royal Air Force was far more concerned with getting to grips with the enemy than with keeping accurate records.

By now, between them, Braham and Gregory had already been awarded one DSO, four DFCs and a DFM. Only two nights later, they struck again. Once again they were on patrol over Germany in the vicinity of airfields from which German night fighters could be expected to be operating against Bomber Command's Main Force. In the bright moonlight, Bob caught sight of a Ju 88 night fighter. He was flying at 22,000 ft with heavy clouds below. The Beaufighter closed to within about 350 yards before opening fire. Strikes were observed on the enemy's port wing but before the action could be brought to a conclusion, all the guns of the Beau jammed. The Ju 88 did not take any avoiding action and no return fire was perceived. It was, in Bob's opinion, a 'sitting duck' and he was confident that, but for the failure of his guns, he would surely have recorded his fifteenth victory. However, as it was, and with the clouds preventing visual proof of a kill, all he could reasonably claim was that the Junkers had been 'Damaged'.

As might have been expected at that height, where the temperature would have been something like minus 40 or 50 degrees C, the official explanation for gun failures was that icing had caused the oil in the firing mechanism to freeze, and not for the first time either. To overcome earlier failures of this kind, special light oils had been used but, in extreme cases, the problem still existed.

Another 141 pilot, F/O MacAndrews, had almost the same experience on the same night. He, too, got his aircraft into an excellent position where it seemed that a long sustained burst would account for the Me 110 night fighter which he had tracked down, but when he started firing all his guns jammed. MacAndrews probably inflicted considerable damage on the Me 110 as he had observed bits flying off his foe. Also the Me 110 was not as stoutly built as the formidable Ju 88. Yet all that F/O MacAndrews could claim was another 'Damaged'.

(MacAndrews, incidentally, was the pilot of the second Beau which survived the near suicidal attack upon the convoy in the Bay of Biscay on 10 April.)

Again, there is nothing in the official records to indicate that Serrate played any part in either of these two attacks nor in any other attacks made by aircraft of 141 Squadron over German-held territory in June 1943. The device was still heavily protected by secrecy and even the HQ combat records keep silent on this matter. Such reports would need to have been typed by low-ranking staff, probably WAAFs, who probably did not have the necessary high level security clearance. On the other hand, using only Mark IV AI, the crews would have to have been very lucky to locate the fast German night fighters without such initial assistance. During the German raids over Britain at night, it was extremely rare for an RAF night fighter, even one equipped with the latest version of AI, to be able to track down even the relatively slow enemy bombers without first being directed towards them by a Ground Control radar station. Serrate in all probability was proving itself a success and Fighter Command had acted wisely in choosing 141 Squadron as the means of proving this new device.

In all, during the last sixteen days of June, crews of 141 Squadron scored five confirmed victories. They could also claim two more as 'Damaged'. Other German night fighters were followed and chased but without hits being registered. Apart from Bob's own score of two confirmed and one damaged, the team of F/O Kelsey and Sgt Smith scored two confirmed victories, and Charles Winn and F/O Scott registered the other success.

Bob's second kill that month well demonstrates his quite exceptional determination to get to grips with the enemy. Few, if any, COs of any squadrons could have flown more during one month. His personal log-book shows that on average he made between two and three flights each *day*, many of them at night. Not all were operational. Some were designated as 'practice' flights, while others were visits to Group or Command HQs. Some were to Drem, others to Desford either for Serrate fitments or to spend a few brief hours with Joan. However, most flights in the latter part of the month were mainly in deadly earnest: night operations over Germany.

These Serrate operations were demanding in every sense. They first required the usual night flying test at Wittering, then an evening flight to whichever airfield had been chosen as a suitable departure point, followed by the long night excursion over enemy territory, ending with a return at around dawn either to Wittering, if that could be reached direct, or else to an airfield nearer the British coast. Return to base was followed by debriefing, and during operations Bob could not have got to bed until well after dawn, yet he still had the squadron to run and was always on call to attend high level conferences. For example, on the night of 19/20 June he flew a Serrate sortie; this required the customary air test at Wittering prior to departure for Ford in Sussex. On the 20th, he squeezed in a flying visit to Joan at Desford and briefly saw his two sons. On the night of 21/22 June he again operated over Germany, this time departing from Coltishall. On this night Charles Winn scored his success. On the next two nights Bob again operated from Coltishall. It is not too surprising that Bob Braham gave himself a day off flying on the following day but doubtless he spent much of the day in the office catching up with the mounds of paperwork which management of the squadron routinely required. In all the CO had flown on twelve separate occasions during the previous four days!

The flight on the night of 24/25 June had come about because Charles Winn's Beau had suffered a burst tyre on take-off. Although Charles got the aircraft down with no further damage – no easy task – it could not be repaired in time for him to operate. Accordingly, Bob and Sticks rushed to Coltishall in time to take part in the operation. Bob's keenness was rewarded. By the time he had completed the operation he had scored his fifteenth certain air victory.

The details of this typical success make interesting reading. Once airborne, Sticks would have to navigate accurately in the dark to the area where he and his pilot were most likely to find marauding enemy night fighters. This involved passing through the formidable searchlight and AA zones which constituted Germany's outer protection. Eventually the Beau reached Gilze, a well-known night fighter airfield. Its flare path was illuminated initially but when the presence of the Beau was detected, this was switched off and a realistic dummy flare path was illuminated nearby. The Germans had by then brought the art of creating dummy airfields and flare paths to a fine pitch, and with excellent results. Ignoring the dummy flare path, Bob continued to patrol above the area. In any case, it was not his brief to fly low and attack the enemy while they were taking off and landing. That was the job of the Mosquitoes and other Intruder aircraft.

While patrolling the area, Bob soon caught sight of the twin exhaust flames from an aircraft well below his height. He was about to investigate this when Sticks drew his attention to an Me 110 which was following them at their height of about 12,000 ft. This, he advised Bob, was closing on them. In all probability, Sticks had deduced this from the blips appearing on the Serrate and/or AI screen. Although rearward detection of enemy radar-equipped aircraft was not the main purpose of the Serrate apparatus, it seems, in skilled hands, to have been of considerable use. Bob again used the tactics which had been successful a few nights before. He allowed the pursuing plane to get almost within its firing range, then he swiftly turned through a complete circle so that their positions were reversed. Now he had the Me where he wanted it, and Sticks could track its movements closely on the aircraft's AI. At a range of 600 yards and closing, Bob opened fire and within seconds the doomed enemy plane was a mass of flames. As it dived vertically to destruction, Bob followed it, giving it another burst, as he mentions in his report, 'for good measure'.

After the attack, Bob wondered if the first aircraft he had seen, the one so blatantly giving away its presence by exhaust flames, had been a decoy. The tactic of using decoy aircraft was known to have been used by the Luftwaffe's day fighters and perhaps was now also being employed at night. On the other hand, it must still have been a surprise for the Germans to encounter RAF night fighters over Germany and it seems doubtful that the enemy had yet become fully aware of this new menace, nor had they had time to work out counter-tactics. More probably, the Luftwaffe felt relatively secure over their own territory at night, *vide* the genuine flare path at first so clearly visible at Gilze.

Before the Me 110 plunged into the ground, Sticks and Bob had both observed bits flying off it. These did not, in this instance, strike the pursuing Beau but many aircraft had been and were still being severely damaged by flying fragments of the enemy. Bob and Sticks had enough fuel left to return to Wittering, but by then it was past three in the morning and there would have been the usual comprehensive debriefing formalities before their night's work was finished. It was quite an eventful 'night off' for Wing Commander J.R.D. Braham and his regular radar operator!

Aircraft being damaged by bits flying off the enemy was but one of many dangers and difficulties that night fighter pilots had to overcome. Others were:

• During take-off
Tyre bursts; engine failure; swing off flare path; attacks by enemy intruding night fighters. These attacks could result in the sudden dousing of the flare path.
• En Route
Radio failure; Serrate failure; AI failure; 'Gee' failure; general lighting failure; difficulties of blind flying by instruments; navigation over the sea and over blacked-out countryside on both sides of the North Sea/Channel; mechanical failure; detection by the enemy's advanced radar chain (Freya) and home radar chain (Würzburg); detection by enemy searchlights; intercom failure between pilot and radar operator.
• In Cloud
Carburettor ice; wing and airframe ice; propeller ice; windscreen ice; ice build-up on additional aerials; turbulence due to cumulo-nimbus clouds and other atmospheric disturbances.

- **At Height**

Oxygen failure; extreme cold; oil in guns freezing; lightning strikes.

- **Combat**

Guns jamming due to cold or incorrect loading causing explosions in breech; enemy firing first; slip-stream of enemy immediately in front; decoy tactics of enemy; being shot at by RAF bombers; being attacked by fellow night fighters; difficulty of correct identification of aircraft being chased.

- **Over Enemy Territory**

Searchlights; AA gunfire; enemy night fighters; misleading information from enemy dummy airfields, etc.

- **Return Flight**

Shortage of fuel; bad weather at base; being fired upon by 'friendly' AA guns, ships or night fighters (due to IFF failure); widespread fog over UK; flap, undercarriage or other mechanical failure; attack by enemy intruder aircraft; sudden dousing of flare path due to detected presence of intruder aircraft.

- **Throughout**

'Sir Isaac' was always waiting. A Beaufighter flying slower than about 100 mph (and at much higher speeds during certain manoeuvres) could, literally, fall out of the sky.

These were some of the many reasons why only a few Serrate operations resulted in the aircrews returning triumphant and why losses NOT to the enemy were so frequent.

It helped that by 1943 nearly all RAF bombers were four-engined types but even here, care with identification 'Friend or Foe' had to be taken as twin-engined Wellingtons were still operational. *Most* twin-engined aircraft visually seen by the Beaufighter crews at night were enemy planes – but not all. On the AI screens there was nothing to indicate how many engines a plane might have. Visual identification was always essential, even over Germany.

As already mentioned, Bob Braham rarely, if ever, took the leave entitlements that all aircrew were generously allowed. However, there was an occasion that summer when he decided to take advantage of an unusual offer. He had detected in himself signs of stress, even becoming short-tempered with his children on the few occasions when he found time to be with them. He was perceptive enough to realize that he needed a break. He could have taken a week or two of leave but, devoted as he was to the challenge to get 141 Squadron into top line shape, he had found that, when with Joan and his sons, even for a short period, his conscience nagged at him. At the back of his mind, he wanted to be back in the thick of the fray. He felt he was needed there. He felt a sense of guilt whenever he was elsewhere, and worried that he might be missing something vital.

The opportunity for a break came when the Royal Navy let it be known that they would welcome a couple of RAF officers on board for a short trip up the east coast in a destroyer which was part of a convoy escort. The journey was to take only a few days and Bob decided to go himself, taking Buster with him as he reckoned that his loyal IO was also due a short break. According to Buster, Bob was soon in and out of every activity on board. He was given the run of the ship and was helpful to the crew, supplying much-needed aircraft recognition. This was important – nearly all Allied aircrews believed that it was the Navy's policy always to shoot first and ask questions later!

Curiously, Bob remarked upon the youth and lowly rank of the naval lieutenant who was the destroyer's captain. What the naval personnel thought of the 22-year-old CO of an important RAF squadron with three broad stripes on his sleeve is not recorded! That Bob's behaviour was generally more akin to that of a boisterous university student than that of a conventional Regular commanding officer might also have surprised the navy personnel.

Although Bob seems to have been actively engaged throughout the voyage and did not let the side down by being seasick, he declared upon his return from the voyage, from Harwich to the Firth of Forth and back, that his few days aboard HMS *Whitshed* had benefited him enormously. He returned to his many responsibilities feeling a 'new man', and with an enhanced respect for the sister Service. It would seem that Bob's nature could instantly enable him to switch on to, or switch off from, his arduous tasks and allowed him to benefit greatly from an occasional change of scene and tempo. Such people are often blessed with the ability, no matter what strains are being imposed, to drop off to sleep the moment the tired head hits the pillow. Not, of course, that Bob allowed himself much time for sleep.

Whatever drove him forwards, his determination to turn 141 Squadron into the finest fighting unit of Fighter Command never flagged. Nothing seems to have dampened his enthusiasm, not even the shortage of sleep which he must have suffered once nightly operations over Germany commenced, despite his many roles, both as a leading player and as principal director and stage manager.

Paradoxically, although he did not have the many extra responsibilities or demands upon his time as Bob did, it was Sticks Gregory who first began to tire. Bob, typically, blames himself for not having detected earlier the signs of operational fatigue which now hit Sticks. Doc Dougall took a hand with Sticks, as he had done with others in the hard-working unit. He was an advocate of allowing aircrews as much rest and leave as possible. Consequently, when Sticks fell ill Bob forcibly grounded his companion in arms despite Sticks's violent protestations. However, he softened the blow by sensibly appointing F/Lt Gregory, an acknowledged navigational expert, to an important ground position as the squadron's Navigation Officer.

Sticks's enforced grounding left Bob without a regular crewman and at Sticks's suggestion Bob tried to get Jacko to join the squadron in his place as Bob lacked the time to start training up a new man. Jacko was still at the OTU at Cranfield but it took only a phone call to 12 Group HQ to arrange for him to abandon his instructing and to join Bob and 141 Squadron for a spell of the 'real thing'. Within days F/Lt Gregory DFC, DFM had been replaced by F/Lt Jacobs DFC.

Before this happened, Bob and Sticks had scored another success and had also been engaged in another very close call. The latter took place on the night of 28 June. Bob appears to have taken along a passenger, S/Ldr Hobhouse, for this operation. As usual by then, the night fighters of 141 Squadron were operating alongside the main bomber stream and on this occasion, having departed from Coltishall, Bob was patrolling at 18,000 ft in the vicinity of Venlo, an enemy night fighter airfield in Holland. He must have been tracked on German radar as the Beau was suddenly attacked by two Ju 88s acting together, one in front and one behind. The rear gunner of the enemy ahead of him gave a number of short bursts of fire, using red tracer bullets, commencing at about 1,000 yd range; he kept firing until the Beau, which was travelling considerably faster than the Junkers, passed underneath it. Bob's aircraft was hit on the port wing and the engine on that side burst into flames, which continued for some minutes. However, with the fuel to the engine switched off, the flames subsided. Bob, now flying on only one engine, took violent avoiding action and dived hard for the clouds, eventually reaching them and escaping from the enemy aircraft. He was able, with difficulty, to nurse his damaged Beau back to Wittering where he landed safely with the one good engine.

The German pilot probably believed that he had shot down the marauding Beau, and no doubt it was recorded by the enemy as a 'kill'. This example illustrated the soundness of the RAF's policy of not allowing its pilots to claim kills in similar circumstances.

This event may be the one recalled by Sticks who relates that on one occasion on an operation with a passenger on board, their aircraft was badly shot up and that Bob only saved the day by taking extremely violent avoiding action. So busy were both Bob and Sticks thereafter that both entirely forgot that there was an extra man on board until they got back to base when, to their surprise, when the hatches were opened at dispersal, an apparently dead body fell out of the plane! First aid was applied and the 'corpse' revived. Having neither seat nor straps, the passenger, who had probably also been affected by lack of oxygen, had been so hurled around the spacious Beaufighter cockpit that he had been knocked unconscious by a number of hefty blows and had not regained consciousness. His silence during the return flight had caused both Bob and Sticks, who had their hands full in coping with the emergency, to forget that they had a third man on board. The punchline of Sticks's story is that when the 'corpse' did revive, the battered officer (Sticks thought that he may have been an Army officer and that he had suffered a broken arm and a broken leg) was so confused that all he could do for quite some while was to mutter over and over again his name, rank and number! In his confusion, all he could think was that the plane had crashed in Germany and that he was now a prisoner of war. Like a dutiful officer, he had learned how to conduct himself correctly as a prisoner!

This kind of 'shaky do', to use the parlance of the day, may have contributed to Sticks's subsequent bout of operational fatigue. However, this one incident did not immediately deter him. By then Sticks had also been awarded a bar to his DFC. This was his third gallantry medal and it was quite likely, at that stage of the war that Sticks was the first non-pilot to have been decorated with a DFC and Bar as well as the DFM.

Bob's sixteenth victory, again flying with Sticks, occurred on another Serrate operation on 9 August. This time they had taken off from Bradwell Bay. They were circling around the German night fighter base at St Trond, Belgium, at 12,000 ft. Eventually, probably with the aid of the electronic devices which the Beau carried, they got on the trail of an unidentified aircraft. However, their supposed quarry was evidently being warned of their presence by enemy radar controllers. It was turning and manoeuvring and trying to get into a shooting position behind Bob's Beau. Whether either could see the other visually, or whether this dog-fight was being carried out purely by electronic gadgets on both sides, is not clear. After many minutes of this unusual night contest, Bob was able to identify his foe as an Me 110. This type was designed as a long-range twin-engined day fighter. It was smaller than a Beau and probably both faster and more manoeuvrable.

As it turned sharply to starboard, Bob was able to turn his Beau inside it and get his aircraft into a deflection shooting position. Two bursts of cannon and machine-gun fire from close quarters were sufficient as by then Bob's deflection shooting was very accurate. The Me 110 was hit several times; it dived, hit the ground and burst into flames. Both Bob and Sticks were able to see the conflagration for the next five or ten minutes. Another aircraft, presumably an enemy one, seemed to mark the place with a flare fired in the air. The 141 Squadron crew of F/O Thornton and W/O Mallett, also on a Serrate sortie, saw both the flare and the burning Messerschmitt on the ground. Bob's own comment in his pilot's log-book refers to: 'very exciting trip, 25 minute dog fight with 1 Me 110. One long burst not far from Liege.' It was his third flight of the night and it was not until nearly four in the morning that he and Sticks got their aircraft back to Wittering, having first had to land at Bradwell Bay to refuel. On the way back to the UK they experienced heavy flak and had been caught in enemy searchlights before reaching the North Sea.

Of the seven other 141 crews which had departed that night, each covering a specific area in the vicinity of an airfield, two had to return because of 'radio trouble' and another had a hatch cover blown off. One did chase an enemy plane for a short while but without success. Difficulties for the squadron were ever present. 'Radio trouble' may well have been an euphemism, no mention of AI or Serrate, or possibly even 'Gee', being then permitted. With several new devices on board, many of which were still suffering teething troubles, many sorties were aborted when one or more of these devices failed.

Their success on 9 August was to be the last for many a month for the experienced duo of Braham and Gregory due to the latter's enforced operational rest. However, for Bob it was soon business as usual. Within two days his log-book shows he had made one night flight on the 11th, three on the 12th and one each on the 13th and 14th, all with F/Lt Jacobs seated behind him to replace the grounded Sticks. A new night fighting Serrate team was about to go into action.

Before recording the successes of this Braham/Jacobs team, mention must be made of the dedicated work of the ground crews who serviced the aircraft with which the aircrews destroyed the enemy. Many of the so-called 'erks' had originally applied for aircrew training but had been rejected, mainly for medical reasons such as colour blindness or traces of sugar in their urine. For these and their colleagues who had not even tried to become aircrew, the war became real and personal when they were able to fight their war mentally through the exploits of the aircraft they serviced and which 'their' pilots flew. A success in the air was 'their' success, just as much as if they had been on board. When a plane returned from operations, the groundcrews always looked first at the wings which contained the guns. The gun ports were normally covered over with fabric and if that fabric had been ruptured, it meant that the guns had been fired. 'Their' plane had been in action. When they clambered up on the wing to help release the crew, the first question was usually 'How did it go?' If the answer was that another enemy had been destroyed, the elation all round would be as genuine among the groundcrew as among the successful aircrew. 'They' had done it again.

With this kind of personal involvement, no effort was spared to ensure that 'their' aircrews flew well-prepared aircraft. The groundcrews never received the extra bacon and eggs that was the standard meal before every operational sortie for the air crews. The ground crews never received the gallantry medals and the public acclaim. They just soldiered on, working in exposed positions in all kinds of weather and at all hours, vulnerable both to the elements and to enemy intruders.

The continued success of the RAF throughout the war owed much to the groundcrews who made it all possible and those officers, such as Bob Braham, who readily made friends with them seemed to make all their privations worth while. They were heartened both by his genial manner and especially by the successes which he brought them. One of Bob Braham's greatest assets was that he treated everyone as equals. It paid handsome dividends too. As 'Barny' Barnard, an AC 1 Fitter 11E, so ably put it : 'Braham was something of a playboy but very popular among the ground crews; perhaps something of a medal collector but none the less useful for that. . . . a great cheer went up among the groundcrews when Braham took the lead [over Cunningham] in night kills.' But perhaps Arthur Smith, another humble 'erk', puts it most succinctly when he writes 'he was always one of the lads'.

Bob Braham seems to have suffered fewer radio and mechanical failures in the air than most did, perhaps because his groundcrew tried that little bit harder for him in return for his consideration towards them. It is appropriate to let Don Aris, who has contributed so very much towards this book in one way and another, have the last word on this subject. He wrote that, as an armourer, he 'serviced the armament of W/Cdr Bob Braham's aircraft for this action [Bob's sixteenth success]. This was not the first time. To arm, service and re-arm aircraft that had destroyed one of the enemy, gave a great feeling of participation in the action . . . albeit without the dangers of the aircrew.'

141 Squadron was growing in strength and confidence. Now, whenever Bomber Command launched a major offensive, their Beaufighters might operate from two or more different airfields close to the North Sea and/or the English Channel. Some would go in one direction, others in another. On the night of 15 August, the squadron put up eight aircraft, all operating from Ford, Sussex. On the following night another seven patrolled around the Paris area. The 15th was a typical night: Charles Winn was badly shot up by the rear gunner of an RAF Wellington but managed to get back safely for a belly landing as both his flaps and undercarriage had been put out of action. F/Lt Le Boutte, the gallant Belgian, was chased by an unidentified aircraft. F/Sgt Rolfe and F/O White and their respective radar operators both had to return early with so-called 'radio' failures. F/Sgt Gregory (no relation to Sticks)

and his crew were picked up by enemy searchlights and shot at. F/Lt Ferguson tangled with both a friendly Mosquito and some of our own AA fire, while F/Sgt Robertson's Beau simply failed to return. It was never plain sailing for 141 Squadron. ('Robbie' Robertson and his RO 'Douggie' Gilliam had attacked an He 177. Return fire hit the Beau and the aircraft caught fire. Both men bailed out and became POWs. Robertson had bullet wounds in his arm and suffered a broken leg.)

On the following night, Bob himself was first off as usual. Again the squadron was using Ford as their forward departure base. After finding no enemy aircraft around the Paris area, Bob, now flying with Jacko, finally chased an enemy aircraft around Melun airfield without catching it; he took out his frustration on ground targets, shooting up the hangars with cannon and machine-gun fire. The hail of return fire missed. Two other pilots had to come back with 'radio failure' but F/Lt Kelsey, with Sgt Smith as his radar operator, had a field day. Near Paris, they saw a V formation consisting, oddly enough, of two Ju 88s and a single Me 110. They were flying at 3,000 ft and so intent were they upon keeping formation in the dark that Kelsey was able to catch the trio unawares and set all three on fire. The leading Ju 88 was seen to crash in flames. It was a clear moonlight night and the newly-fitted night camera gun – yet another gadget to operate – was used. Kelsey could only claim 'One Ju 88 destroyed and two other planes Damaged', but it seems more than likely that all three were destroyed; the Me 110 in particular was unlikely to have survived any kind of determined assault by a Beaufighter.

The next night was a memorable one for both W/Cdr Braham and for the RAF, and for the Allied war effort as a whole. On the night of 17 August 1943 Bomber Command launched a massive raid on the German experimental aeronautical establishment at Peenemunde on the Baltic coast. Thanks to intelligence reports, probably via Ultra, aided by aerial reconaissance photography carried out by unarmed Spitfires of the Photographic Reconnaissance Unit

(PRU) – the resulting prints being interpreted by Constance Babington-Smith and other WAAFs, aided by information from some valiant Poles and friendly Swedes – the RAF had learned that at Peenemunde the Germans had almost perfected two of Hitler's much vaunted weapons of mass destruction. They were a flying bomb (the V1) and a high flying rocket which would penetrate the stratosphere before descending at speed far in excess of the speed of sound upon an unsuspecting public (the V2). Peenemunde was also developing the first German jet-powered aircraft. The place had never been attacked before and it lay deep inside Germany. For this important maximum effort, Bomber Command mustered nearly 600 long-range bombers carrying nearly 2,000 tons of bombs. If Peenemunde could be wiped out, people in Britain would be able to live in greater comfort; although, of course, no word of this great raid nor of the RAF's discovery of the birthplace of Hitler's secret weapons, was breathed to any but a very few in Britain.

Although 141 Squadron had been operating during the two previous nights, thanks to dedicated efforts of the ground crews, Bob Braham was able to muster ten aircraft to go to the aid of Bomber Command. Due to the location of Peenemunde and the distance to be flown, the Main Force would have to overfly Denmark and head more or less directly towards their target. There would, however, also be spoof raids apparently heading for Stettin and Berlin in attempts to divert the enemy night fighters. Bob's ten aircraft were to position themselves first at Coltishall. Naturally, he himself would participate. Doubtless also he had attended various high level secret briefings in advance of the operation.

Bob also decided to use a new tactic for this very special operation. Instead of sending his Beaufighters to circle around the various German fighter bases at height, he decided to lay them in two lines between the known German fighter centres and the route over Denmark which the Main Force of bombers would have to take. Range, or lack of it, was always one of 141 Squadron's major problems. The length of time when the Beaus would be in a position where they were most likely to find themselves 'customers' to chase was so limited that, not for the first time, Bob divided his slender forces into two groups. One group was intended to intercept the Ju 88s and Me 110s as they were coming out to tackle the British bombers while the other group would take off later, timed to link up with the returning Bomber Command aircraft. As was his custom, he himself would be first off. This way he would be around after completion of his own sortie to greet and help debrief the others on their return. He spared himself nothing. He hoped to be there to congratulate personally any team which had scored a victory.

Bob Braham admits in *Scramble* that by the time he came to lead his flock against the unseen enemy on the night of the Peenemunde raid, he was exhausted. He had operated for several successive nights and had had little sleep. Notwithstanding his reduced physical state, Bob and Jacko had a most successful night. First, they sighted an Me 110 which was jinking as if it had been warned by control that it was in close contact with an enemy plane. However, Bob soon had its measure and, closing to within about 300 yards, slightly below and nearly astern, he swiftly despatched it with a short burst of fire. Me 110s seldom survived a blast from a Beau. For 'good measure', Bob gave the stricken plane another short burst on its way down and he and Jacko had the satisfaction of watching it burn in the sea.

Soon after, again probably thanks to Serrate, Bob and Jacko caught up with another Me 110. This one had initially been chasing their Beau and must have been under German radar control although the night was brightly moonlit. Bob found himself closing on this Me 110 at a fast rate. As a result, he was only about 50 yards behind it when he opened fire. The result was spectacular. The enemy night fighter blew up and disintegrated. It was so close that, as he fired, Bob had to pull up to avoid ramming it. In *Scramble*, Bob explains that one reason for his being so close before opening fire was that, in his highly fatigued state, he could hardly keep his eyes open.

Whenever he peered ahead, they misted up and smarted. One man from this Messerschmitt baled out and Bob's fiendishly aggressive spirit almost got the better of him again; he turned in order to shoot down this parachutist and 'finish him off'. It was only thanks to Jacko's intervention that Bob was deterred from committing this 'crime'.

Generally, pilots of both the RAF and the Luftwaffe obeyed the unwritten law that aircrews dangling helplessly under parachutes should not be attacked. However, there were some instances on both sides when a pilot's excitement got the better of him. Likewise, air sea rescue boats and Red Cross planes generally, but not always, were allowed to carry out their life-saving missions. Again both sides respected such humane services. However, from a strict military point of view, it made sense to prevent a skilled pilot who had baled out from operating again and research shows that in this case many British lives were subsequently lost because Jacko curbed Bob's over-zealous aggression on this occasion.

Don Aris has researched these particular encounters in great detail. He discovered that both the Me 110s shot down by Bob that night belonged to a crack German night fighting unit, IV/NJG 1, based at Leeuwarden in Holland. The first Me 110 was commanded by George Kraft, a night fighter ace with fifteen victories to his credit. Although one of his crew was rescued from the sea, the pilot's body was washed up some time later. The second Me 110 was flown by a still greater ace, one who already could claim over a score of victims. In this case both the auxiliary aircrew were killed, but the pilot, the figure whom Bob had seen parachuting earthwards, survived. He was Heinz Vinke. After eighteen hours 'in the drink', he was eventually rescued. He later crewed up with the surviving crewmen of the first Me 110 shot down by Bob that night and together they went on to shoot down many more RAF bombers. When Vinke was finally killed in 1944, he had become one of the top aces of the Luftwaffe's night fighter force, with up to fifty-four claimed victories. By then he had been decorated with the Knight's Cross with Oak Leaves.

The number of victories scored by the enemy seem high by RAF standards, but it has to be remembered that RAF bombers nightly presented the Luftwaffe with hundreds of large and relatively slow targets to attack; also, of course, the German method of determining what was a 'kill' and what counted as a 'Probable' or a 'Damaged' was not necessarily pursued with the punctiliousness that Fighter Command employed. Another factor which gave the Luftwaffe fighter pilots huge scores (their day fighters' claims ran into hundreds in a few instances) was that the Luftwaffe did not normally automatically rest a pilot after he had carried out a certain number of operations. Many of their top pilots simply went on and on without any operational rest until they were killed, although a few, like General 'Dolfo' Galland, were promoted to such a high rank that they were given other duties to perform rather than flying against the Allied Forces.

IV/NJG 1 had been scrambled to intercept what they were advised was a force of enemy bombers. It must have come as a surprise to find themselves tangling with the night fighter pilots of 141 Squadron. In all they sent up five Me 110s that night and lost three of them to the Beaus of 141 Squadron. The third loss came about when Bob's squadron scored another success that night in their efforts to protect the Peenemunde raiders. The combination of F/O Harry White and F/O Mike Allen, a pair who were fast beginning to make a name for themselves, also shot down two Me 110s. At the time they could claim only one as a certain 'kill', which they misidentified as a Ju 88. Their other attack was on an Me 110, but they could only claim this as being Damaged. However, postwar research has identified this as the third plane lost that night by the elite night fighting unit of IV/NJG 1.

It is a sad commentary on the state of serviceability of the various gadgets on board the Beaufighter at the time that two more of the tiny force returned early due to radar, radio or R/T trouble. Part of the equipment on board was experimental but the serviceability record of the special equipment seems appalling. Sadly, it also has to be said that some of the early returns were unnecessary. Even without some of the sophisticated equipment on board, pilots like Bob Braham would carry on regardless. Others decided to 'live to fight another day'. One crew, for example, returned after an inconclusive combat with an enemy night fighter because they thought that their Beau had been hit and damaged, but immediate inspection failed to detect any damage.

It is also noticed that many Beaus returned to base on completion of their assignment after having spent about 3½ hours in the air. The squadron record book, on the other hand, shows that Bob Braham, Charles Winn and others managed to extend their time aloft to up to an hour longer. Fuel preservation, accurate navigation and the confidence to land in almost any weather conditions enabled them to stay over enemy ground for the additional time. All such skills helped. Much depended upon the confidence and experience of each aircrew. An extra hour, or even half hour, may not seem very significant but when it is appreciated that much of the 3½ hours would have been spent going to and returning from the combat area, any additional time doubled or even trebled a crew's *offensive* period.

During a lull in operations, when a spell of bad weather prevented Bomber Command from operating, Bob arranged a squadron security exercise. Half the crew members would play the parts of Germans who had been dropped by parachute by night while the others would defend the airfield. It was carried out with typical Braham enthusiasm. The area around the airfield came alive as men with blackened faces crawled about, trying to reach the airfield in order to put chalk marks against parked aircraft to indicate that they had been sabotaged. Bob placed two such marks but ended up, along with most other 'German parachutists', as a prisoner in the Guard House. Sticks became a *real* casualty. He let go of a thunder flash too late and burnt his hand quite badly. Otherwise the exercise was popular and fortified the squadron's spirits. Braham, though in many respects hardly a conventional squadron commander, was nevertheless a stickler for certain disciplinary actions. He would never allow a crew to operate until he was personally satisfied that their recognition of aircraft at night was near perfect. They all had to pass a stringent test which he had devised using epidioscope projections. He also insisted that everyone who flew, including 'unofficial' passengers such as Buster Reynolds, had to take part in a swimming pool in a realistic dinghy drill practice.

Soon a few Mosquitoes began to arrive to replace the Beaufighters. It had long been recognized that 141 Squadron would be able to operate more efficiently if they had aircraft with a longer range and endurance. The Mosquito was the obvious choice. This 'wooden wonder' was superior to the Beau in both range and speed. But the Mossie, produced by De Havilland's almost as a private venture, and using wood instead of the aluminium alloys that were otherwise generally employed, was much in demand. Fighter and Bomber Commands and units of the USAF all wanted to get hold of these aircraft. As a fighter, it almost equalled the speed and manoeuvrability of a Spitfire but had twice the range. For Bomber Command it could carry about two tons of bombs to Berlin and get back at a fraction of the losses which were being incurred by the bigger, heavier and much slower types. Coastal Command also welcomed the Mossie as a long-range fighter with which to protect their large anti-U-boat aircraft over the Bay of Biscay. Later, armed with forward-firing rocket projectiles, Coastal Command also used it to attack ships and submarines. Fighter Command also quickly realized that it would make a superb night fighter with sufficient range to make their bomber support units – both Intruder and Serrate operations – doubly effective.

Even the PRU relished the Mossie's speed and range for high flying photography. The Mossie was even being used as a high-speed commercial transport on swift runs, defying all German defences, to neutral Sweden where it picked up much-needed ball-bearings. It also picked up VIPs in Sweden, one such being the great Danish nuclear scientist, Professor

Niels Bohr, whose expertise was needed to enable the Allies to produce an atom bomb before the Nazis could do so.

As one would have expected, Bob Braham was one of the first to try his hand at flying the squadron's new Mosquitoes, although these were largely elderly examples which carried none of the specialist equipment that 141 Squadron needed. Like almost every pilot who flew a Mosquito, Bob was immediately impressed by its performance, handling and load-carrying capabilities. Used as a day fighter aircraft, it was nearly as powerfully armed as the Beaufighter. It carried the same four 20 mm cannon and four machine-guns. The guns were mounted in the nose, but for night fighting they had to be removed to make room for the radar and other gadgetry. However, by 1943 most German planes had been fitted with armour which could absorb a lot of machine-gun fire. Cannon fire was needed to ensure destruction.

A sad sight that almost every crew member of 141 Squadron had to learn to accept was one which they saw regularly when operating Serrate sorties alongside their Bomber Command comrades: a large aircraft falling in flames. The chances were that they were British planes. Some crews saw as many as five go down during a single sortie. Some aircraft were caught and held in the glare of the searchlights and then set on fire by the Germans' effective radar-controlled AA guns. Others would fall to the guns of the Luftwaffe night fighters. Sometimes blazing aircraft would fly on gamely for some minutes before plummeting to certain destruction. In each there was a crew of up to half a dozen men.

A more heartening sign for the crews and the CO of 141 Squadron appeared in the shape of senior officers who were briefly posted into the unit in order to learn about the new and experimental form of operations. This suggested that they were proving the new method to the satisfaction of the Command and that other similar squadrons would soon be formed with the visiting officers in command. One such pilot was W/Cdr 'Jumbo' Gracie, a pilot who had been in the forefront of the Spitfire defence of Malta and who had left that island with a reputation second almost to none. He was destined to take command of 169 Squadron which would soon be equipped with Beaus and Mossies modified to carry out Serrate and Intruder sorties against the German night fighters.

Bob seems to have become rather frustrated during September 1943. Success in the air had not come his way for quite some while. On one patrol over the Coulommiers area beyond Paris, having found no enemy night fighters to stalk and destroy, on his way back to base he decided to attack surface transport instead. The Fighter Command order which stated that successful night fighters and squadron leaders should not expose themselves to risk on this kind of operation was conveniently forgotten. Bob, with Jacko behind him, attacked a train close to Paris, causing its engine to explode. He then went down to attack another on the Dieppe–Paris line. In this attack he flew too low and hit some trees, causing considerable damage to the lower fuselage. However, he managed to retain control and landed back safely.

Low flying was something that Bob had experienced before, and with similar results. Eddie 'Tosh' Marsh, an airman who serviced the aircraft of A Flight, 29 Squadron, when Bob was a squadron leader supplied a description of the state of Bob's Beau on its return from one sortie: 'I got him parked and could see his cannons had been fired so I climbed inside to undo his straps; he told me . . . about his latest success. When the armourers opened the bomb doors which housed the Hispano cannon, they almost got drowned with sea water and covered with seaweed!'

You can't fly much lower than that.

Derek 'Steve' Stephens also remembers what it was like to go low flying with Bob Braham in a Beaufighter. Steve was the regular radar operator of 141 pilot Doug Gregory. On one occasion, Gregory and Stephens were on board a Beau which Bob was flying from Predannack to West Malling. On arrival the weather was poor and light was fading fast from the evening sky. The clouds were 'on the deck'. They were being guided home by their 'Mother' radar beacon situated on the station and Steve said, 'Bob knew West Malling well and asked me as the navigator to bring him in from the south on a heading of 320 degrees in order to use the gap in the Downs . . . We found the gap OK but ended up at 90 degrees to the runway in use and close to touchdown. I never wish to experience again the low level tight turn and side-slipping with full flaps and undercarriage down, culminating in a landing half way down the runway and a ground loop at the end . . . Bob was a wonderful pilot – he could fly anything but was particularly expert in handling the Beaufighter, not every pilot's dream aeroplane.'

The operations by crews of 141 Squadron on the night of 16 September speak for themselves. Six aircraft departed from West Malling on Serrate operations over France. They encountered no enemy aircraft. The first one saw an aircraft hit by flak and go down in flames. The next saw an aircraft hit by cannon fire and flak. The third was first chased by a single-engined fighter and, after evading this, was fired upon by a Lancaster bomber. The fourth returned early with oxygen failure, as did the fifth. The last of the six never reached the French coast having suffered from intercom failure. The job was unnerving, frustrating and dangerous. It needed Bob's kind of determination.

On the previous night a Beau piloted by F/Lt Ferguson, on patrol over France, reported that he had been hit by flak, that one engine had failed and he was experiencing trouble with the other. Bob, also airborne, heard the report and ordered him to bail out over the Channel before total disaster overtook him. Nothing more was heard for about 24 hours and another crew was posted as missing. Then a Typhoon pilot reported seeing a dinghy in the Channel. Eventually a Walrus amphibian plane landed alongside the dinghy, ignoring a known minefield, and picked up F/O Osborn, the stricken Beau's radar operator, whose father, advised by telegram that his son was missing, had come to Wittering in order to get the latest news. He was overjoyed. Sadly Ferguson, the pilot, was never again seen. It was surmised that he had probably hit part of the aircraft when he bailed out. This was another all-too-common occurrence.

Bob Braham managed to find time to fly up to Desford to see Joan and his sons at least once a month. The station had a Tiger Moth biplane and if nothing else was available, Bob would take this. On such occasions, as often as not, he would stay the night. As is clearly shown in *Scramble*, throughout his wartime service Bob was torn between his love of family and enthusiasm for his unit.

Serrate was now proving itself. By the end of September, there is even a rare mention of it in the Squadron's Operational Records Book which refers to aircraft 'fitted with Special Apparatus for detecting and homing in on the enemy AI transmissions'. It also says that 'so far these activities have resulted in the destruction of thirteen enemy aircraft, the probable destruction of one more and the damaging of six,' adding that, 'the Beaufighters, as well as destroying enemy planes, also divert the attention of their night fighters'. It ends with the hope that, 'with the re-equipment of the squadron with Mosquito aircraft, their additional manoeuvrability and range will produce even better results'. However, apart from a few worn out Mossies which had arrived solely so that pilots could start to familiarize themselves with this type, no progress toward re-equipment of the squadron had been made.

Bob's sense of frustration was further tested on the night of 23 September. On patrol over the St Tronde area, he and Jacko had picked up the trail of an unidentified aircraft at 17,000 ft and were closing in to identify and attack it if it was hostile when the 'radio' packed up. This is clearly a reference to the aircraft's AI, as immediately it happened they had to abandon the chase. It did not help Bob's humour that both on the way out, and even more so on the way back to base, their aircraft was engaged by heavy flak. The Beau was also held in the glare of about twenty searchlights and for a while Bob was unable to extricate it from this exposed position. Its destruction by gunfire seemed only a matter of time. Bob then tried the ploy of firing a flare from the Very pistol on board whereupon all searchlights were promptly doused. Later they ran into more flak. Other 141 Squadron aircraft that night also suffered 'radio' failure, witnessed planes being shot down in flames, were caught in searchlights for what seemed agonizingly long periods and were shot at by the enemy's AA guns.

Bob's spirits must have been revived by two incidents which followed soon after this particularly frustrating flight. First he was awarded the rare distinction of a bar to his DSO. The citation read: 'Since being awarded a second bar to the Distinguished Flying Cross, Wing Commander Braham has undertaken many sorties at night during which he has destroyed a further five enemy aircraft. He is a brilliant leader, whose excellent skill, gallantry and unswerving devotion to duty have been reflected in the fine fighting qualities of the Squadron with which he has obtained notable success.'

Within a day of this award, Bob led the Fighter Command detachment in a big Battle of Britain parade and march through the streets of London and past Buckingham Palace where King George VI took the salute. With such highly publicized fighter pilots as 'Sailor' Malan, Al Deere, John Cunningham and the like available, the choice of Bob Braham must have come as a surprise to many. It is probably about that time that the Press, alerted to both his numerous decorations and his honoured position in the Battle of Britain parade, descended upon him but Bob would have nothing to do with them. At an earlier stage of the war, his father, who seemed delighted to be interviewed by the Press about his famous son, had given a ridiculous portrait of Bob which had caused him much embarrassment. Some of the details which his father had poured forth to the eager journalists were 'that his son was a quiet sort of chap, clever and deeply religious. He loves reading, history, Thucydides is his favourite author. He drinks no spirits and likes a pipe.' The Revd Dr Braham went on to tell a story about how Bob had once been challenged by a drunken navvy to a fight and how he had brought him home to the vicarage where they had fought in the attic: 'John had broken the navvy's nose. There was blood all over the place. A week later they were going off to the cinema together.'

Much of this is pure invention, and his father had even agreed to be photographed with his RFC wings and First World War medals sewn on to his surplice. Bob was much annoyed by this headline interview which appeared in the *Daily Express*, then Britain's best selling newspaper. Buster Reynolds, when the journalists arrived to interview Bob, did his best to persuade Bob to meet them, but in vain. In the end, Buster had to do what he could to pacify them. However, from that day on, denied as they were of a good front page story, the Press lost interest in W/Cdr J.R.D. Braham, DSO*, DFC**, the young pilot ace whose father had told them that he was known as 'the Destroyer', although there is no shred of evidence to support this.

Bob Braham was not publicity conscious, yet there seems to have been a certain competitive awareness that John Cunningham and he had become rivals. In *Scramble* he mentions the moment when he equalled Cunningham's top score of enemy aircraft destroyed at night and the moment when he surpassed this. Without doubt his devoted ground crews and his fellow aircrew members were constantly comparing his total with John Cunningham's. Members of 141 Squadron naturally resented the amount of publicity which was being lavished on the 'other man' while their own hero was receiving almost none. It was galling for them to be extolling the accomplishments of their CO at home in pubs and elsewhere only to encounter disbelief.

The memorable period in London around the time of the big Battle of Britain parade when, for a change, Joan was able to bask briefly in her husband's fame and enjoy his company, ended Bob's period of lack of success in the air. The very next night, flying again with Jacko, he scored his official nineteenth air victory. It was his eighteenth at night and it was this one which brought him equal with 'Cat's-eyes' Cunningham. Once again, he was on a Serrate operation from Coltishall.

After crossing through the heavy belt of searchlights and

enemy flak over Holland, the pair proceeded towards their assigned area near Bremen. Reaching that port, they soon picked up the trail of an aircraft which Bob recognized as a Dornier. Just as Me 110s and Ju 88s had been converted into night fighters so also had a few Dornier 215 bombers. A dogfight ensued. Closing to within a few hundred yards, Bob gave the Dornier a three-second burst from both cannon and machine-guns. Strikes were seen on both wings and the Dornier dived with smoke and flames pouring from it until it crashed and burned about 10 miles west of Hanover.

Immediately after this successful encounter, Jacko and Bob obtained a contact on another aircraft but were unable to match its speed. A Mosquito might have helped here. Just then another aircraft, probably an RAF bomber, burst into flames nearby and went down. On the return journey they again had to get past the heavy band of enemy AA guns and efficient radar-assisted belt of searchlights. Also as usual, one of the 141 Squadron aircraft had to return early, this time due to engine trouble. During this latest success, Bob records that he used the cine camera during the combat period (which in all had lasted for ten minutes), but no record of the results are known. Bob had also employed his now established practice of following the burning enemy aircraft down and of giving it another short burst 'just to make sure'. Perhaps he could recall at least one occasion when he himself had been apparently shot down in flames, but had managed to put the fire out and get his Beau back to base.

Two nights later, again flying with Jacko, they flew to Coltishall and later took off on another Serrate operation. This time the area which he had been detailed to patrol was around the enemy night fighter airfield at Twente in Holland. They carried with them a passenger, Major McGovern USAAF. By then American squadrons had come to share the airfield at Wittering with the RAF and Bob's 141 Squadron. The arrival of the Americans caused quite a few initial problems due to the fact that, as one airman put it, 'They seemed to have almost unlimited transport, better equipment and uniforms [It would have been hard to find uniforms worse than the RAF's thick serge which the majority wore], were better paid and had masses of cigarettes.' The RAF men had henceforth to share the local pubs with their American brothers and there was always the feeling that, with their extra money, smart uniforms and cigarettes, they might all too easily win the hearts of the local girls. However, the determination that both air forces constantly displayed overcame most of the difficulties. The Yanks were new to British ways and customs but soon mucked in happily enough.

The American USAAF unit at Wittering operated a Group of Lightning P-38 twin-engined fighters. (An American Group was roughly equivalent in size to an RAF Wing.) The actual units were their 77th and 79th Fighter Squadrons, both of which settled in at Wittering's satellite airfield of Kings Cliffe and the 55th Fighter Squadron which shared Wittering with 141 Squadron. As was so often the case, a number of 141 Squadron's 'Specialist' maintenance men, i.e. radar mechanics, were Canadians who could challenge the Americans at such sports as softball.

Major McGovern, Bob's passenger on the night of 29 September, was about to see how efficient his British buddies were. First the Beaufighter had to find a way past the enemy's formidable searchlight and AA gun belt. That alone must have been an eye-opener to the major. Then, over the Zuider Zee, they saw an Me 110 flying straight at them. Bob turned sharply and a dogfight ensued with each trying to out-turn the other as well as trying to gain height so as to make the other more visible against the backcloth of the waters of the Zuider Zee.

The Me 110 and the Beau were well matched in speed and manoeuvrability and it took all of Bob's skill and experience to get the better of a worthy opponent. However, after about ten minutes of turning and climbing Bob, now at 18,000 ft, managed to get the Messerschmitt into the position where he most wanted it. A three-second burst of fire from close range proved sufficient. The enemy fighter exploded in a mass of flames and dived straight down with burning debris coming from it. After plummeting into the Zuider Zee it burned for several more minutes on the water. The American passenger, who through the protracted dogfight must have had a job staying on his feet, must also have been favourably impressed. But the trip was not over. The search for more 'business' continued and within a short while a Ju 88 was detected and chased. This, too, was turning and climbing. Both enemy pilots were, no doubt, being advised by their Ground Control of the presence and position of Bob's Beau. The Ju 88 was larger than the Me 110 but less manoeuvrable. Bob was soon able to get behind it and opened fire at a range of only 500 yards. After about two seconds, all the guns jammed. Both aircraft were at about 18,500 ft so the extremely cold outside temperature may have been responsible. Nevertheless, the Junkers was hit on the fuselage and on both wings and went down with flames flickering from one engine. A frustrated Bob Braham, unable to fire, could only watch it go. No return fire was experienced and Bob was convinced that but for the gun stoppages, he could have finished it off, although Ju 88s generally soaked up punishment better than most German types.

The excitements of the night were not yet over. As they neared the English Coast, although by then they were in contact with friendly ground stations, Bob's Beau was first illuminated by searchlights and then briefly fired upon by Bofors guns whose shells came perilously close. Bob's hasty firing of the correct 'colours of the day' which identified him as friendly caused the ground fire to cease immediately.

Although Bob Braham had no idea at the time (other than perhaps the difficulty he had experienced in getting into position behind the aircraft before destroying it), post-war research shows that the Me 110 which he eventually shot down that night was flown by another top German ace night fighter, August Geiger of NJG 1. This German also had dozens of RAF night bombers to his credit. If, as seems likely, the majority of RAF aircraft were shot down by only a relatively few night fighter aces of the Luftwaffe,* Bob's destruction of

* This certainly was the case in the RAF.

another Luftwaffe night fighter ace must have saved the lives of scores of bomber crews.

The official Squadron Records Book goes out of its way to mention that, 'with his 19th confirmed night victory, Wing Commander Braham, DSO, DFC, had overtaken John Cunningham and was now Fighter Command's ace night fighter pilot.'

All in all it was a dramatic sortie and the American major had something special to relate to his colleagues and the folks at home. It is also significant that the night was one when the weather in the UK was deemed to be so poor for flying that, although 141 Squadron had initially intended to send seven aircraft over Germany via Coltishall, only Bob Braham and one other crew actually departed. The others were then cancelled. Because of bad weather at Wittering, Bob had to land back at Coltishall. Those remarks about Bob's 'unswerving devotion to duty', in the citation of his bar to the DSO, had been shown to be aptly chosen.

These two great efforts with F/Lt Jacobs were to be Bob Braham's swansong with 141 Squadron. Within days, he was posted away. This 'threat' as he saw it, had been hovering over him for some time. He had led the squadron for nearly a year and had transformed it. He had never for a moment spared himself. He had, but for a few precious moments and never for more than an occasional night, put aside his private and family life. He had taken no long leave. In *Scramble* he admits that he had once again become short-tempered and he must have been displaying obvious signs of operational fatigue to those familiar with the symptoms. Nevertheless, Bob protested vigorously against the order that he should hand over his squadron to another and instead attend a largely Army Staff Course at Camberley. A far-seeing career-minded officer, and one who had only had a Short Service commission, could have been greatly encouraged by such a prestigious posting. To be hand-picked for a Staff College course meant that those at the top had their eyes on him and were lining him up for higher appointments. But to Bob's weary mind a posting away from his first command, from the unit which had become almost an integral part of his mind and body, was like the amputation of a limb.

Wing Commander Braham had found companionship and satisfaction beyond all belief in bringing 141 Squadron not just up to scratch as he had first been asked to do, but to a high pitch in the vanguard of a new form of aerial warfare. It probably irked him that he knew that within a few weeks his war-weary Beaufighters would be replaced by the more efficient Mosquitoes and that with these aircraft the squadron's chances of success deeper inside Germany would be much enhanced. In every respect except sheer ruggedness and fire power, the Mosquito was superior to the Beau – much as Bob loved this large and powerful night fighter.

Before leaving squadron life, as Bob Braham was now about to do for the rest of his war, it is perhaps appropriate to give Bob's wise comments on one aspect of RAF life indulged in by the aircrews, which caused adverse comment and some eyebrow raising. The aircrews lived hard and drank far more than was either good for them physically or would have been tolerated by the officers and NCOs of the other front line Services. The aircrews were wild. They played pranks and caused damage that went beyond the bounds set by Army and Navy officers and NCOs, especially those who had served in peacetime when officers were expected to behave as 'gentlemen', and NCOs were veterans and venerated. Every 'gong' that Bob, or anyone else in the squadron was awarded, was inevitably followed by a great 'thrash'. If the award was a DFM, then the party would be held in the Sergeants' Mess; if it was a DSO or DFC, then it would be held in the Officers' Mess. In both cases the 'thrash' would extend to the pubs around the station. Generally, as Bob expresses it in *Scramble,* 'drinking was a means of escapism or a way of hiding fear. Some others,' as he puts it, 'adopted the attitude of "let's enjoy life to the full for tomorrow we may die".' The worst fear of most aircrew was not of being hit or killed but of showing fear in front of others. If parties at times got out of hand, fuelled liberally by alcohol to the point where property was damaged, cars wrecked and persons injured, it was because 'under the influence' those fears were momentarily banished. Bob also mentions 'the terrible responsibilities which were thrust upon young men, some no more than boys.' Bob himself handled these manfully but they weighed heavily with some of his age.

The risk of not surviving even one tour of operations was very real. The statistics are horrifying. The chances of living through an operational tour were:

Torpedo pilot	17½%
Night fighter pilot	39%
Day fighter pilot	43%
Bomber pilot	44%

Night fighter pilots, therefore, had less chance of survival than the bomber pilots whom, nightly, they saw falling in flames. Until Serrate operations commenced, relatively few 141 Squadron aircraft were lost to the enemy, although quite a few were lost from other causes. Between 1939 and 1945 the squadron lost thirty-eight aircrew in flying accidents and forty-six killed on operations (not that all losses on operations were due to the Germans). Weather, engine and other failures also claimed victims with 'Sir Isaac' often an accomplice. The pattern of 29 Squadron was typical in that the kills were largely accounted for by a small number of pilot/radar operator combinations. During this early period of experimental Serrate operations, almost all the positive victories were scored by Braham with either Sticks or Jacko; Kelsey with Smith, and White with Allen. It would seem that there had to be some kind of magical chemistry between the pilot up front and the radar operator with his various electronic gadgets.

Don Aris, the devoted armourer, recalled: 'Wing Commander Braham was with 141 Squadron from 22 December 1942 to 1 October 1943. In just over nine months he turned it into a first rate unit. He trained and led it into entirely different types of operations from its previous role. As well as the normal duties and responsibilities of a Commanding Officer, he took part in 63 separate sorties. These included scrambles and patrols on Home Defence both day and night; Ranger operations over NW France; Instep and Reconnaissance patrols over the Bay of Biscay and 26 Bomber Support operations over Germany, Holland, Belgium and France. His 26 Bomber Support operations took place between 14th June 1943 and 29th September 1943, a lot of operations in a short time bearing in mind that these were a completely new type of operation for himself and his crews . . . the Serrate equipment and the Gee navigation equipment had to be learned and mastered. . . . These Serrate operations which he started and largely developed had, by the end of the war, resulted in the destruction of some 200 enemy night fighters by the squadrons of Bomber Support of which 141 was the first.'

Mention should also be made of his many visits to both Group and Command HQ to discuss tactics. He even went to RAF Kenley for a few days in advance of his role as leader of the great Battle of Britain parade in order to be instructed in marching drill and parade orders. In his personal pilot's log-book, which is beautifully neat throughout (and is now a prize exhibit in the RAF Museum at Hendon), he wrote at the foot of the page after his last operation with 141 Squadron: 'The end of very happy and exciting days with 141 as CO.' In *Scramble* he writes: 'My association with my "first love", 141 Squadron, was now broken for good, and with it comradeship such as I have never known since.' Elsewhere in his autobiography, he gives full praise to the help that he received from both Dickie Sparrowe his adjutant and from Buster Reynolds, whom he refers to as 'my spy', this being the commonly used term for all squadron intelligence officers.

W/Cdr J.R.D. Braham made despairing, but ineffective efforts to continue with 141 Squadron. He was truly reluctant, although aware of his own state of fatigue, to sever the umbilical cord which linked him to his first command. He appealed personally against the posting right up to the AOC of the Group but Air Marshal Sir Roderick Hill would not relent. Also, having a few days in hand before having to report to the Staff College at Camberley, Bob commenced to badger his replacement CO for 'just one more operation', but firm orders had come from Group that 'Braham was not to fly any more combat missions.'

Proof that he and 141 Squadron had successfully developed a form of night operations never before attempted in warfare is evidenced by the fact that at the time when he was being retired from the fray, two other squadrons were being formed to carry out this task. All three squadrons would soon be flying Mosquitoes deep into the heart of Germany. More significantly still, these three night fighting squadrons and others engaged in different forms of Bomber Support would all soon be transferred to the newly created and very secret 100 Group. Moreover the control of this Group would be handed over to Bomber Command itself whereupon 141 Squadron would then cease to be in Fighter Command.

Some idea of how sorry the squadron was to lose its dynamic commander can be gauged by the words in the unit's official record book dated 1 October 1943: 'W/Cdr Braham DSO, DFC, officer commanding the squadron has today been posted to HQ No. 9 Group, pending a Staff College course. . . . The whole Squadron, while wishing W/Cdr Braham every success, feels very much the loss of a man who has been everything that a Squadron Commander should be. He joined the unit at a time when it was at its very lowest ebb. By his magnificent example and good organization, and despite the fact that all the experienced crews were posted away, the morale and work of the Squadron started to improve immediately. He succeeded in communicating a fine offensive spirit which showed itself to such effect, while the Squadron was at Predannack, that they were specially chosen from all the night fighter squadrons of Fighter Command to undertake the present extremely important tasks. During the nine months he has led the Squadron, he has succeeded in destroying eight enemy aircraft and damaging two others. While at Predannack he shot up a Motor Torpedo Boat in a convoy and on another occasion seriously damaged a submarine, both in the Bay of Biscay. Over France in Ranger operations, he seriously damaged a train and a lorry. He has succeeded by his last victory in beating the score of W/C Cunningham and leaves the Squadron as the Night Fighter Ace Pilot.'

It is to be hoped that Joan was shown these words as she had, during his period in command, almost had to surrender her man to the squadron which Bob had come to love . . . and which in time had come to love him. Her sacrifice had not been in vain. Yet this was not to be the end of Bob Braham's personal crusade against his hated enemy.

13

Just One of the Lads . . .
A Ruthless Killer

Many renowned pilots who, in spite of their protests, are forced to take a job on the ground after a distinguished wartime spell of fighting, virtually disappear from the public scene. But it was not so with Wing Commander Bob Braham DSO & Bar, DFC & two Bars. Nothing, so it would seem, would ever keep Bob on the ground for long. He was not only determined to keep flying but he HAD to be flying offensively against his country's enemies.

However, before returning to the operational saga of Bob's accomplishments against his sworn enemy, it seems appropriate to pause a while and look at this remarkable person's character and characteristics, as seen by those who knew him at various times.

John R.D. Braham was not born with any outstanding natural gifts in the scholastic, mental or athletic fields. He was not, like Rhys-Davies, a great ace of the First World War, a brilliant classical scholar. He was not a gifted natural ball-player as were Douglas Bader, Laddie Lucas and several other air aces. Bob had not from early childhood, lived, breathed, studied and almost worshipped every aspect of aerial combat as had George Beurling, the great Maltese fighter ace. Yet Bob Braham, by 1943, had become a rare genius at the most difficult art of night fighting in the air. How? If any man epitomized the saying 'Genius is 10 per cent inspiration but 90 per cent perspiration', that man was Bob Braham. An outstanding characteristic which shines throughout his career is Bob's unquenchable energy. Another was his ability to put his whole being into whatever task confronted him. Jimmy James, Guy Gibson's talented radar operator, commented: 'Gibson's conversation covered a wider range of subjects than Bob's, whose mind was focused entirely upon war.' Yet if one compares their school records, Bob's accomplishments probably were superior. Mention has already been made of Bob's ability to talk naturally, with no hint of a patronizing tone, to all and sundry, including the humblest of erks. Rank and status meant as little to him as they did to the great Maltese reconnaissance pilot ace, Adrian Warburton. In both cases it earned these two pilots (who between them were awarded five DSOs & seven DFCs!) the undying devotion of those who looked after their aircraft.

Bill Geddes, a recently promoted groundcrew sergeant, was on duty at Lasham in early 1944 when a couple of unknown senior officers from HQ 2 Group arrived to 'borrow' a Mosquito of 613 Squadron in order to depart on a daylight Ranger operation. Bill was caught at an awkward moment: normal operations having been cancelled owing to unsuitable flying weather, he had allowed all his men to go to the NAAFI. However, Bob soon put him at ease and between them they successfully got the Mossie airborne. Bob's opening remark, 'Any of your Mossies will do,' established an early rapport. Thus reassured, Bill helped to 'shoe-horn' Bob and his navigator into their seats and away they went with a parting friendly grin from Bob. On their return some hours later, having shot down a four-engined Heinkel 177, Bob was again helpful and friendly.

This was the one and only occasion when Bill Geddes met Bob Braham; remarkably Bill said, over fifty years later, 'When I think of Mosquitoes, I think of Bob Braham.' This is quite a tribute, coming from a man who strapped scores of pilots into dozens of Mosquitoes over quite a long period. To get the two-man crew side by side into the narrow Mosquito was literally a 'shoe-horn' operation. As one unabashed airman cheerfully advised a Mossie pilot: 'A Mossie is a bit like a virgin, Sir. Difficult to get into but very satisfying when you've got there!'

Even later in the war, when he was a POW, Bob – who by then had acquired high rank, a reputation in the RAF second to none and a 'fistful of medals' – seems to have been as unassuming as ever. Having been forcibly removed from the front line, Bob seems to have reverted to being the almost shy private person of his school days. Jack Bushby, who knew Bob Braham in Stalagluft III at Sagan, remembers him as being 'unassuming and shy to the point of withdrawal'. He also recalls that when a discussion arose about post-war prospects, Bob commented: 'Me? Why? What can I do? The only thing I know is how to drive aeroplanes and shoot down other aeroplanes. Not much call for that in Civvy Street.'

On their first meeting, Bob had made a good impression on Jack. Each compound of Stalagluft III consisted of a long barrack block. However, for senior officers, at the end of each block there were 'VIP' quarters, 'a comfortable roost for two', as Jack puts it. Bob, as a wing commander, and at that time the most highly decorated pilot in the RAF, was offered a bunk in one of these more comfortable small rooms. But he refused it, being, as he put it, 'perfectly happy to be found a place in one of the larger rooms' where he could mix with its inhabitants in what was called a 'combine' among a number of inmates who shared rations, food parcels and so on.

Jack says that 'a wing commander who preferred to be among the boys created quite a sensation at the time'. Jack also recalls that Bob had so many rosettes, each signifying a bar to his DSO or DFC, affixed to his medal ribbons on his tunic that 'they looked as if they were held firm with drawing pins'.

Jack also recalls a curious post-war incident concerning Bob. He was going through a job lot at the Blackburn Grammar School which Bob had once attended when he found a portrait in oils. The headmaster didn't recognize the person: 'Some old boy or other. Don't really know who.' The portrait was about to be dispatched to some dark corner. 'Fortunately,' recalls Jack, 'I at once recognized it as a startlingly good portrait of Bob Braham,' even though at that time Jack was unaware that Bob had been a former pupil of the same school. 'Needless to say,' Jack adds, 'It is now given a place of honour.'

Jack Bushby, who only knew Bob when they were both POWs, described Bob as 'not only a great fighting pilot but also a thoroughly nice guy'. Another colleague, Jim Carter, recalls an incident in a pub near Ford, Sussex, which illustrates another side of Bob's make-up. At the time, Bob was the squadron commander: 'We joined 141 Squadron in February 1943. Braham had recently taken over the unit. We arrived early one evening and within minutes were whisked away to a pub in Littlehampton where the squadron was holding a party. As we entered the large room, the sight which greeted us was that of three or four shirt-sleeved bods standing on a stage and bombarding about ten or twenty uniformed Other Ranks with bread rolls, buns and anything else that came to hand. We discovered later that the ring-leader was none other than our CO, Bob Braham. He had a boyish sense of fun and was not afraid to let his hair down in public. He possessed the common touch . . . which was to pay dividends when the groundstaff personnel – the erks – reacted to him with what amounted to hero worship.' He adds: 'After he had been posted away, he used to come back to visit the squadron and almost 100 per cent of the erks assembled, mostly in their own time, to welcome him when he flew in.' Yet in contrast, comments Jim Carter, he was deadly serious about operations. On one occasion he recalls that, when only Sticks and he had been successful on a night operation, he wanted to know why: 'He quizzed each other aircrew individually in front of the whole squadron and, believe me, it was worse than flying on operations. We, my radar operator and I, were able to advise that we had tracked down three aircraft but that all had proved to be friendly. He apologized and admitted that he had not studied our Intelligence Report sufficiently. . . . He was firm and fair but did not suffer fools gladly.' Jim Carter also recalls that after a Ju 88 had dived out of the clouds and strafed the airfield at Ford in daylight, Bob was seen taxiing a Beau furiously across to a take-off point with a pair of legs flailing dramatically out of the rear hatch as his RO desperately attempted to get on board. Sticks only just got himself into his position on board the Beau before Bob took off after the fast-disappearing intruder. Bob considered the attack by the Ju 88 on the airfield as an invasion of his personal territory and field of responsibility. He *had* to take off to try to eliminate the attacker if at all possible.

George Jones, Paddy Englebach's radar operator, recalled that after Sgt Blackburn's tragic death, 'Bob called everyone together about the Aussie and Blackburn and told the pilots that anyone who did any beat-ups would be instantly court-martialled.' George also speaks well of Bob's fairness towards George's pilot, Englebach, who was having difficulties with the Beaufighter on take-offs and landings. After Englebach had damaged his Beau's propeller tips on several occasions, Bob resisted attempts to have him grounded. Bob described him as a 'gutsy little chap' who deserved another chance. Thus reprieved, Paddy Englebach made the grade and survived the war, but he was shot down by a He 219 on a Serrate operation on the night of 27 June 1944 and became a POW. As George Jones commented: 'Bob displayed patience as well as fairness.'

Armourer LAC Claxton writes: 'From the time that Braham joined us in 141 at Ford, the general atmosphere changed for the better. . . . His leadership seemed to inspire everybody and the squadron went from strength to strength. . . . I did not consider him to be a disciplinarian but felt that his personal style of leadership earned him the respect of all squadron personnel and in this way achieved results. . . . the number of aircraft destroyed increased considerably.'

Bob's brother-in-law, Ron Dabney, who was a Navy man, saw Bob from quite a different viewpoint; although they seldom met, largely because they served mostly in different continents, their relationship was always good. Ron Dabney comments upon two facets of Bob's character: 'He was always a very forthright individual and, having reached a conclusion or decision, he was a difficult man to budge . . . he always fought shy of publicity and was without pretences and arrogance. . . . I could never induce him to talk about his wartime exploits but he was always good company socially.'

Fred Pedgeon, an airplane mechanic of 29 Squadron, remembers Bob Braham as a 'friendly helpful chap'. The airfield at Wellingore became a sea of mud during the winter of 1940, so much so that aircraft could only be refuelled in a few places where the ground was firmer. This caused queues and delays. Fred recalls one occasion when Bob, after a long and tiring patrol, still had the energy to leap out on to the wing, grab a hose and do his own refuelling, much to the amusement and admiration of the groundcrew.

'Doc' Dougall, the likeable 'Mad Irishman', commented upon another aspect of Bob's personality: 'We had the boxing gloves on when he was not flying – just knocking hell out of one another. He could use his fists well.' The Doc also added: 'Bob was a true leader, never asking any of the aircrew to do a job which he had not already done.' On one occasion during a visit to Joan at her parents' home in Leicester, Bob's father asked the the Doc to help him to persuade Bob to stop flying as 'they were afraid of losing him'. The Doc replied that 'it would be easier to turn the sea tide with a pitchfork'.

Norman Franks, the well known wartime aviation author and researcher, relates a story told to him. After the war, Bob had a job at the Air Ministry and he used to walk to work with a civilian raincoat over his RAF uniform and medal ribbons, and without a hat, so that he could remain unrecognized. If true, this was another sign of his avoidance of publicity and public acclaim. Did those medal ribbons exacerbate a natural tendency towards shyness?

Doug Gregory, a 141 Squadron pilot (no relation to Sticks), confirmed Bob's brilliance in the air, and praised his fantastic flying; he also recalled that Bob was full of praise for Steve Stephens, Doug's radar operator, for his excellent navigation. Doug still occasionally flies at air displays where he is careful to apply the lesson learned from Bob about low flying: that it is essential to concentrate on flying the aircraft within the limits of its performance and very accurately . . . and not to bother about the effect it may have on others on the ground.

Jim Hartley first met Bob Braham a few years after the war. An NCO pilot flying single-seat Hornets from Linton, he was asked to take a visitor from the Air Ministry in formation with him on a low-level cross-country flight over Holland and Germany as far as Switzerland and back. The unknown visitor appeared in a Mae West which concealed all rank badges and, during the long and interesting formation flight, called Jim Hartley 'Sergy' throughout. The trip was a typical low-level flight, involving some quite close formation flying with Jim in the lead. It was quite shaky at times such as when they ran into sea fog when flying in close proximity and only a few feet up. It was only after they were safely back at base that the visitor, Bob Braham, removed his coat, and Jim saw his rank insignia and rows of medals. Bob explained to Jim that, although he had a desk job at the Air Ministry, 'he liked to keep his hand in'. As Jim puts it, 'there was a bloke who knew the continent backwards and he was thanking *me* for a nice trip. I felt pretty good as praise from him was praise indeed. . . . he was a gentleman by any standards.' This seems to confirm that Bob's self-effacement and friendly attitude towards all and sundry, regardless of rank, was still the same several years after the war had finished.

Sticks Gregory stresses the importance that Bob always gave to meeting personally the people on the ground who controlled them in the air. Sticks also adds a new twist to the post-war Bob Braham story. He relates that: 'After the war he was OK but very unsettled, as his wife has confirmed. In Joan's words, his period as a POW had changed her husband. 'He was never quite the same spontaneous person again. He resigned from the RAF and was going to join the Rhodesia Police Force.' Sticks confirms that Bob resigned from the RAF and was applying to join the Rhodesian Police. 'My wife and I spent a weekend with Bob and Joan in Leicester, and I realized that he was very unhappy at leaving the RAF and his friends and that he would really like to remain in the RAF. I was on the Staff Group at Watnall and, during the Monday morning conference, I informed the SASO [Senior Air Staff Officer] of this. He rang Air Chief Marshal Sir Basil Embry. I was instructed to get Bob for an interview as soon as possible. He was very soon back in the RAF.'

Years later Bob Braham *did* resign from the RAF but only to join immediately, obviously by pre-arrangement, the RCAF without loss of rank. Sticks (and others) put this final resignation down to financial and parental worries: 'He was always short of money. He wanted to educate his three boys to the best standard he could afford. The pay of a wing commander in the RAF did not match these intentions. In Canada the pay was excellent and Bob was able to carry out his educational plans for his boys.'

Sticks recalls another event that is very significant in the light of what later transpired (and which incidentally is at odds with what Joan Braham believes). During 1962 Bob went to stay with Sticks and his wife. 'He complained of very bad headaches and I arranged for the station medical officer to give him an examination. This he did but couldn't find anything to cause the headaches . . . yet years later he died of a brain tumour.'

Curiously, Joan has said that, apart from the occasional hangover, she never knew her husband 'even to have a headache'. Somehow he must have kept the complaint from her and doubtless, keen as he was to continue to fly, he would have been at pains to keep such knowledge from any RAF or RCAF doctor for fear of being grounded.

Sticks has also commented on the differences between Guy Gibson and Bob Braham: 'Bob was popular with everyone in the squadron while Guy was only popular with a few.' Sticks rates Guy 'as the person with the most guts and courage of anybody I ever knew', but adds 'Bob Braham came very close indeed; in fact, upon reflection, I will say now that he was his equal.' Fred Pedgeon recalls an occasion at West Malling when Guy Gibson was asked to scramble quickly, and took off straight from dispersal across the airfield, so eager was he to get at the Hun. 'Gibbo', as he calls him, 'was always chafing at the bit' if he was obliged to delay take-off.

R.M. Holdsworth is another man who knew Bob Braham only after the war, when Bob was at the Central Flying Establishment at West Raynham, Norfolk, in some senior capacity. 'I always found him an extremely pleasant person to talk to, with no side. He would not suffer fools gladly and, fortunately for the ground staff, would talk with us. He was also rather fatalistic. When I was strapping him into a Meteor, he said to me: "It's no good, I would only be killed by the tail when leaving the aircraft".' Holdsworth adds that this was before the advent of the ejector seat. Jack Hoskins DSO, DFC, himself a distinguished pilot who rose from the rank of sergeant pilot to acting wing commander in less than three years, met Bob in 1961 when they were representing their respective air forces of RAF and RCAF and living in Paris while on SHAPE (Supreme Headquarters Allied Powers Europe) duties. By this time Bob had been in the RCAF for some time. 'He was always good company,' writes Jack. 'He had an ebullient nature and, although wearing RCAF uniform, could just as well have still been in the RAF. He was quite gregarious and respected by all, having a natural rapport with Germans, Italians, Norwegians, USA personnel serving alongside . . . he was forthright in his opinions but not aggressive . . . his sense of humour would, I am sure, lighten many a dark tense moment and it would not be at other people's expense.' Jack is in good company when he writes 'Bob deserves a bit more recognition.' Air Marshal Jimmy James (not the previously mentioned radar operator Jimmy James) met Bob after the war when he was a group captain; Bob was then in the RCAF. Jimmy James was representing the RAF which at that time had an interest in the Canadian CF 100 Arrow project, which Bob was flying regularly. The RAF was considering purchasing this advanced jet fighter which Bob was helping to prove. Jimmy was the Director of Research (A). 'The fact that this ambitious project of AVRO (Canada) was not taken up by either the RAF or RCAF was no fault of Bob Braham's.'

The other Jimmy James (real name Richard) was the radar operator who flew successfully with Guy Gibson in 29 Squadron. He has a very strong impression of Bob. 'He was so utterly obsessed with killing the enemy that I thought it spilled over into his subconscious mind.' He recalls that at squadron parties when they had reached a stage of 'anything goes', 'Bob used to dash around "shooting" people with his fingers in the gun position and making staccato noises.'

Jimmy James supplies an interesting physical portrait: 'blond hair, steely blue eyes which often narrowed when in the mood, a really determined set to his mouth and lips . . . suddenly he would be transformed. The eyes would crinkle and his mouth would form into a mischievous grin and you saw him for what he was – a charming young man . . . and very young.'

Jimmy also adds: 'his achievements simply surpassed those of any other Allied airman'. High praise indeed from one who flew for nearly a year with Guy Gibson VC. For those who doubt that Braham surpassed all others, his personal log-book is now in the RAF Museum for all to study.

In Jimmy James's view, both Guy and Bob were superb pilots but Bob was the better shot (as Gibson himself acknowledged). James considers that Bob was more aggressive but adds that 'publicity seeking was never in Bob's mind'; he mentions one incident when Guy, in his cups, made remarks indicating that he intended to become 'some kind of national figure' (which, of course, he did by leading the Dambusters to glory). Jimmy James recalls that Basil Embry once remarked, when referring to Bob Braham, 'I never met anyone to surpass Bob Braham's sheer aggression and fighting spirit.' That remark, coming as it did from a man whom many consider the most aggressive leader in the RAF, is high praise indeed. Laddie Lucas CB, DSO, DFC, another distinguished wartime pilot (and much else as well), has given an interesting description of both Bob Braham and Basil Embry in the foreword of this biography.

Yet when Laddie did meet Bob, he found him quite a different character to the one which he had imagined: 'He was quiet, almost reticent, content to listen and to keep his judgement and opinions to himself . . . but it was the pair of startling blue eyes, set below a fine crop of very fair hair which stuck in the mind.' Laddie Lucas was soon to learn about Bob's habit of descending upon Mosquito squadrons and 'borrowing' one of their aircraft for a daylight Ranger operation over Europe. He learned also of the understanding that Bob and Basil Embry had reached which enabled Bob to collect a willing navigator from HQ once every week in order to carry out an official Ranger operation. Bob had been heard to say: 'It is the only thing which keeps me sane.'

Laddie, in essence, has accurately described the two conflicting Bob Brahams, the Jekyll and Hyde wartime personalities. One was a quiet, pleasant, private person but the other was a man who, for as long as the war lasted, was bent upon killing on behalf of the RAF as many of the enemy as was humanly possible. Laddie Lucas had trained as a *Daily Express* journalist before the war, so who better than he to observe these conflicting traits?

Air Chief Marshal Sir Basil Embry described Bob Braham in the following terms: 'I have never met anyone to surpass his sheer aggressive fighting spirit and one who was more determined to come to grips with the enemy in the air.' He goes on to describe Bob as a 'great individualist'. However, with respect to Sir Basil, whom others regard as having what he terms 'aggressive fighting spirit which could not be surpassed', he may have done Bob an injustice in describing him as an 'individualist'. Bob was much more than an individualist; he was also a leader. He made an instant impression on almost everyone he met and he inspired others to follow in his footsteps. He is kindly remembered to this day by the sergeant who once, and only once, helped him to get a Mosquito ready. He made an instant impression upon the girl whom he spied across the crowded pub floor. He also made a lasting impression on the man who shot him down, Robert Spreckels.

Robert Spreckels met Bob only briefly during the war in conditions which limited what either man could say. As a prisoner of war Bob was allowed briefly to meet the pilot who had shot him down. Their conversation also had to pass through an interpreter. Yet after the war, Spreckels spent years trying to find Bob Braham. . . . Not until 1956 did Spreckels learn that his 'victim' was still alive and it was some time after that before they actually met. When after so many years they did meet again, they became instant friends. Bob could only be described as an 'individual' in the sense that all night fighters fought their battles on a one-to-one aircraft-against-aircraft basis, not in formations. However, each victory was a product of at least two persons: the pilot and the radar operator working together, and, in many cases, a third man, the Ground Controller. Surely the evidence is that Bob Braham was just as much a leader as any other Fighter Command leader from Douglas Bader downwards? Bob led in his own simple way: by example, but one only has to compare 141 Squadron's achievements before and after his arrival to discover what a dynamic and effective leader he was.

'Tosh' Mellersh CB, DFC, now a retired Air Vice-Marshal, tells of an incident when Bob, wanting to borrow one of the Mosquitoes of the unit where he was stationed, first had it cleaned down with Dunk and then polished with floor polish in order to make it slip through the air a few miles an hour faster. 'Tosh' also believes that Bob Braham's wartime achievements were 'underrated and stood higher than those of much better known chaps'. Tosh knew Bob when Bob was a deputy Flight Commander of 29 Squadron. Tosh was then aged only 19.

It also appears that Tosh was the driver of the car which once put Bob into hospital! Regarding Bob Braham's character, 'Tosh' writes: 'He was a popular and likeable chap; not over-blessed with intelligence but absolutely straightforward and down to earth . . . he was in his happiest mood after he had scored a "kill" in the air. The Ground Controller once had to tell him, as there were WAAFs present in the Ops

Room, to control his language or switch off his R/T.' That may have been the occasion when Bob Braham decided to broadcast to all within R/T range his version of "I've got balls that jingle, jangle, jingle . . .". In those days one did not swear in public, nor in the presence of the fairer sex. The overgrown exuberant schoolboy with the mischievous grin was, it would seem, never far from bubbling to the surface.

As a young pilot Freddie Newton joined 141 Squadron when Bob was its CO. He remembers being given a warm welcome by Bob who, he discovered to his surprise, was about as young as himself. He remembers Bob's almost suicidal attack upon the German MTB in the Bay of Biscay and adds: 'This action was regarded as very much a "press on regardless" attack, even by the standards of the time.' Freddie is among the many who considered it a great honour to have served under Bob. 'His one aim was to get at the enemy and all of us would have followed him at the drop of a hat wherever he went. He was highly popular, cheerful and put everyone at ease . . .he didn't have to drive us because he knew we were with him and his example was a spur to us all. He had terrific energy and easily got bored . . . when things were quiet, he would wrestle with anyone in the Mess, just to let off steam.'

Freddie recalls that when a visiting American pilot saw Bob's medal ribbons with all the rosettes attached, he remarked: 'Gee, that guy sure has got his "gongs" riveted on!' Newton ends with: 'It was a privilege to be on 141 Squadron with Bob and I remember him with affection.'

Arthur Smith's recollections cover a post-war period at West Raynham. 'No one could believe that he possessed three DSOs and three DFCs. I spent two years under his command and he was just one of the nicest people I ever met.'

G.A. Jones describes Bob as 'a magnificent leader' and makes the point that Bob was always first to depart on sorties against the enemy. 'Steve' Stephens, who describes himself as a very raw Nav/Rad crewman, relates that 'Cunningham and Braham were in competition for the top night fighting honours', and adds: 'Unfortunately "Cat's-Eyes" got all the publicity but because of this and Bob's press-on attitude, squadron morale was never higher. The team would have followed him anywhere.' Steve actually suffered injury at the hands of Bob Braham when he was sideswiped by a staff car driven by him. He 'still retains a scar from my broken nose'.

Ian White is another man who writes generously about Bob: 'I regard him as being one of the best exponents of night fighting techniques and the leader in the field of the offensive use of night fighters in Bomber support . . . in ranking terms, he must rate alongside Cunningham, Aitkin, Chisholm etc.'

Charles Widdow's personal views of Bob Braham are derived from the period when he was CO of 29 Squadron and Bob was one of his relatively junior pilots. Charles had been posted to restore the squadron's morale. 'He was still developing his killer instinct,' yet Charles soon came to regard F/O Braham as: 'One of my anchor men upon which to build the squadron . . . a young, keen and able pilot and a charming personality.' Time seems not to have changed him. Brian O'Reilly, who knew Bob when he was working for SHAPE, has written: 'Bob Braham was probably the best liked in the section by all parties and he was a pleasure to work for.' Brian O'Reilly adds the information that his main task was to devise and co-ordinate the "paper" air exercises throughout the NATO area'.

Another man who knew Bob at SHAPE was a fellow Englishman in the RCAF, Bruce Micklewright. Bruce had a Canadian T-33 unit at Marville and Bob used to visit there and go flying with Bruce. Although it was not necessary for him to do so, Bob used to get his Instrument Rating renewed by Bruce. They also went on official visits to such places as the weapons range at Deccimomamu, Sardinia. On such flights they could admire the unmatched scenery of the Alps from above. Bruce would act as Bob's personal pilot and almost his unofficial aide-de-camp. Bob was then a Group Captain and the year was 1963.

Bruce remembers enjoying looking with Bob at some wartime photos which Bob's camera gun had taken during a 'beat-up' of a French airfield, almost certainly on one of his

Ranger operations in Mosquitoes. The daylight photos include a Frenchman with a donkey cart. The donkey was more alert than its owner and in an early frame is bolting as the Mossie roars down. However, in a later frame the Frenchman has not only chased after the frightened animal but is yards ahead! It has been computed from the time lapse between shots that the Frenchman must have broken the world 100-metre record! Throughout the sequence of photographs, a flak tower can be seen firing at Bob but it was the French sprinter that Bob most remembered.

Sir Peter Wykeham, now a retired Air Marshal with a string of decorations, writes: 'I am with you heart and soul on the object of your work and I share your surprise and indignation that Bob never achieved the renown he deserved.' Much the same sentiments were expressed by Laddie Lucas when he wrote: 'Not enough is known about Bob save to those who were with him in 141 or in 2 Group. . . . Perhaps this book may help fill the void.'

Air Commodore A.S.G. Lee, SASO of 12 Group, in a book called *Special Duties*, writes: 'In a lifetime of flying and being among flying people, the one who stood out most prominently was W/Cdr J.R.D. Bob Braham.' Lee added: 'He had never met a man with such quietly determined cold blooded courage as he . . . Had the Victoria Cross been awarded to airmen for a long succession of acts of deliberate courage, then Braham should have had that ribbon also on his tunic to go with his three DSOs and three DFCs.'

14
On the Ground . . . Mostly

Being selected to attend such a high level Army Staff course was an honour given to only a few RAF officers and even fewer non-Regular RAF ones. Someone at the top must have had his eyes on Bob Braham. A promising and permanent career for Short-Service officer W/Cdr Braham now beckoned. The selection may have caused a few raised eyebrows since Bob had never attended the RAF's own prestigious Staff College at Cranwell. However, Bob Braham didn't see it in this light. To him it was a hindrance: he wanted nothing more than to be back in the air fighting his hated enemy.

Although most of those attending the Staff Course at Camberley were senior Army officers, there were a few other RAF officers and a smattering of men from other countries and Services. The course was divided into a number of syndicates which studied various Army tactical situations, with the RAF officers serving as air advisers to the various syndicates.

Bob was not the only one who took the course with rather less seriousness than it warranted, and soon he and a few cronies found themselves a friendly pub, the Cambridge Arms, which supplied them with as much of the weak wartime beer as they could drink, even after official closing time. While others burned the midnight oil studying, Bob and his friends were enjoying themselves in the pub.

An indication of the importance of the course was that among the many very senior officers who gave lectures were General Montgomery, the victor of El Alamein, and General Anderson who commanded the British First Army in the

Anglo-American victories which had resulted in the capture of Algeria and Tunisia by May 1943. Most of the Army students saw the course as a stepping stone towards their ambition to become the future generals and field marshals of the British Army. The various merits of 'Monty' and General Anderson were much debated, with Bob siding with the large group who preferred General Anderson. They pointed out that he had had a difficult and complex task, working alongside French and American forces, whereas the more cocky and confident Monty had a relatively free hand. Bob, with his profound dislike of every form of personal publicity, was not one to fall under Monty's spell.

Not too surprisingly, Bob Braham found that many of his Army colleagues were more staid, hidebound by tradition and sober than was generally true of RAF officers; by this stage of the war, nearly every RAF Mess was full of people who, before the war, had not belonged to any Service. The Army officers on the course were delighted to be there and were anxious to show their merit. Bob, in contrast, was there unwillingly. However, once the ice was broken, he soon struck up friendships with several of the Army officers. These friendships were cemented when Bob discovered that some of the aircraft at nearby RAF Farnborough could be easily borrowed. He took several of his new-found friends on a number of flights. He also made several visits to Joan and their two sons, all still living in Leicester. Joan had, not unnaturally, suggested that for the duration of the course at least, she should move closer but Bob refused. He remained convinced that war and family life should not mix. He rigidly kept the two interests apart.

The aircraft which Bob borrowed at Farnborough were a mixed bunch. They included Tiger Moths, a similar Avro Tutor biplane, Mosquitoes from 605 Squadron, a Percival Proctor, an Airspeed Oxford and even a single-seater biplane fighter, the obsolete but delightful to fly Gloster Gladiator. On one of his flights to an airfield near Leicester he managed, unofficially of course, to give Joan her first trip in the air, much to her enjoyment.

The Staff course was a long and demanding one. It had already been running for over two months when 141 Squadron decided to hold a party in late January 1944 in honour of its former and much respected CO. A model of a Beaufighter was specially made for the party. Bob had arranged for a number of his friends at Camberley to attend this big 141 Squadron 'bash'. They were to be flown down in the spacious Oxford to West Raynham, Norfolk, the new home of 141 Squadron. Bob accompanied them, as 'fighter escort', in the Gladiator.

The men of 141 Squadron seem to have got their hands on an abundant supply of drink and the party, wild even by RAF standards, was an eye-opener to Bob's more formal Army friends, especially when alcohol removed all inhibitions. Several Very cartridges were let off and fire extinguishers sprayed around. The Mess was partially wrecked, glasses smashed and furniture broken, and the next morning the sooty bare footprints of the forty-year-old squadron 'spy' Buster Reynolds were clearly visible on the ceiling! Nursing their hangovers, Bob and his Army colleagues hurried back to Camberley early next morning before the inevitable 'inquest' by the Station Commander could gain momentum. Damage had to be paid for.

Throughout the long course, Bob kept his eyes open for the future and, during visits to various HQs, angled for a flying job that would enable him to get back into the air.

In the mean time, much was happening in the world, in the country, in the RAF and in 141 Squadron. The gloomy picture that the Allies had faced on almost every front in October 1942 had, by January 1944, changed dramatically, and all for the better. Victory followed victory on every front and in every theatre of war. Stalingrad and Alamein had seen the once invincible German armies smashed into retreat and surrender. These successes had been followed by the conquest of Algeria and Tunisia and the surrender of about 400,000 Axis troops in North Africa. Moreover the Allied air forces and navies had ensured that the defeated troops could not escape to fight again, as the British had done at Dunkirk. The tide had turned, and the conquest of Sicily followed. This was the first Axis territory in Europe to fall to the Allies and it led to the collapse of Italy and the ignominious end of the strutting dictator Mussolini. After that, the Allies had to fight for every inch as they slogged up the length of Italy but their steady advance continued. Meanwhile the Russian armies were rolling back the Germans on every Eastern front and their massive armies and Stalin tanks were entering Europe. The once deadly U-boats had been defeated in the Atlantic by a combination of Allied naval forces and the long-range planes of Coastal Command. Throughout, the German mainland was being pounded from above by an ever-increasing number of heavy bombers of Bomber Command and by the now almost equally large USAAF. Their formations of B-17 Flying Fortresses and B-24 Liberators penetrated deep into Germany in broad daylight, protected by swarms of their long-range P-47 and P-51 fighters.

The USAAF's initial problems had been overcome. After the early slaughter of their heavy bombers on daylight raids such as those upon the ball-bearing factories of Schweinfurt, when their casualties were enormous, they had produced the peerless P-47 and P-51 escort fighters. The latter had the fighting abilities of the Spitfire combined with enough range to accompany the bomber pilots to Berlin and beyond. An American design of moderate success, the P-51 had been transformed by the change to the British Rolls-Royce Merlin engine. P-51 pilots, aided by the P-47 Thunderbolts, shot down German day fighters in their hundreds. Also, the well-protected American bombers were able, by 1944, to hit vital targets with the accuracy that only daylight bombing made possible.

This effort by the US Eighth Air Force aided the RAF in at least two ways. The Luftwaffe could no longer spare many Me 109s and Fw 190s to fight at night alongside their Ju 88 and Me 110 night fighters. Most single-engined fighters were desperately needed to protect the German homeland from the US Fortresses and Liberators which the Germans could see all too plainly. In addition, the decision to concentrate many of the

American bombing attacks on the German oil and synthetic oil production was effectively denying the Luftwaffe not only the fuel needed for daily flying operations but also the fuel needed for essential flying training. By 1944, the large numbers of Luftwaffe pilots lost were not being fully replaced, and those pilots who were hurriedly trained and thrown into action were far less thoroughly taught than in the past when fuel was plentiful and the demand for replacement less urgent. Huge formations of the USAAF's twin-engined B-25 Mitchells and B-26 Marauders were also attacking in daylight industrial and strategic targets nearer the English Channel.

To complete the global picture of successes, the Japanese were being driven remorsely back towards their homeland as the Americans, having smashed the Japanese navy, recaptured island after island in the Pacific, while the British Fourteenth Army, brilliantly led by Field Marshal Slim, was remorselessly defeating the Japanese first in Burma and then in Malaya. Soon Singapore would be within Slim's sights.

However, despite these promising months when victory after victory was achieved, the task of recapturing Europe itself from the grip of the Nazi warlords remained truly formidable. A huge German army stood guard on the other side of the Channel, entrenched behind massive concrete walls which millions of slave-labourers had painstakingly created. The walls bristled with guns and the beaches were laid with mines and barbed wire. The same slave labourers had enabled the Germans to continue to produce tanks, guns and planes at much the same rate as before in spite of the massive raids on their towns and factories by the RAF and the USAAF. This miracle of production was carried out on the same scale and with the same determination as that which Britain had displayed in 1940 when its factories were being devastated day and night by German bombers.

Talk of the forthcoming cross-Channel invasion which clearly had to come soon dominated English conversation, and nowhere more so than in the army syndicates at Camberley. Many of the Allies had half expected the invasion across the Channel to be launched in 1943 soon after the many victories of late 1942 and early 1943. The Russians had virtually demanded that it be attempted then but only a small experiment, the ill-fated Dieppe raid, had taken place. That small but costly endeavour showed that there were many difficulties to be overcome before any serious cross-Channel invasion could be launched with any chance of success. Stalin had to be content with the successful landings in north-west Africa.

The whole structure of the RAF was being radically changed. Air Marshal Sir Arthur Tedder, whom many regarded as the best brain in the RAF and whose talents eventually resulted in his appointment as deputy to General Eisenhower, the Supreme Commander of Allied Forces in Europe, had instituted a new Tactical Air Force (TAF) composed of bombers, fighters and coastal aircraft. The TAF was created to assist the great cross-Channel invasion and was already in action, attacking daily the sites of the V1 terror weapon and generally disrupting every form of enemy road, rail and water transport in all the areas where an invasion was likely to take place.

Only very few people knew exactly when – and more importantly where – the invasion would take place. It was rightly said that the fate of Western civilization would depend upon the outcome of this gigantic endeavour which had to be mounted in 1944: if it was further delayed into 1945 or beyond, then the successful Russian armies seemed likely to become the masters of all Europe. Many openly wondered, with good reason, whether the Russians would make better European masters than the brutal Nazis.

141 Squadron was also undergoing dramatic changes. By 1944 it was fully equipped with Mosquitoes and was thus able to penetrate deeper into Germany in pursuit of the German night fighters whose blips appeared on their Serrate and AI screens. The Germans had countered this threat by developing their own airborne radar detection sets. RAF and Luftwaffe night fighters were henceforth equipped with sets which could detect each other's radar transmissions, as well as with an

array of gadgets which would make life more difficult for pursuers. The experimental operations using Serrate, which Bob Braham had personally proved to be feasible and which his squadron had brought to fruition, had now become part of the RAF's standard tactics. Along with two other Mosquito squadrons, 141 Squadron had formed the kernel of 100 Group. The Group's motto was 'Confound and Destroy', and as much effort was put into the former aspect as into the latter.

In 100 Group every form of deception was employed. The German night fighter defence systems on the ground and in the air were being constantly tricked, bamboozled, lured in the wrong direction and interfered with by a score of different ploys. Their radar and radio frequencies were jammed. The Allied boffins were having a field day. 100 Group became a vast enterprise carried out at considerable cost. Some American units were also involved in this war of deception and by the time the war ended as many as twenty-five units had become involved in 100 Group's secret work. But it worked. The crippling night losses were reduced and Bomber Command, using bigger and bigger bombs, dropped with ever-increasing accuracy, thanks largely to the latest navigation devices dreamed up by the back-room boys, were nightly pounding the German cities and reducing them to rubble. Goering's boast that no enemy plane would ever penetrate German defences was made to look even more ridiculous.

As the British people waited with bated breath for the day when the cross-Channel invasion would be launched, many more backroom boys were busy preparing elaborate hoaxes to mislead German intelligence, with the result that the enemy never knew the precise location until D-Day arrived. Even after D-Day and the landings along the Normandy coasts, the German High Command remained convinced that a second invasion would be launched across the Straits of Dover, or even in Norway. At this time, every German soldier was desperately needed in the Normandy area in order to contain the Allies' initial precarious bridgehead there. While the Germans were being forced to give ground around Caen and

St Lo, sixteen of their divisions – well over half a million men – sat idle opposite Dover awaiting a second invasion that never came: proof that the elaborate hoaxes had succeeded.

Bob Braham meanwhile was pulling every string he could to ensure that, when his long Staff Course did eventually end, he would be able to return to the fray. His forte as he saw it was flying aircraft and shooting down the enemy, and his record showed that few could equal him at this, especially at night. Earlier in the war Bob had been compelled to be idle on the sidelines while the daylight Battle of Britain had raged overhead. Then he had had to play a very minor role in the inadequate night fighter version of the Blenheim. He had welcomed the Beaufighters with open arms. By 1944, with the hard work done and his skills honed to perfection, he was raring to be in at the kill in the magnificent Mosquitoes.

The Luftwaffe by 1944 was being slaughtered by day and night. Bob did not really care whether he tackled them in darkness or in daylight – all he wanted to do was get at them and join in the slaughter as often as possible. When his course ended, which Bob seems to have passed in spite of his lack of interest in it, Bob emerged with increased respect and personal regard for some of his 'pongo' brethren. They in turn seem to have learned something new from Bob. It is recorded in *Scramble* that, on the final day of the course, Bob and his new friends said 'Goodbye' to the prestigious Army College Staff Course at Camberley by washing down the portraits of the distinguished generals, which graced the main building, with a fire hose!

Bob's quest for a flying job, almost *any* flying job, proved to be in vain. On an exploratory visit to the new 100 Group HQ, he learned that the AOC definitely wanted him, with all his unique experience, but only on the ground as a member of his staff at HQ. This was a disappointment but the AOC's view was understandable. However, during the visit, Bob found himself discussing tactics with the Group's SASO, Air Commodore Roderick A. Chisholm DSO, DFC, a renowned night fighter with almost as great a reputation as Bob himself. However, the two men found their views about the best use of Serrate-equipped aircraft were at sharp variance. Accordingly, Bob decided not to accept any appointment with 100 Group and instead left it to chance to see what the Air Ministry would decide for him. What turned up was a pleasant surprise.

Air Vice-Marshal (later Sir) Basil Embry decided to pay a call upon the Army College with the express intention of finding out whether Bob Braham would like to join him at the HQ of a new Group which he had just taken over as AOC. This was part of the new Tactical Air Force. Embry's 2 TAF comprised twelve squadrons of light bombers, half of them Mosquitoes. They would be specifically used to attack, by day and night, German surface transport and other targets of opportunity in preparation for, and subsequent to, the long-awaited D-Day. Basil Embry was the RAF leader whom Bob most respected. They had much in common, especially in spirit. Air Vice-Marshal Embry wanted Bob to help train the Group in night operations. Bob was the ideal choice owing to his experience as a night Ranger pilot and his subsequent Serrate victories.

Bob Braham, however, still had his sights on taking command of an active squadron. The two men knew and respected each other and a compromise was eventually reached. W/Cdr Braham would fill an important post in Basil Embry's Group HQ but would also be allowed to go roving over enemy territory on just one flight per week, provided that he could find himself a suitable navigator from personnel in Group HQ to accompany him. Each flight had to be approved by the AOC in person and none was to overfly Germany.

Bob had been grounded for a full three months. Would that period away from the firing line have blunted his enthusiasm or taken the edge off his finely honed skills as a fighting airman? Few pilots went through the war without having 'second thoughts', when the very real dangers of the job would rise up and almost dominate every waking moment. Would Bob Braham, posted to a Staff appointment in the HQ of No. 2 Light Bomber Group of the Tactical Air Force, be so affected?

Time alone would tell.

15
Staff Officer

Several RAF Group HQs were housed in splendid country house mansions. The HQ of the No. 2 Light Bomber Group, Tactical Air Force (2 TAF) was no exception, being based at Mongewell Park, Berkshire. The Group's squadrons, however, existed in much more spartan surroundings, the Mosquitoes being largely based at Lasham (107, 305 and 613 Squadrons) and at Hunsdon (21, 464 and 487 (RNZAF) Squadrons). However, many of the men were already living under canvas in preparation for the day when they would move over to France behind the invasion fleets.

As well as bombing all the German V1 'Doodle Bug' sites, the Mosquitoes were already attacking almost anything that moved on *both* sides of the Seine river, both by day and by night. The policy was that for every bomb dropped west of the Seine, where the Allies intended to invade, an equal number had to be dropped east of the river in order to keep the Germans guessing. The attacks on surface transport were carried out at night as well as by day and Bob Braham was given the title of Wing Commander Night Operations. His job was to see that the squadrons knew how to attack effectively at night and that their training should be efficiently directed towards this demanding task. He seems to have taken office on about 21 February 1944 and would probably have been granted a short spell of much-needed leave between that date and the end of his course at The Army Staff College which finished on the 11th. However, he seems to have partially ignored the leave (as usual!) as there is a record of him flying with Jacko in a

212

Mosquito on a low-level cross-country exercise on the 19th. Joan and their boys continued to come a poor second place while the war against Germany still raged. Fortunately, Joan, wisely and proudly, accepted this position although, reading between the lines of *Scramble*, Bob himself clearly had pangs of conscience about his unfair treatment of his family.

His personal pursuit of the war had become almost an obsession. His RAF masters were honouring and promoting him and he considered that even a day away from his job was akin to letting down those who had put such trust and faith in him. Bob seems to have had it planted firmly into him, probably by his father, that a 'job worth doing was worth doing properly'. And Bob Braham's idea of 'properly' was to set an almost impossibly high standard.

The presence of Jacko, flying again with Bob, was not just a lucky coincidence. It seems that part of the 'deal' which Bob had arranged with Basil Embry was that both Jacko and Sticks should also be posted to Basil Embry's HQ. If so, it made sense. Both Jacko and Sticks knew as much about night flying over enemy territory as Bob himself; there was the added advantage for him that when he set out on his weekly operations, he could count upon finding at HQ at least two skilled crew members who would not hesitate to accompany him. By then Jacko had received a bar to his DFC.

Air Vice-Marshal Embry was gathering around him a collection of bellicose Staff officers. His deputy was one of the famous Atcherley twins: both David and his twin brother Dick were notorious. Both were renowned RAF pilots . . . and playboys before the war. One had been selected to take part in the successful High Speed Flight which had held the Schneider Trophy and the world speed record in Supermarine float-planes, which had reached nearly 400 mph several years before the war. The Atcherley twins believed in flying hard and playing hard, and might almost be said to have set the pattern which the fighting Commands of the RAF followed during the war. Although most Group HQs were fairly staid institutions, it would seem that No. 2 Light

Bomber Group, TAF, continued to enjoy life in the light-hearted manner of the squadrons.

Sticks didn't arrive at 2 TAF HQ until early March, but Bob was quickly into action without him. On 28 February Bob and Jacko went to Lasham and there 'borrowed' a Mosquito of 613 Squadron for a daylight Ranger deep into France. On this sortie they reached Bourges (about 150 miles south of Paris) where they shot up a petrol lorry which they left in flames. The weather was poor and they ran into a snow storm, not the nicest thing to encounter at low level. Although it must have been a full and tiring day, beginning with a flight to Lasham in an Oxford from Benson (the nearest airfield to Mongewell Park) and ending with a return flight to Benson, Bob tackled it with the enthusiasm of a schoolboy. In his personal log-book he wrote that it was 'bloody good fun'. In all he made five flights that day as, probably due to the poor weather, he first landed at Ford before taking the aircraft back to Lasham. Judging by his log-book comment, the long Staff Course had not diminished Bob's enthusiasm for operations.

These daylight operations were unconnected with his job at HQ. The Mosquitoes of 2 TAF were a type that he had rarely flown before, and they were not equipped with AI or Serrate or any other of the boffins latest 'toys'. However, they did carry Gee navigational equipment. Jacko flew with Bob solely as a navigator in order to ensure that they did not get lost or run out of petrol. These Mossies would have been armed with the usual four 20mm cannon plus four machine-guns in the nose. Mosquitoes never carried defensive guns: their 'defence' lay in speed.

To Bob, who had not flown on operations for about four months, it must have been exhilarating to be at the controls of the splendidly fast Mosquito flying at almost nought feet, waving at Frenchmen in their fields, but always on the look-out to blast away at anything which he regarded as a legitimate target. It is well known that French morale was boosted by such operations. The French were well aware that the long-awaited invasion was bound to begin soon and their gallant underground organizations were preparing themselves so that they too could play a part in the liberation of their beloved country.

Sticks seems to have arrived at HQ on 4 March. One wonders if he knew what he was letting himself in for! The very next day he was once again flying alongside his former CO of 141 Squadron, and helped him destroy his twenty-first confirmed 'kill'! They took off at 1310 hours and again set course for the Avord-Bourges area south of Paris. The poor weather which had restricted all other activities at Lasham that day seems to have also affected Bourges and Orleans. With nothing to shoot up at those airfields, Bob proceeded to the airfield at Châteaudun. Here he caught sight of a large four-engined Heinkel 177 apparently flying a circuit at about 800 ft. Without any opposition Bob was able to close up to within about 300 yards and fire a long burst. The Heinkel soon burst into flames and spun in. It burned on the ground for many minutes while the Mosquito crew watched.

Bob's principal enemy that day was the weather. On the way back, still hugging the ground on the look-out for anything worth shooting at, the Mossie ran into another snowstorm. This, however, didn't prevent Bob from shooting up the only source of ground fire which he experienced during his long flight, in the neighbourhood of Pont-de-la-Percée. Bob noted in his personal log-book that they had covered 900 miles during the course of the Ranger sortie.

The He 177 deserves a mention since it was seldom seen over the UK. It was produced as a long-range four-engined aircraft which would patrol over the Atlantic to discover and report Allied convoys for the German U-boats to attack. Its engines were mounted in pairs one on top of the other, each pair driving a single four-bladed propeller. It therefore looked like a twin-engined aircraft. Its teething and engine troubles were endless and the Luftwaffe pilots lost so much faith in it that they regarded it as the '*RAF*'s best plane', because so many had crashed with fatal results. Although it was first developed quite early in the war, it never became a serious menace to the Allies. It was a poor substitute for the efficient Fw 200 Condor which it was designed to replace.

Exactly one week later Bob, again flying with Sticks, carried out a similar Ranger in a Mosquito of 613 Squadron based at Lasham, probably first flying there in the Group's Oxford aircraft. Again the weather was cloudy. Indeed, it seems that Basil Embry, whose personal permission Bob had to obtain for every sortie, only allowed him to fly when the forecast weather conditions were bad enough to offer him good cloud protection. While allowing Bob Braham to operate, Embry was doing what he could to protect his ace pilot. However, on this sortie, which covered nearly 1,000 miles over the now familiar area south of Paris, Bob and Sticks for once came off second best. They could discover no enemy activity around any of the several airfields which they orbited but, breaking cloud on the way home north of Bayeux, they ran into accurate machine-gun fire which hit their starboard engine. As the oil temperature of the glycol-cooled engine was rising rapidly, Bob had no option but to switch it off before it caught fire and return to base as best he could on the remaining one, a feat which he accomplished safely.

Two days later Bob, accompanied by Joan and his father, attended at Buckingham Palace where the king pinned on to his lapel the second bar to his DFC and the bar to his DSO. Jacko was also there to receive the bar to his DFC. Bob had to stand in line *twice*. The king's aide had, unusually, got into a muddle and, when Bob first presented himself before His Majesty, the correct decorations were not readily to hand, so he had to 'go round again'. These ceremonies were well staged. The guests assembled on gilded chairs while the recipients were led away and briefed. Small, almost invisible, hooks were affixed to the lapels of their uniforms. King George would appear and the men would line up in a prearranged order and step forward when their names were called. In the background a military band would be playing popular tunes. His Majesty might, or might not, stop for a brief chat with a recipient. On these occasions, he would be relaxed and ask well-informed questions without a trace of stutter. He would wear a certain amount of make-up so as to be more clearly visible to the crowd of relatives watching the proceedings. As soon as one recipient turned away out of sight, a hand would reach out and swiftly remove the decoration from its hook! It was then placed in its silk-lined case and later returned.

It was another ten days before Bob could again get the required permission from Basil Embry to go Ranging again. Doubtless, as soon as a week had elapsed from his last sortie, he had been agitating daily. For Bob, this weekly flight was his treat of the week. 'The only thing which kept me sane,' he recorded in *Scramble*. He did not relish ground appointments. But to make up for lost time Bob, this time flying with the Group's Navigation Officer, S/Ldr Robertson, destroyed *two* enemy aircraft – his twenty-second and twenty-third confirmed kills. Again he flew first to Lasham to borrow a Mosquito from 613 Squadron, but this Ranger sortie was different as the route took him over Denmark where the Luftwaffe kept many operational aircraft. Since Lasham is in Hampshire, Bob first flew to Coltishall in Norfolk so as to be nearer the target area. Soon he had overflown most of Denmark and was patrolling the east side of that country. In the vicinity of Aalborg he caught sight of a Ju 34 and a Ju 52 flying in close proximity. Aalborg is in the north-east of Denmark, not too far away from Sweden, and the German pilots could not have been expecting to be fired on by their enemy in this relatively safe area, far distant from any battle zone. Both types of Junkers were military transport, rather than fighting, types, and neither aircraft made the slightest effort to defend itself. Both were soon dispatched by bursts of cannon fire. The Ju 34, a single-engined type, winged over and crashed in flames but the Ju 52, a larger three-engined type, attempted to crash land in marshy ground where it turned over and crumpled on to one wing. Bob, who always tried to make certain of an enemy's destruction, made a final attack upon the wreck as it lay upside down on the ground. Strapped into an armed aircraft, Bob Braham was in the business of killing Huns and was totally ruthless about it. During these attacks he had used 320 rounds of cannon shells and had also activated his camera gun. Initially he thought the Ju 34 was a Me 109 flying with its wheels down but subsequently realized that it was a Ju 34, a type only rarely seen by RAF crews. (It seems likely that the recognition was due to the films taken during combat.)

A pattern emerges to Bob's Ranger operations. Clearly his first priority was to shoot down enemy aircraft and he reckoned that the best way of finding them, without any radar or control guidance to help him, was to circle around known enemy airfields, such as Aalborg. Most airfields were likely to have aircraft airborne on training or test flights at various times of the day and it was obviously the best place to be for one intent upon destroying them in the air.

It was near another airfield that Bob scored his twenty-fourth victim on his next rationed flight on 4 April. He again borrowed a Mosquito from 613 Squadron, but this time he must have first flown to Predannack (or another airfield in the west country) before setting out, once again with Sticks Gregory, to 'look for trouble' in the Bordeaux area. Perhaps he was looking for another He 177. They were known to operate from the big airfield at Merignac in that area. Since each He 177 carried a large crew of up to ten, they represented a most satisfactory 'kill'. However, Bob's 24th victim was in sharp contrast to the large four-engined He 177: it was a single-engined trainer biplane, almost the German equivalent of the RAF's Tiger Moth! It was diving and zooming over a range of hills behind Bordeaux but whether it was on a private beat-up mission or on a practice bombing exercise is not known. Whatever, the fire from the Mosquito's multiple cannon and machine-guns caused the small Bucker 131 Jungmann to disintegrate so rapidly that Bob had to fly through the fragments. Not finding any other aircraft to attack, Bob then had to be content with blasting a camp and a lorry near Bordeaux. This trip covered 1,250 miles in all. More 'good fun' appears in his log-book.

The loss of a training bi-plane was not great in simple terms of enemy aircraft destroyed, but both this sortie and the previous one over north-east Denmark may well have caused the enemy to move personnel, guns and planes to these seldom-attacked areas in order to be able to counter future Ranger attacks. The already overstretched Luftwaffe would have been further overextended by such movements.

On their next Ranger, nine days later, Bob and Sticks encountered more worthy opposition. Again they headed for Denmark, this time in a Mosquito of 305 Squadron, a Polish unit based at Lasham. In order to take off closer to the enemy, they first landed at West Raynham, Norfolk, to refuel. After crossing the North Sea, Bob espied a He 111 which was orbiting some hoardings near the lighthouse at Esbjerg. It was at low altitude, about 300 ft, and Bob had little difficulty in blasting it with a three-second burst of fire, whereupon it crashed into the sea with one engine on fire and exploded on impact. Later he proceeded to his Aalborg hunting ground where he caught sight of a twin-engined Fw 58, another small enemy type rarely encountered by the RAF. A burst of fire soon set its starboard engine on fire and the aircraft dived vertically into the ground. As Bob broke away in his Mosquito, two Me 109s were sighted approaching from the south. The cloud level was at 1,000 ft and Bob was able to hide in its folds and make good his escape. Some light flak was also fired at him. Bob flew back direct to Benson, near his Group's HQ, returning the Mosquito to its owners at Lasham the following day.

Basil Embry's policy of only allowing Bob to operate when the cloud base was expected to be low enough to provide him with a safe line of retreat had proved correct. As it was, one of the Me 109s, a type which had a slight speed advantage over the Mosquito, had managed to get close enough for a short but ineffective burst of fire. It would have been most unwise for Bob to attempt to fight it out with even one Me 109. Single-engined fighters always had an advantage over the less manoeuvrable, slower and heavier twins.

Rather surprisingly, Air Vice-Marshal Basil Embry then

allowed Bob Braham to take part in a low-level strike on an important enemy railway marshalling yard about 15 or 20 miles west of Paris on 22 April. By then, perhaps, Embry was one of the very few who knew the Allies would be attempting to land in the Normandy area within only six weeks time and every target west of the Seine needed to be attacked. Although Bob again picked up a Mosquito from the Polish 305 Squadron, the other eight Mosquitoes of the attacking force were from 107 Squadron, also based at Lasham. Bob carried two 500 lb bombs fitted with an 11-second delay fuse, giving just enough time for a low-flying aircraft to clear the area before detonation, and another couple of 500 lb bombs fused to explode six hours after being dropped. Bob Braham had never dropped bombs before and had never had any practice at this precise art (apart from one attempt during the brief period when two Beaus of 141 Squadron had been fitted experimentally with bomb-racks).

The raid resulted in several significant hits on rolling stock and railway repair shops, as well as blocking several tracks with craters. Bob, as the 'new boy', was sent in last to attack. He dived from about 3,000 ft to about 200 ft. Being last man to attack, he received most of the flak. German flak was always well aimed* and in this instance four of the eight aircraft were hit. Although the flak was both intense and accurate, Bob's personal log-book describes the sortie as 'quite good fun'.

Exactly one week later Bob and Sticks were again Ranging in a Mosquito of 305 Squadron, this time over central and south-west France, operating direct from Lasham. Embry had evidently relaxed his cloud-cover proviso as the weather was clear with good visibility and there were no friendly clouds into which to escape. North-west of Poitiers the pair went down to attack two German road vehicles and as Bob was pulling up he sighted an Fw 190 flying on a reciprocal track at

---

* Unlike that of the allies, German AA defence was in the hands of their air force, the Luftwaffe.

about 300 ft. This formidable single-seater fighter appeared to be on a special mission: it seemed to be carrying what looked like a rocket under each wing with an additional fuel tank slung under the fuselage. With a burst of power it sped away at about 300 mph. Bob gave the enemy a long burst from 600 yards in an attempt to slow it down and the tactic seemed to work as evidence of a hit was observed and the Focke-Wulf fighter did slow down. This enabled Bob Braham to get in a good burst from nearly dead astern, whereupon the Fw 190 caught fire, stalled and crashed in flames with the wreckage spread over three fields. It was W/Cdr Braham's twenty-seventh confirmed victory, and a prized one too. Fw 190s were not often destroyed by Mosquitoes, being both faster and more manoeuvrable, and the signs are that this one was engaged on special trials with rockets and a long-range tank. The successes in daylight by the USAAF's B-17s and B-24s had forced the Germans to resort to extraordinary countermeasures which included using day fighters to fire rockets at the big formations. By this time, the huge American daylight raids were causing mortal damage to German property and morale. The Luftwaffe was compelled to try almost anything to thwart them: fighters armed with rockets, experimental jet aircraft and even a rocket-powered plane, the Me 163. By then, the USAAF raiders were escorted throughout their sorties by up to a thousand of the efficient and deadly P-51 Mustang fighters which were at least a match for any fighter that the Luftwaffe possessed.

Although Bob Braham was maintaining that flying his 'ration' of Ranger operations was the 'only thing which kept him sane', the evidence suggests that he was also doing a valuable ground job at Basil Embry's HQ. The job was difficult, too. Because the specific role of the Mosquito squadrons controlled by 2 TAF was to destroy German surface transport at night once the invasion started, Bob had to persuade the squadrons to get themselves ready for this important night role. However, the Mossie crews, who had previously been operating largely on day Ranger and similar operations, disliked night flying. For some, it interfered with other 'night operations' with girlfriends; operationally it also carried additional risks. 'Sir Isaac' was known to hover over all night take-offs and landings. The Mosquito pilots did not feel the same need for concealment that darkness provided for the heavy bomber crews. The crews of 2 TAF wanted to continue with their exciting day operations.

Bob, often accompanied by Sticks, visited every squadron to impress upon them the importance of the role which would soon be theirs. He assured them from personal experience that night flying was, once a pilot got used to it, no more dull nor dangerous than daylight operations. However, night flying never became popular with the Mossie crews of 2 TAF.

Initially they flew at night against enemy airfields. These were easy targets to locate and the crews who found hangars and aircraft to shoot up began to take a more favourable view of their new tactics. However, locating a large airfield was much easier than searching for enemy vehicles along the network of narrow French roads. Some attacks were tried against surface transport at night but the success rate did not satisfy Bob or the Group. These problems led to the introduction of the 4.5 inch parachute flare. Dropped from about 2,000–3,000 ft, these would illuminate a wide area of countryside for several minutes during which period the Mosquitoes could dive down and attack anything visible on the roads with withering fire. Each aircraft was also fitted with bomb racks which could carry up to four 500 lb bombs. These were also dropped at night on suitable targets exposed by the flares. However, the flares did not last long enough for the aircraft to lose enough height to be able to attack at low level. This led to the suggestion that one aircraft should drop the flares while another, already in position at low level, carried out the actual attack. All this required intensive re-training and a high degree of cooperation between flare-dropper and attacker.

The Group also controlled several RAF squadrons of USA-built B-25 Mitchell light bombers. They were larger aircraft with greater carrying capacity than the Mosquitoes. They could carry dozens of flares. Consequently, tactics were developed whereby a high-flying Mitchell would drop a succession of flares, turning night into day, while the Mosquitoes below did the attacking. This suggestion was, as might have been expected, furiously resisted by the Mitchell crews, some of whom were American. They realized that their role would make them vulnerable to enemy night fighters and they did not relish carrying out a supporting role while British Mosquito pilots had 'all the fun' of the low-level strafing. However, like it or not, the Mitchell units had to comply. Their dislike for their less glamorous role was greatly worsened when, on the first attempt to serve as flare droppers, two of their aircraft were shot down; to make matters worse, it transpired that both had been shot down by British night fighters which had mistaken them for the similar-looking twin-engined, twin-tailed Dornier fighter/bombers.

The training of the squadrons to make them capable of effectively attacking German surface transport at night immediately after D-Day was an important task since Basil Embry's Group was the only one charged with this particular responsibility. Since the many squadrons of Typhoons and other daylight fighters would quickly make it impossible for German troop movements to take place safely during daylight after D-Day, the success in holding the initial Allied bridgehead depended in part on the night attacks on enemy roads and railways which 2 TAF could make with their Mosquitoes and Mitchells.

Given a job to do, whether he liked it or not, Bob Braham was the type who made sure that it would be carried out efficiently. He even records in *Scramble* that he and Sticks were actually booed by a unit to which they had gone to explain the tactics which they would have to learn in order to operate efficiently at night. Mosquito pilots loved their aircraft. They were confident that they could roam across Europe in daylight shooting up any target that caught their eye. To forgo this great pleasure and turn themselves into night attackers of elusive ground targets went much against their feelings, previous training and experience.

After Bob Braham's twenty-seventh victory in the air, there are signs that his judgement was becoming impaired. He had scarcely taken any leave since the war began and had been flying, almost always leading from the front, for much of the previous two years or so; he must have been extremely tired. In *Scramble* he admits to finding himself becoming short-tempered with his family on the few occasions when he visited them. By spring 1944, as it became increasingly obvious to almost everyone in the UK that the invasion was about to be launched, a general edginess permeated the country. 'Let's get on with it. Let's get it over and done with,' was a widely voiced impatient cry. It probably also irked Bob that he had to travel around his Group trying to sell them a change of policy, knowing that, in their shoes, he would have been equally resentful of it.

Eight days after his success against the Fw 190, Bob Braham collected a navigator from Group, F/Lt Walsh, and borrowed a Mosquito from 21 Squadron at Gravesend. Since he had elected to go Ranging over Denmark again, he first flew to West Raynham in Norfolk. By this time 141 Squadron were based there and it was just like old times having the aircraft refuelled by his former ground crews. Bob and Walsh spent the night at West Raynham, and doubtless Bob received a hero's welcome.

The next day was partially cloudy but with good visibility. Bob was soon across the North Sea and heading for his happy hunting ground in the Aalborg area. Nor did he have to wait long. Before reaching Aalborg he caught sight of a Ju 88 flying just beneath the clouds. For the next ten minutes Bob did his best to catch and shoot down this enemy aircraft. The chase went in and out of the broken clouds with the German rear gunner firing back at times. Bob managed to get in four fairly long bursts, mostly at a range of about 400 yards and using deflection shooting. The third burst set the enemy's port engine on fire and the fourth, from close range, set the aircraft well alight. It dived and crashed in a ball of fire 8 miles west of Roskilde. This was Bob Braham's twenty-eighth air victory.

Bob was almost out of ammunition and decided to call it a day and return to West Raynham. By the time they landed, they had been in the air for more than five hours and had flown over 1,100 miles. Don Walsh DFC, a former RAF Mitchell navigator, much enjoyed this outing with Bob. In fact, Walsh had first sighted the Ju 88. He was to see much of Bob during the next year but under far less favourable circumstances.

Bob Braham's next sortie was only five days later. By this date, 12 May 1944, many people expected the invasion to have already begun. But only a dummy run had been carried out to test the arrangements along the south coast. Bob used the same departing arrangements. After borrowing a Mosquito from 107 Squadron at Lasham, he flew for an overnight stop at West Raynham where his former 141 Squadron personnel refuelled the aircraft while Bob and Sticks enjoyed a night in the Mess with their old squadron friends. The next morning found Bob and Sticks Ranging in the Aalborg–Copenhagen area. By then the countryside must have been familiar to them. However, the presence of the Mosquito had been detected at an early stage of the flight and near Samsos Island, a ship fired at the aircraft. Near Hurning, an Fw 190 was sighted and Bob gave chase. However, he soon found himself being hotly pursued by an Me 109 which dived and fired a burst which scored several hits, rupturing the fuel lines on the port wing. Fuel began to leak out. Happily for Bob, the Messerschmitt was not seen again. Bob ignored the damage to his aircraft and continued to chase after the Focke-Wulf. At about zero feet – so low in fact that he flew into and bounced off a mound – and at a range of only about 100 yards, Bob was able to fire a killing burst into the enemy. The starboard elevator of the Fw 190 flew off, followed by bits from the cockpit. A fire ensued; billowing smoke enveloped the enemy aircraft which abruptly reared up and stalled. An explosion erupted from its engine and, almost colliding with Bob's Mosquito, it crashed in flames about 10 miles from Aalborg. Bob soon turned for home but his already damaged aircraft was again hit, this time by a hail of ground fire as he crossed the coast.

The fuel used up during the engagement with the enemy aircraft was considerable and Sticks quickly calculated that they had no hope of being able to reach England. Bob feathered one propeller as he could fly more economically on one engine. It was only then that he became aware of how hard they had bounced off the ground during the pursuit: the tips of the feathered propeller were noticeably bent back!

About one hundred miles from the nearest home airfield, with the fuel gauges registering near zero, Bob climbed briefly in order to broadcast more effectively his emergency state. His 'Mayday' call was received and Bob was pleased to get acknowledgement and to learn that the Air Sea Rescue services had been alerted and would be putting to sea heading in his direction. However, Bob had been unable to pass a positive position of where he might have to ditch. This made the chances of any ASR boat finding the ditched Mosquito only slight. Accordingly, when Sticks sighted some boats that appeared to be trawlers, Bob decided to make the most of this good fortune. The cockpit hatch was jettisoned. The two men tightened their shoulder harnesses and Bob brought the aircraft down into the sea about half a mile ahead of the leading trawler. At a speed of about 125 mph, the 'wooden wonder' smashed into a slight swell and amid expensive splintering noises soon came to a stop. Neither Bob nor Sticks was hurt – they weren't even wet. The Mosquito had broken in half and the tail section drifted away. Sticks and Bob sat briefly on the shoulder of the cockpit but decided that since their portion contained the heavy engines, it would probably soon sink. They decided therefore to 'abandon plane' and to get themselves into their one-man dinghies. Up to this point both men had stayed relatively dry but, as Bob started to inflate his dinghy, a movement of the sea caused both men to fall off their perch into the water. Bob, after some difficulty in inflating and righting his dinghy, managed to crawl into it, wishing that he had practised this awkward manoeuvre. Sticks meanwhile had lost his dinghy and was bobbing about in the water a few feet away. Bob managed to paddle across to reach him; he tried to haul him aboard but their combined weight nearly dragged under his single dinghy. However, it had just sufficient buoyancy to keep them afloat until a rowing boat from the nearest trawler appeared. It could not have come too soon.

Sticks had swallowed a lot of sea water and, once on board the trawler, was in no state to appreciate the mammoth glass of rum which was thrust upon the two men. It was a powerful drink and it almost made Bob immediately keel over. In Sticks's case he had to rush to the heads where he was violently sick. Grateful to their rescuers, Bob and Sticks, now wrapped in blankets, gave the trawler crews most of their equipment as souvenirs.

The ships were, it transpired, small RN minesweepers and they used their 20mm Oerlikon guns to sink the two parts of the Mosquito which remained afloat despite their damaged condition. Soon a fast naval MTB appeared and the airmen were transferred to this and were soon heading at 30 knots towards Grimsby. About midway, the MTB made contact with the RAF Air Sea Rescue launch and once again Bob and Sticks were transferred at sea. A doctor on board the launch checked them over and they were given dry clothes.

At Grimsby the CO of a nearby RAF Bomber Command station personally picked them up in his car and took them back to his Mess where they were wined and dined in style. Although both were now clad in civilian clothes, no doubt the CO was aware that between them they could have displayed the ribbons of two DSOs, five DFCs and a DFM! However, all the weary pair wanted was an early bed, and they were reluctant to be welcomed as heroes.

Some idea of the high regard in which Bob and Sticks were held in 141 Squadron can be measured by the fact that when it became known on 12 May that they were missing, Mosquitoes from 141 Squadron were taking off within minutes to search probable areas where they might have ditched while others were standing by at immediate readiness. Almost all squadron activities were directed towards a thorough air search.

Bob was rightly apprehensive about the kind of reception

he would receive from his AOC. Although he had requested permission for the Ranger operation, by the time he took off Basil Embry had neither said 'yes' nor 'no'. His apprehension was heightened when his AOC refused to see him until he was more correctly dressed in RAF uniform. Bob did get a dressing-down which made him feel thoroughly ashamed. He had great admiration for his AOC and felt that in his enthusiasm he had abused his trust. However, Bob *had* destroyed his twenty-ninth enemy, an FW 190 too, and that counted for much in the eyes of his fighting AOC. David Atcherley was also present during Bob's reprimand. In the end, after all was said and done, Sir Basil eased the tension by saying, 'The matter is now forgotten. Have a beer with me at lunch time.'

Bob was Basil Embry's favourite pilot and the one who most mirrored his own fighting spirit. It was impossible for the Air Vice Marshal to be too severe with a man who had done no more than he himself had done in the past, and would do again in the future. Bob and Sticks finished a memorable day in the Group's most popular local pub, the White Hart, always known as 'Clemmie's' because of its friendly owner, Mrs Clements.

It may be significant that Sticks never again flew with Bob Braham. No pilot could have had a more faithful or reliable radar operator/navigator but . . . both had already done more than enough. Sticks, with his DFC & Bar and DFM, was probably one of the most highly decorated radar operator/ navigators in the entire RAF (he later received the DSO). If he saw the events of 12 May as a warning, who could blame him? It should also have warned Bob Braham too, but it didn't. By then, operations against his hated enemy had become almost addictive for the much decorated wing commander.

On 25 May, flying with S/Ldr Robertson, Bob Braham, now with twenty-nine certain kills to his credit, set out on yet another Ranger operation. Once again he borrowed a Mosquito from 21 Squadron at Gravesend and flew to West Raynham to have it topped up by his former crewmen of 141 Squadron before heading for Denmark. However, as he approached the enemy coast, he ran into poor weather, with continuous drizzle and low cloud. For once, he allowed discretion to rule and he turned back. This was his fifteenth Ranger operation since taking over his staff job at HQ but curiously the flight does not appear in Bob's personal logbook. In the course of these operations he had shot down nine enemy aircraft, bombed an airfield from low level and shot up several other targets of opportunity. Few pilots on *continuous* operations had achieved more in such a short period.

Soon after his ditching, Bob was among the few who were informed of the invasion plans in detail. Thereafter, he was forbidden to operate anywhere near enemy territory in case he was captured and forced to reveal the secret information. So great was the secrecy concerning the when and where of the invasion that the mail of everyone who knew the great secret was censored, even Bob's.

Every activity within the Group was now focused sharply upon the day when the Allied troops would set sail in a vast modern armada towards the Normandy beaches. The first troops went ashore in the early hours of 6 June 1944, a day which will go down in history. During the night of 5th/6th, ninety-eight Mosquitoes of the Group attacked road and rail transport over the length and breadth of Normandy. It was towards this end that all their training had long been directed. Every Mitchell of the Group that could be got into the air also participated in similar attacks, some acting as flare droppers.

On the night of 6 June, not only was Bob Braham operating against enemy road and rail links at night but also Basil Embry himself! When the AOC had last flown, indeed if he ever had, a Mosquito, is not known but disguised as 'Wing Commander Smith', he was determined to play his part. Whether or not *he* had anyone's permission to go night Ranging under a disguised name over Normandy is also not known. Not to be outdone, G/Capt. David Atcherley also decided to take an active part. He persuaded Bob to take him as his navigator in spite of having one arm in a cast as the result of an accident. It also soon transpired that he did not know how to operate the Gee navigating aid. In Bob's view, the injury to his arm would have prevented the deputy AOC from getting out of a Mosquito either in the air to parachute to safety or, if obliged to ditch, at sea. But such fine points had never deterred the Atcherley twins from joining in whatever fun or flying was available. David and Bob did not find any really worthwhile targets to shoot up but did fire several bursts into what seemed to be troop transports and also dropped the 500 lb bombs they were carrying. The action of the Deputy AOC was typical of the aggressive spirit which Basil Embry had infused into all his staff officers at HQ. Most had, of course, been picked by him in the first place.

Bob flew again a week later and once more a week after that, both times in Mosquitoes of 305 Squadron. It seems likely that he was again being limited by a 'once a week' edict from his AOC. On each occasion he took with him S/Ldr Robertson, the Staff Officer who had been with him when they had shot down the Ju 34 and Ju 52 over Denmark. On the first of their June 1944 operations, they attacked a vehicle and bombed a bridge but Bob ruefully reports that he would never have made a good bomber pilot because he missed it completely. On the later mission, when the weather was foul, they still managed to shoot up a train with good results.

This was the last time during the war that W/Cdr J.R.D. Braham DSO & bar, DFC & two bars, took off and returned safely to the UK. From his next flight, another week later, he would not return. He took off in a Mosquito of 21 Squadron on 25 June 1944, but he was not to see England again until 6 May the following year. He and his navigator F/Lt Walsh would spend the intervening months 'in the bag', as involuntary guests of the Luftwaffe in one of their Stalagluft prison camps. The operational career of Fighter Command's most decorated pilot was coming to an end.

16
Last Flight and POW

The imminent promulgation announcing that W/Cdr J.R.D. Braham had been awarded a second bar to his DSO meant that for the remainder of the war, Bob Braham would be the most highly decorated RAF fighter pilot of the war. It must, however, be pointed out that bomber pilot Leonard Cheshire with his VC, two DSOs and three DFCs was the most highly decorated of *all* RAF pilots. It is also difficult to equate Bob's unique decorations with those of G/Capt 'Tirpitz' Tait and Basil Embry, both of whom received *four* DSOs, as well as other decorations. However, Tait and Embry, like Cheshire, were primarily bomber pilots. The citation for this second bar to his DSO again reflects the aggressive qualities which Bob Braham invariably displayed towards the enemy:

> Since being awarded a Bar to the Distinguished Service Order, this officer has taken part in many sorties, including numerous successful attacks on rail targets and on mechanical transport. In air fighting he has destroyed many more enemy aircraft, bringing his victories to at least 29; this officer has displayed the highest qualities of skill and leadership and his achievements are a splendid testimony to his courage and fighting spirit.

Although Sticks seems to have absorbed the lessons of 12 May, when their Mosquito was first hit by an Me 109, hit again by ground fire crossing the coast and was obliged to ditch in the North Sea (where Sticks had all but drowned), clearly Bob

Braham was not so affected by these traumatic events. To Bob, it was inconceivable for a trained pilot in the RAF not to be flying actively against his country's enemies; it was akin to an actor being in the spotlight on stage but not playing any part. He felt that come what may – and it was widely acknowledged that his good fortune could not last for ever – he HAD to continue to fly sorties against the enemy. Guy Gibson was much the same. He was shot down and killed when flying a Mosquito quite unnecessarily at a time when he was holding down a ground job. Bob knew that his vast experience gave him a much greater chance of returning from a contest in the air than that of any raw recruit flung into the battle straight from an OTU. Perhaps he was aware that he had a reputation to maintain. Many wartime aces reached a point where, like it or not, the reputation which they had established travelled before them and more or less compelled them to continue in the same aggressive manner as that upon which their reputation had been built. They were living on a pedestal from which they were not able to climb down, even if they had wished to do so.

Whatever thoughts were in Bob's head, the evidence is that on 25 June, nine days after his previous flight with S/Ldr Robertson over Denmark, W/Cdr Braham, this time flying with the Australian navigator F/Lt Walsh DFC, again took off in a Mosquito to see what targets they could find. Once again, strongly defended Denmark was their destination. The aircraft belonged to 21 Squadron which had just moved to Thorney Island and Bob, as was his custom when heading for Denmark, first flew to West Raynham so that his former crewmen could refuel and, if necessary, re-arm it prior to departure: an extra chore for them but one which they were proud to perform.

The weather was far from ideal for such a risky flight. A pilot who was less tired or less determined might well have refused the flight or turned back at an early stage and reported 'lack of adequate cloud cover', without attracting any adverse comment, but Bob Braham was never cast in that mould. In all probability they had spent a pleasant night at West Raynham, leaving at around 8 a.m. For obvious reasons, Bob Braham's personal log-book (which never flew with him, as was the rule) cannot be relied upon for accurate data of his last flight of the war, nor can his recollections in *Scramble* which he wrote many years later. Good fortune now deserted Bob. At the end of his 300-mile trip across the North Sea, approaching the Danish coast, the Mosquito passed over two German flak ships, or small destroyers. From then on it was a near certainty that the progress of the flight would be continuously monitored on German radar. This was soon confirmed. By then, Bob had learned that a slight whine emanating from his radio set indicated that his aircraft was being monitored by German radar. On this trip, the radio whined almost continuously although they altered course frequently to try to make the Germans lose contact.

Ranger operations depended much on surprise but this element had been removed. Moreover, he was returning to an area where several times before he had strafed transports and shot down enemy aircraft. It was an area which contained many Luftwaffe bases. The enemy may well have been almost waiting for Bob's 'weekly' hostile visit. Over Denmark the clouds had almost entirely disappeared and, much to Bob's credit, he realized that it was sheer folly to continue the sortie and he decided to turn back. It was perhaps, in retrospect, a decision that he should have made at an earlier stage of the flight. Although turning back was anathema to Bob, he could probably still have made it back safely but for chance again taking a hand. As he crossed back over Fyn Island, he caught sight of an imposing building flying a big swastika flag. A staff car was visible driving away from it. This, to Bob, suggested the possibility that some important Nazi might be in it. With guns blazing Bob dived to attack it. In a short time the car was overturned and blazing. Who was inside and how they fared is not known.

Shortly thereafter, having accurately pin-pointed his position to the enemy, Bob discovered that he was not alone in the air. Two Fw 190s had come to dispute the airspace with him. Cloud cover was now extremely scarce. Bob knew only too well that his Mossie was no match for the faster and more manoeuvrable Fw 190s. He had shot down two single ones but were they in skilled and experienced hands? To try to fight it out with two would be asking for serious trouble. Noting a patch of cloud above, Bob pulled sharply up to try to gain its protective cover. Long before he could reach it, it became all too clear that his aircraft was not going to be able to hide itself in its folds. The Focke-Wulfs were closing in.

The only avenue of escape left to Bob Braham was to try to outfly them in a dog-fight. One Fw pilot attacked from ahead and fired. Although close, he missed but the second one made no mistake. His first burst of fire hit the Mosquito's port engine and wing, causing fire to break out on the port wing. The next burst smashed in a side window and shattered the instrument panel only inches in front of the two men. Miraculously neither was hurt and Bob retained control. He dived for the water below and pulled out at a bare 100 ft. He had been in similar positions before and knew what to do. He stopped the damaged engine and operated the engine's fire extinguisher. Unfortunately the fire continued to burn. Also it was soon apparent that the enemy was clearly a man who shared Bob's own philosophy of continuing to fire at apparently doomed aircraft 'for good measure'. Another burst of fire riddled the Mosquito but again neither crewman was hit. However, Bob realized the damage to his Mosquito meant there could ultimately be only one end to the contest. Accordingly he decided that, while he still had some control over the Mosquito, he had to crash land immediately. With one wing coming down in the water and the other on the beach, the Mosquito, with terrible rending sounds, hit the ground at 150 mph, and bounced before slithering to a halt. Bob had made no attempt to put the wheels down. In that soft sand the plane then might easily have cartwheeled over if he had done so.

Bob and Don Walsh immediately got away from the burning aircraft before the fuel tanks exploded. They had been fortunate that no such explosion had occurred upon impact caused by their rough arrival. Almost as soon as they had dived behind a friendly sand dune, the Mosquito exploded. Any thoughts of escape were soon removed from their minds. Although they had clambered out unhurt and had taken cover in the dunes, they had crashed close to a German radar station and armed troops were running fast towards the two airmen.

Even before they saw the enemy troops, they had experienced a scare. Bob genuinely thought that their last moment had come when the victorious Focke-Wulf pilot had dived at them, roaring over their heads at a mere 20 feet. But instead of finishing off the British airmen with a burst of fire, the pilot had waved a greeting at them. It was an action that astonished Bob, as he had come to regard his enemies almost as monsters, rather than as human beings. Also had he not, only minutes before, shot up a German car leaving it upside down and ablaze in a ditch? Moreover he had earlier strafed the wreckage of a Ju 52 which he had shot down. If the victorious pilot had shot at Bob and Don, Bob at least, would have regarded it as no more than his just deserts. He had never hesitated to kill Germans in the air or on the ground.

The Fw pilot's wave, so obviously a friendly one that Bob actually waved back, was to have repercussions for Bob. It was the first sign that his life was to be spared, and that the enemy pilot was a chivalrous man, one whom he might even learn to like. Although a few shots were fired by the armed troops advancing upon the crashed pair, none hit them. They were soon captured, marched off and searched. The discovery of the German Mauser pistol which Bob always carried and which he had remembered to bring from the plane was not well received. In his heart, given even half a chance, Bob was prepared to fight it out with his captors and then hope to find a friendly Dane with whom he could shelter before finding a way of escaping to neutral Sweden. However, there clearly was no such prospect. Also, again rather to their surprise, Bob and Don were taken to a barrack of sorts where they were given a welcome cup of German synthetic coffee.

Soon Luftwaffe officers arrived in a car to collect Bob and Don. This was fortunate. Contrary to popular belief at the time, RAF prisoners of war were, on the whole, fairly treated by the Luftwaffe. It was to their advantage that RAF POWs were usually incarcerated in prison camps run by the opposing air force. Airmen, even retired ones such as many of the staff in the Luftwaffe-run camps, always harbour a certain regard for other airmen. It is true that about fifty escaped RAF prisoners had been recaptured and murdered in cold blood in March 1944 but the murderers were nothing to do with the Luftwaffe. Indeed, Luftwaffe personnel were almost as horrified as were people in Britain.

By some unrecorded 'gentlemen's agreement', Herman Goering, who had been an ace pilot during the First World War, had let it be known that most RAF prisoners would be kept in the hands of the Luftwaffe and would be reasonably treated in return for similar treatment of Luftwaffe airmen who became prisoners of the British. Despite all the indiscriminate bombing carried out by both sides, this agreement remained good throughout the war.

After a night spent in the guardroom of the nearby airfield at Esbjerg, Bob and Don were taken by train across Denmark and Germany to the main Luftwaffe interrogation centre at Oberursel, near Frankfurt. It was a long train journey which lasted a day and a night due in part to the train having to halt during air raids. No bombs fell near the train but the men guarding the prisoners with automatic Schmeisser pistols made it obvious that they regarded the British airmen with hatred. Both soldiers and civilians shouted abuse at them and threatened violence. To Germans, all captured British airmen were assumed to be 'night bomber terrorists'. During the night, drunken German soldiers tried to force a way into the reserved carriage in a train that was already overfull. One drew a bayonet and seemed determined to attack them. Bob admits that his knees were trembling. Fortunately a young Nazi SS soldier, in his distinctive black uniform, shouldered his way into the carriage and with authority barked an order. Immediately this restored the situation. Thereafter the Nazi sat close to the prisoners and their guards. His presence was clearly as disquieting to the guards as it had been to the drunks. Although the arrogant young man had been instrumental in saving Bob and Don from a nasty situation that might all too easily have resulted in injury or death, he none the less displayed open contempt for the two British airmen. By 1944 the Allied bombing campaign had reached such a height and aroused such hatred among the German people that the fate of all captured airmen depended largely on whose hands they fell into. They were safest in those of the Luftwaffe.

At Oberursel Bob was kept in solitary confinement for about two weeks and was extremely poorly fed during this period. This was standard treatment, intended to make airmen almost glad to talk to anyone during interrogation. It also weakened them physically. During this period Bob was frequently interrogated. He became so physically weak that he tended to black out if he sat up suddenly. The Luftwaffe intelligence service had prepared files on every prominent RAF member, often based on news items concerning local heroes in British local papers. These filtered back to Germany via neutral embassies and other sources. Bob Braham was surprised to discover that almost every detail of his RAF career and much of his private life was known to his interrogators. Such information often unnerved men who then went on further to 'spill the beans'.

The pilot of the Fw 190 who had shot him down, Robert Spreckels, paid Bob a surprise visit. Spreckels had been highly praised by his superiors who had been quick to advise him that he had shot down a famous RAF ace. On his own initiative Spreckels had requested that he might meet his victim: his forty-fifth such victim as Spreckels himself was an ace. Bearing in mind the considerable distance between the northern base where Spreckels was stationed and Frankfurt, Spreckels must have been very determined to meet Bob Braham.

The two met under strained circumstances. For one thing, neither could speak the other's language and they had to converse via an interpreter. Also Bob had to be on his guard not to reveal any secrets about his aircraft or the mission.

However, he welcomed the tea and biscuits provided for their talk. Strangely, an immediate affinity developed between the two men of the opposing air forces. They were of similar age and outlook. Both wished the other good luck and parted with Bob promising to buy Spreckels a whisky once the war was over. Bob's firmly-held conviction that the war would soon be over and Germany totally defeated, seemed to come as rather a surprise to the young German. Spreckels had been brought up on Nazi propaganda and the idea of Germany losing the war never seems to have crossed his mind, in spite of the Allies by then being firmly established ashore in France and with the Germans' Eastern front crumbling. As far as Spreckels was concerned, he was winning the war and his dozens of victories proved it. The two men parted with a warm handshake. Bob, of course, had every reason to be grateful that his victor had not shot at Don and himself during that low pass over their crashed Mosquito.

The principal German interrogator was Hauptmann Koch and he had also interpreted for the two airmen. A personal aide of Goering's who spoke good English also visited Bob and questioned him about Spitfires and British defences as he was about to resume operations in Ju 88s. Bob's sensible advice to him was to remain as Goering's personal aide and to stay on the ground and well away from Spitfires for as long as possible!

Several other unusual incidents occurred during Bob's brief stay at Oberursel. One was the unofficial communication channel which he and the POW next door established via tapping on the walls in Morse code. Another was when Koch informed Bob that he had been awarded a second bar to his DSO! This had been announced in Britain within a day or two of Bob being reported missing. This made Bob Braham the most highly decorated fighter pilot of the RAF, and he was to remain so to the end of the war, being the sole recipient of three DSOs and three DFCs.

Before departing for Stalag Luft III, a regular Luftwaffe-run POW camp where many RAF aircrew were incarcerated, Bob was given the usual Nazi propaganda treatment. During a friendly walk in the woods with Koch, the German argued that it was all wrong that Britain and Germany were fighting each other and that they really ought to be allies fighting against the Russians and world Jewry. Bob might have countered this by enquiring why it was then that Hitler in 1939 had formed the alliance with Stalin and thus indirectly started the Second World War by attacking Poland.

It is also worth recording that Spreckels had told Bob, without apparent rancour, that his parents had been killed during an Allied bombing raid. His philosophical attitude may have been because both realized that they were fighter pilots who, by and large, did not normally associate themselves with the 'bomber boys'! Spreckels dismissed the death of his parents with 'It is the war.' This further enhanced Bob's regard and respect for the young German war ace who in so many ways seemed similar to himself and to his RAF comrades whom Bob had known during his period of service.

After interrogation at Oberursel, Bob and Don were moved to Stalag Luft III at Sagan, Germany. Sagan was close to the Polish border and was then in Prussian Silesia. Border changes after the war mean it is now in Poland and is called Zagan. Stalag Luft III was the main POW camp for officer aircrew of the British, Commonwealth, Allied and American forces. The approximate number of prisoners held in the camp when Bob Braham was there was 10,500 officers and other ranks. Over 90 per cent were officers and the remainder were a mixture of RAF and Army other ranks who, along with aircrew NCOs, had volunteered for duty as orderlies. The camp was under the control and jurisdiction of the Luftwaffe and consisted of six compounds:

North Compound: British and American prisoners
South Compound: American prisoners
East Compound: British prisoners
West Compound: American prisoners
Centre Compound: American prisoners
Belaria Compound: British and American prisoners

It was also the famous POW camp from which three officers escaped in 1943 after using a vaulting horse to conceal the digging of a tunnel. This was written about by one of the escapees, Eric Williams, in his book *The Wooden Horse*. It was also from this camp that seventy-six officers had escaped from North Compound by tunnelling in March 1944, three months before W/Cdr Braham's arrival. After being recaptured, fifty of them were shot in cold blood by the Gestapo. This atrocity had obviously depressed the spirits of the prisoners; in addition to threatening to shoot all future escapees, German reprisals included the suspension of all inter-compound activities including sport and entertainment. It also resulted in the almost total abandonment of escape attempts although there was still an escape committee, and a partly excavated tunnel was in existence when the camp was evacuated in January 1945.

W/Cdr Douglas Bader, the legless ace and a prisoner of war since August 1941, had been in this camp but by W/Cdr Braham's time, Bader had been moved to the infamous Colditz prison Oflag 1VC. Another Fighter Command ace, W/Cdr Bob Stanford Tuck, a prisoner since January 1942, was also in the camp but during Bob Braham's time he was in Belaria Compound.

As far as can be ascertained, Bob Braham was in North Compound. The nominal roll of the compound has not been discovered and is believed to have been lost during the evacuation. However, the rolls of East and Belaria Compounds do not list W/Cdr Braham, making it likely that he was in North Compound.

North Compound comprised fifteen wooden huts and other buildings including cookhouse and latrines; the compound itself was a quarter square mile allowing adequate space for exercise and games. It held about 2,000 men, of whom approximately 600 were Americans. The living conditions were tolerable with a large library of books and educational facilities. Entertainments were organized by the prisoners and there were also sporting activities although inter-compound activities had been stopped by the time Bob Braham arrived.

The food rations in Stalag Luft camps, supplemented by Red Cross food parcels – one per man per week – were normally sufficient to sustain a healthy life. However, by the time that Bob Braham came to the camp, the interruption of communications in Europe after the invasion and the worsening war conditions in Germany meant that the Red Cross supplies had been reduced to half a parcel per man per week. Moreover the German rations had also been reduced. This resulted in some malnutrition.

By mid-January 1945 the Russians, advancing from the east, had come almost within striking distance of Sagan and the prospect of having to move the prisoners became a distinct possibility. The German camp Kommandant refused to confirm to the Senior British Officer in North Compound, G/Capt. D.E.L. Wilson RAAF, that they would be moving but, on his own initiative, Wilson gave instructions to the men to be ready for the move at any time.

Abruptly, at 21.00 hours on 27 January 1945 and without any prior notice, the Germans gave orders to vacate North Compound immediately. The prisoners were told they would have to march. No destination was given and neither rations nor water were issued. Each prisoner was given one Red Cross food parcel and was permitted to take anything he could carry. Snow had fallen and some inmates, in anticipation of the evacuation, had made rough wooden sledges. At 01.00 hours on Sunday 28 January the prisoners began to leave North Compound. The last man left the camp at 03.15 hours. The very sick and injured were left in the prison hospital.

The weather was atrocious with thick snow lying on the ground. It was intensely cold and further snow fell during the march, soaking the men's clothing which then froze. Two horse-drawn wagons carried the kit and rations of the German guards and a small ambulance accompanied them for the first few miles. However, this was not seen again after the morning of the first day. No provision was made for any sick men or stragglers, nor for food and water. There were 2,000 men walking in a column straggling over three miles in length;

anyone who fell out was likely to die of exposure. No recognized rest period was given and the prisoners still did not know their final destination. The guards were mostly elderly men who were more concerned with looking after themselves than their prisoners. In some cases, when the prisoners bartered items from the Red Cross parcels for food and water from the civilian population, the guards even took the food from them.

They reached Halbau at 08.00 hours on 28 January after having marched ten or eleven miles, and a halt of one hour was given. They then marched a further seven miles to Freiwalden where they were supposed to stop for the night. However, the townsfolk objected to the presence of the prisoners in the town and they were made to march a further four miles to the village of Leippa.

At Leippa, which they reached at 17.00 hours, after having marched over twenty-one miles, they found only one barn into which some 700 men crowded. The rest had to wait out in the open in the snow for four hours on a bitterly cold night. Finally other barns were found but some men still had to sleep on straw in the open. They had been on the march for up to sixteen hours.

The march resumed at 08.00 hours on the 29th and at 11.30 hours a halt was made at Priebus where water was obtained from civilians. Muskau was finally reached at 18.00 hours after a march of seventeen miles. Here billets were found in a cinema, a glass factory, a riding school, a stable, a laundry, a pottery and a French POW camp. At Muskau 523 officers and men of the USAAF left to join another column of American prisoners and 1,050 British officers and men from East Compound arrived. A much-needed rest of three days was given to all the prisoners at Muskau.

At 22.45 hours on 1 February they started marching again. Fifty-seven members of North Compound were too sick to march and were left in Muskau, together with 566 men of the East Compound.

The POWs could hear gunfire from the battles raging to the north-east and the roads were full of German refugees. By then, the prisoners also looked more like refugees than a military column. They wore a variety of clothing, with pots and pans dangling from any convenient strap or string. Some were pulling sledges, others pushing prams or wheelbarrows bartered from locals. Many sick men dropped behind and had to be rounded up and helped along by their friends. Most of the guards abandoned any attempt to control the prisoners and straggled alongside them. However, one guard fired at a party who stopped to rearrange their kit and others allowed dogs to harass them. At the village of Jamlitz one party met members of a German Panzer Division just out of action and these men generously shared their rations with the hungry prisoners. This may also have surprised and favourably impressed Bob Braham. At 06.00 hours on 2 February the column reached Graustein where they halted until 11.00 hours; local farmers provided hot water for them. As the column approached Spremberg the guards became more efficient and aggressive, one officer prisoner being hit by a rifle butt. Spremberg was reached at 15.00 hours, where soup and hot water were provided in the reserve depot of 8th Panzer Division. At 16.30 hours they marched a further two miles to Spremberg railway station, but some of the sick remained at the Panzer reserve depot. At the station they were allocated cattle trucks with forty or fifty men being crammed into each truck. All the trucks were filthy and many were littered with manure and human excreta. Before leaving they were issued with bread and 1,500 Red Cross parcels but no water.

The train stopped at Falkenberg at 13.00 hours on 3 February but they were not allowed off and no food or drink was provided. A train full of German wounded from the east had recently arrived and they, not unnaturally, were given all the supplies. The train stopped at 07.30 hours on 4 February on the outskirts of Hanover where the first water for thirty-six hours was issued. The train reached Tarmstedt station, near Bremen, at 17.00 hours on Sunday 4 February after a journey of some 300 miles.

After detraining, the column marched the few miles from

Tarmstedt station to the POW camp at Marlag-Milag Nord, arriving at 18.30 hours. Here each prisoner was searched, the men being divided into groups of twenty; meanwhile the rest of the column waited outside in pouring rain. The last prisoner was searched at 01.30 hours on 5 February.

Most of the prisoners were undernourished even before they started on the exhausting march and train journey. Many had already been prisoners for three or four years and some for over five. On arrival many of them, variously suffering from frostbite, dysentery and vomiting, collapsed. The final wait in the rain after eight days of marching and travelling under atrocious conditions with little food or drink proved the breaking point and more than 70 per cent of those reaching Marlag-Milag Nord suffered from gastritis, dysentery, influenza, colds and other illnesses.

Bob Braham's robust frame and abundant energy enabled him to stand up to the demanding conditions better than most. It helped that he had been in Stalag Luft III for a shorter period than most. The only physical damage he suffered was the loss of both big toe nails due to a combination of frostbite and the long hours of marching in boots not designed for that purpose.

The column that reached Marlag-Milag Nord contained 1,916 officers and other ranks. The camp had previously been used to house Royal Navy other rank prisoners but they had already been evacuated. At the time of their arrival there were only twelve wooden huts, two kitchens, two washhouses and two latrines. The huts had been practically gutted and there was neither light nor stoves and only 460 beds. Even after a fortnight the men had only wood straw for bedding and no provision for drying clothing or blankets.

On the second and third days after their arrival, the Germans kept the whole camp on parade in rain and bitter cold in order to establish their names and numbers. The camp was administered by the German Navy and conditions were crude and far below the standards of the Luftwaffe camp at Sagan.

The Senior British Officer of Stalag Luft III North Compound during the journey to Marlag-Milag Nord and for the first weeks was G/Capt D.E.L. Wilson RAAF. His heated arguments with the Germans over living conditions and Red Cross parcels resulted in his dismissal by the Germans and he was moved to Spangenberg. G/Capt L.E. Wray AFC, RCAF, who had been Senior Administration Officer then became Senior British Officer and he maintained the high standards of caring for the prisoners set by G/Capt Wilson.

By early March the camp had been cleared, the huts repaired and the whole camp cleaned, principally by the prisoners. W/Cdr Braham's name appears on the list of prisoners at this time: his POW number was 6623 and he was billeted in hut 20. As there were only twelve huts when they arrived it must be assumed that more had been erected. However, the conditions were still very bad. The barrack huts were overcrowded, the lighting was poor and there was not enough fuel for either warmth or cooking. Fuel had to be supplemented by the prisoners gathering wood. However, the five weeks or so at Marlag-Milag Nord gave the prisoners a respite ahead of further moves.

The British Army advance across North Germany continued. As the leading troops approached Bremen, south-west of Garmstedt, the Germans decided on 10 April that the prisoners must again be evacuated. One rumour was that they would be moved to Denmark and there used as a bargaining counter in any surrender terms.

The weather was now fairly warm and pleasant and by this time most of the ardent Nazis had either fled or had left to make some futile last-ditch stand. It was obvious to almost everyone that the end of the war was in sight and the general atmosphere was much better than on the previous march. Gradually the prisoners were able to exert their influence. As they marched towards Schleswig-Holstein, the pace became more leisurely, with only about four or five miles being covered each day, the prisoners themselves deciding when to stop.

The RAF intake was now joined by a British Navy contingent from an adjacent POW camp. Together they marched from Tarmstedt to Lübeck, a distance of about 85 miles. The RAF and Navy took it in turns to lead, with one Service resting as the other strolled by.

The Senior British Officer, G/Capt Wray, by forceful representation and non-compliance with orders, practically assumed control of the march although a few guards still maintained an aggressive and bullying attitude, notably Unteroffizier Krause who twice opened fire upon prisoners committing minor transgressions. In one of the incidents early in the march, F/Lt Bryson was shot and killed. After the war Krause was arrested and punished.

A more tragic incident occurred when the column was shot up by Allied aircraft; three men were killed and seven injured, all Navy prisoners. Apart from the damp and discomfort of having to sleep in fields and barns, the conditions for the tired and undernourished men were not too intolerable. The knowledge that the war was all but over was a constant boost to their morale.

On arrival in the Lübeck area, G/Capt Wray found the proposed camp so unacceptable that he refused to allow the column to enter the town. He was able to persuade the Germans to provide better accommodation in the barns and outbuildings of a very large estate. Assistance was also provided by the Red Cross which delivered food in trucks driven by American and Canadian prisoners who carried on even during air raids.

On 2 May 1945 one British patrol car reached the area and this was sufficient to persuade all the guards to surrender to the car's occupants. The prisoners were now free. They were full of praise for the Red Cross, the International Young Men's Christian Association and the Canadian Prisoner of War Relatives Association, all of which had done everything within their power to ensure that the men were fed and housed in accordance with the Geneva Convention.

The Luftwaffe in general abided by these rules and were honest in allowing the prisoners to receive Red Cross parcels even when this meant that at times the prisoners were better fed than their guards. James Goodson, the American fighter ace who was also a POW in Stalag Luft III but was part of a different march during that cold January, has written in his splendid book *Tumult in the Clouds* a very detailed and understanding account of the conditions pertaining at that time. In some instances, a genuine rapport sprang up between prisoners and certain guards and Goodson describes how, when the snow and cold made marching almost impossible, there were occasions when guards and prisoners helped one another along, the guards' rifles being stacked away in a lorry which was also pressed into service as an 'ambulance' for those prisoners unable to continue.

Goodson spoke German well and he relates that, towards the end, he was practically ordered to escape in order to make contact with the nearest American ground forces so that the guards could surrender. He describes the Red Cross parcels as 'real life-savers' and tells how the goods therein, unobtainable in Germany, were at times exchanged with the locals for additional clothes, footwear and so on. With the advancing Russians almost breathing down their necks, prisoners and guards seemed to be of one mind: to head further west, away from the Red Army, as speedily as possible.

James Goodson also comments on the infamous murder of the fifty Air Force escapers who were shot after being recaptured. He believes that one reason for this outrage was that by 1944 Germany was so full of non-German workers and so deficient in genuine leaders (who were all fighting at various fronts) that the Nazi hierarchy was afraid to have escaped prisoners loose within Germany because, with so many hostile workers all around them, the escaped prisoners might well have acted as a catalyst and provoked an internal insurrection. All that the enormous numbers of forced labourers lacked was leadership. After that notorious incident, the German guards at Stalag Luft III almost begged their prisoners not to try to escape, pointing out that the risk was too great. Many of the Luftwaffe officers in the camp regarded the killing of the fifty escapers as a stain upon Germany's honour. They had no wish to see it happen again.

There was welcome news for Bob. Upon his release he learned that Basil Embry and his HQ had reached Belgium and before being flown back to Britain he spent a happy day with his old comrades in Brussels. Basil greeted Bob with the remark 'You stink!' This was all too true as by then Bob had been walking and sleeping for weeks in the tattered remains of his uniform, unable even to wash thoroughly. A long luxurious soak in a hot bath soon solved the problem. Bob had not been able to touch alcohol for months and, at the party to welcome home the 'lost' hero, he was incapable after a couple of drinks and had to be put to bed.

The next day, nursing a hangover, W/Cdr J.R.D. Braham DSO and two bars, DFC and two bars, was on his way home as a passenger in a Mosquito. It had been almost a year since he had departed in another Mosquito under quite different circumstances.

The war in Europe was over. What did the future hold?

17
After the War

Even before repatriation, Bob Braham and others in Stalag Luft III had realized that postwar Britain would be very different from the wonderfully united Britain of 1940. As in most POW camps, the inmates of Stalag Luft III had managed to make and conceal a radio set on which they were able to listen to BBC news broadcasts. They were sickened when they heard the news of renewed strikes and labour unrest. To them, strikes simply meant delays in the delivery of the war material which could set them free. By early 1945, well before Germany's surrender, the unions and politicians were already manoeuvring for positions. The national government which had served the country so well was about to break up, with Winston Churchill, the great architect of victory, reduced to leader of the Opposition. At this time the Black Market was thriving, and the spivs who ran it were becoming rich and powerful.

Generally, as Bob admits in *Scramble*, his return to his family, still living with Joan's parents in Leicester, was a joyous one, but he still had doubts about the future of the country which he loved and which he had served so well. Joan Braham found him 'difficult to live with at first. He was short of temper even with the family he loved. He had lost much of his spontaneity.'

It is known that he became depressed and disillusioned when he learned in Stalag Luft III that the wife of a close colleague had deserted him for another man while her husband lingered in captivity.

It seems likely that Bob Braham had been so obsessed with his RAF activities during 1939–44 that he had retained the impossible idealism of youth until he was faced with almost unlimited time to dwell upon the realities of life, firstly as a POW and then in the immediate postwar period. However, his own future seemed assured. On his return, he was granted a permanent commission in the RAF, an honour that many Short Service Commissioned Officers would have welcomed. Moreover, he had a very important asset in the rat-race for peacetime promotion in the Services in the shape of Basil Embry, already rising rapidly towards the top of the tree. Already Sir Basil, who always thought the world of Bob, had become an air marshal and was soon to be promoted to an even higher rank. One step behind him was David Atcherley, now an Air Commodore, who was being groomed by Basil Embry to follow him upwards. Bob was almost ideally placed to follow behind David.

On his return, Bob was granted an immediate six weeks of leave. During this period, Joan and he found themselves their own home in Leicester, in Kirby Road. Bob's initial mood of uncertainty in himself and his disillusion with some elements of postwar Britain brought him once more into conflict with the Press. He was essentially a shy man and had avoided all contact with the media. The absurd interview which his father had given years before still rankled. Almost on the day of his return to his family, they came nosing around, hoping for a colourful story about the most highly decorated fighter pilot in the RAF, but he would have nothing to do with them. When they persisted, Bob physically threw them out. This may explain why the name of Bob Braham, perhaps the RAF's greatest ace, remains generally unknown to this day. Journalists do not relish being ejected.

Unlike most others who returned to the RAF after the war, Bob did not appear to have to drop rank once the war was over. Moreover, he was given appointments which would have delighted most other pilots retained in the RAF.

As soon as the war ceased and the big task of getting the

men overseas flown home was completed, the atmosphere in the RAF changed dramatically. During the war the object was to fly as much as possible. Now the politicians made repeated attempts to reduce the RAF's flying hours to a minimum. The RAF was drastically cut down in size and those who were fortunate enough to be retained had their hours kept to a low figure due to the costs and petrol involved.

W/Cdr Bob Braham was, however, able to fly an interesting number of different, and often new, aircraft types. Among several other postwar postings, he went to the Night Fighter Development Unit at the Central Flying Establishment (CFE). This form of test flying was very much in line with Bob's inclinations and it is noted from his log-book that he made several flights to bases in Belgium, sometimes accompanied by F/Lt 'Jacko' Jacobs, who served as his navigator. Bob had several Belgians in his unit when he commanded 141 Squadron, notably the extremely courageous Lucien Le Boutte. Before long, Bob was to receive a further decoration, the Belgian Order of the Crown with Palm – one of Belgium's highest awards. He also received the Belgian Croix de Guerre with Palm.

Among the new types that Bob flew was his first jet-powered aircraft, the Gloster Meteor. The fact that he had languished in a POW camp for the best part of a year had not dampened his enthusiasm for flying. Even on that first flight home in a Mosquito, nursing a hangover, he commented in *Scramble* how good it was to be airborne again.

By March 1946, the strength of the CFE was cut by 50 per cent. Even development flying was feeling the pinch. In addition, rationing, which everyone had hoped would be relaxed almost immediately hostilities ceased, was if anything tighter than ever. Clothes, food, petrol, coal and other resources were all severely rationed. It was generally a depressing and unsettling period and, perhaps due to unrecognized wartime fatigue, few people seemed willing to work while many seemed to think that, having won the war, they should be paid a lot for doing little. It is not too surprising that in this mood of disappointment and uncertainty about Britain and its future, Bob decided to resign from the RAF and apply to join the Rhodesian Colonial Police. However, as has already been explained, Sticks got in touch with Basil Embry who soon had Bob back in the RAF as a flight lieutenant although he retained the rank and pay of an acting wing commander. This renewal of his RAF career encouraged Bob to rent a furnished bungalow at Chorleywood, Herts., for his family. At that time he held a non-flying post at the Air Ministry.

For the next six or seven years Bob held a number of interesting RAF posts. Sometimes he had ground jobs, at others a commanding officer's flying position. It would have been more than enough for most career-minded officers but Bob, with the memories of the war in his mind, found the postwar RAF 'dull'. Yet his log-books show many flights to Germany, to Malta and to the airfields of all the British aircraft manufacturers – Warton, Hatfield, Gloucester, Bristol and so on – where new jets were being developed. It is also known that even when assigned to a Staff post on the ground Bob Braham would still find ways of visiting squadrons and 'borrowing' their aircraft. He was also flown to America and Canada on four occasions, where he took every opportunity to fly their latest jet fighters. His popularity among the Americans was such that on one occasion they specifically asked for him by name when they wished to test one of their latest types.

In due course Sir Basil Embry became C-in-C Fighter Command, with Air Marshal David Atcherley still one step behind him. By this time Fighter Command, with its fighter-bombers, had become dominant in the RAF. From time to time Bob himself held positions at Fighter Command HQ but principally his work involved the development of new aircraft types and tactics. His experience as a night fighter made him the ideal choice for the development of various all-weather planes and tactics.

Bob's AFC was awarded in 1951; the lengthy citation listed a large number of his postwar accomplishments. 1951 was also the year when his father died. By then Joan had given Bob a third son.

Sadly, David Atcherley was killed in a flying accident in 1952. It must have been a difficult year for Sir Basil Embry as Bob again decided, this time finally, to resign from the RAF. He was increasingly disillusioned with Britain, and worried a lot about how he could afford to educate his three sons at private schools, on his wing commander's salary. He considered that they would have a better chance in Canada and he was able to arrange, before resigning from the RAF, to be taken on by the RCAF without loss of rank. Canadian pay was considerably higher and that country seemed, in 1952, to offer a brighter future for the rising generation than did Britain. Canada was striving to establish itself as a major aircraft manufacturing country and it seems almost certain that they grabbed at the opportunity to have the services of such a renowned pilot and test pilot as Wing Commander Bob Braham. Among their projects was the CF-100, an advanced military machine with a worldwide sales potential. Bob was to take part in much of the development flying of this type.

The family sailed to Canada on the liner *Empress of Scotland* on 6 June 1952. Bob was at once appointed Staff Officer for Operations and Training at Air Defence HQ at St Hubert, an airfield near Montreal. The Canadians also seem to have been less penny-pinching about allowing their RCAF pilots to fly and it is on record that during the next twenty months, Bob flew 193 times. The Lockheed T33 Silver Star and the North American Sabre F-86 were the jet-powered types most used but he also flew the even faster CF-100 on thirty-nine occasions. As well as flying to a great number of Canadian and US bases, Bob also visited the Canadian F-86E squadrons in Britain, taking the opportunity to spend the night with his in-laws, still living in Leicester.

His next appointment was to command the All-Weather Fighter Operational Training unit at North Bay, 200 miles north of Toronto, where he chiefly flew the CF-100. This aircraft could exceed Mach 1 and was heavily armed. In one such aircraft Bob took part in a formation display at a major air show. He also paid visits to Germany where Canadian squadrons were based as part of the NATO defences. On one occasion, coming in to land with a pupil in a CF-100, a flap broke off; Bob immediately took control and with great skill pulled off a safe landing. For this he received a Canadian commendation.

In 1955 an appointment at Air Defence HQ at Ottawa followed. However, Bob continued to find opportunities to fly many times during most months. He principally flew the CF-100 or the T-33 Silver Star. Although he was an acting director at Ottawa, Bob did not always see eye-to-eye with his colleagues and must have welcomed the appointment, in 1957, to take command of an active Canadian squadron of CF-100s. 432 Squadron, known as 'Cougar' Squadron, was based at Bagotville, Quebec. This happy period lasted from October 1957 to July 1960. It was, however, marred by a serious accident. When flying in formation, Bob's CF-100 was hit by another and one wing broke off. Bob ejected but the canopy did not detach. As a result Bob was catapulted through the canopy. He suffered a broken back and head injuries, but was flying again within two months. The head injuries did not at the time seem serious but may have accounted for his premature death some years later. In all, during this period, Bob made over 500 flights in CF-100 aircraft.

As had been the case before, Bob Braham relished the chance to command a fighter squadron where he could fly as often as he wished. His enthusiasm rubbed off on others and under his leadership Cougar Squadron flourished. They even adopted a live cougar as a mascot during Bob's period of command.

In July 1960 Bob Braham was appointed as Senior Operations Officer at SHAPE (Supreme Headquarters Allied Powers in Europe). This involved moving himself and family to Paris. Both Joan and he came to like this ground job. His obvious genuineness and his habit of treating everyone, including the once-hated Germans, with bonhomie made him an excellent ambassador, as Jack Hoskins and others have asserted. Joan liked Paris and the fact that the boys were able to continue their education in a good private school. With Bob no longer risking his neck daily in the air, this was one of Joan's happiest periods. They lived in a large and lovely villa just outside Paris, provided for them, fully furnished, by the Canadian Government.

Bob was never able to live for long without wanting to fly, and even here he managed to get several flights in a number of aircraft including the English Electric Lightning and the Lockheed F-104 Starfighter. These aircraft were capable of twice the speed of sound and he flew them up to 50,000 ft. He also flew a T-33 Silver Star, a type which he always seems to have been able to get to fly. His flights took him to Germany, Sardinia, Belgium and Luxembourg as well as England where he visited the 1962 Farnborough Air Show.

In Paris Bob Braham was promoted to group captain, which increased his pay and his ultimate pension. However, by then his sons had received the education which he so much desired for them and the eldest, Michael, left Paris to complete his training at the Royal Military College in Kingston, Ontario. Later he joined the Navy, rising to the rank of captain. Robert, the next son, became a colonial police officer, much as Bob had often wished to be. Robert left Paris to serve in the Southern Rhodesia Police. Later he joined the famous Royal Canadian Mounted Police, as also did the third son, some years later.

However, the highlight of the SHAPE posting was the long-awaited reunion with Robert Spreckels, the Fw 190 pilot who had shot Bob down in 1944. Their brief meeting at Oberursel during Bob's initial period as a POW had been, from start to finish, unusual and was to carry unusual consequences. In the first place Robert Spreckels must have shown great determination to meet his opponent. The distance between Spreckels's base in Denmark and Oberursel near Frankfurt is several hundred miles and it had to be accomplished at the time when Germany was under a constant rain of bombs day and night. Equally strange was the immediate affinity which sprang up between the two young men. In an instant upon meeting Spreckels, all Bob Braham's hatred of his enemy seems to have vanished. In 1944 they could only converse through an interpreter and Bob was on his guard as he half expected Spreckels to try to prise from him information about the secret activities of 141 Squadron and other Bomber Support operations. As Bob describes in *Scramble*, Spreckels seemed to be very like many of the keen pilots he knew and admired in 141 Squadron. Spreckels was also enormously impressed by Bob. After the war, he made numerous attempts to find out if his victim had survived, though Bob was only one of dozens of RAF pilots whom Spreckels had shot down. Years later, on a visit to England, Robert Spreckels first learned that Bob had survived. By then he was in a shipping business at Hamburg and somehow he persuaded the German consul in Bath to try to locate Bob and a letter from Robert eventually reached Bob. It had been redirected first by the Air Ministry in London, then by Air HQ in Ottawa. It was by then 1956 and Bob was at AF HQ at Ottawa. From that first letter, a correspondence followed but it was not until Bob was moved to Paris that an opportunity arose for the two pilots to meet. After seventeen years, Bob was finally able to buy Robert the long-promised Scotch. By then Spreckels had become familiar with the English language so no interpreter was required. As Bob affirmed in *Scramble*, 'Robert Spreckels became, in spite of world tension and hatreds, one who is counted among my company of close friends'.

This seems to be a fitting point to end this tale of one of Britain's finest wartime heroes. If this book helps to bring W/Cdr J.R.D. Braham DSO and two bars, DFC and two bars, AFC and other foreign decorations from the shadows into the limelight, it will have achieved its purpose. The life story of such a remarkable man deserves to be remembered beyond those who knew him. Such men inspire others and it is Britain's good fortune that, in her hours of peril, men of this high calibre rise from relative obscurity and fearlessly give their all in order to preserve the qualities of life that many in Britain hold so dear.

May it always be so.

Epilogue

In 1964 the SHAPE appointment came to an end and the Braham family returned to Canada. Joan wrote: 'Domestically it was something of a shock coming back after four years in the luxury of Villa Fontenella.'

After nearly a year at the National Defence College of Canada, which included visiting military bases in the USA and the Far East, often flying as co-pilot in a Canadair Yukon, G/Capt. Braham served at Ottawa as Director of Air Force Operations. During this period, two and a half years, he flew various missions to Europe, Africa, Asia and frequently to America. However, he became increasingly disillusioned with the Canadian policy which threatened to amalgamate all that country's fighting Services under one and put all into a common drab uniform. Even the abolition of air force ranks was threatened. G/Capt. Braham spent the late months of 1967 on a mission to bases around the world, operating as pilot or co-pilot of Yukon transport aircraft. It was to be his last Service flying.

In 1968, unable to accept willingly the unification of all Canadian Armed Services, he resigned from the RCAF. He was aged only 48 and a good future would have been assured. However, by that time, there was also talk among the politicians that the days of the manned fighter were over. Worse still, the Canadian Government had lost out in its endeavours to build their own fighters. The excellent CF-100's replacement, the CF-105 Arrow, had been cancelled when Canada decided to purchase American aircraft instead. These matters may also have influenced Bob's decision to resign from the RCAF.

Bob Braham had always been interested in history and he joined the Historic Sites Department of the Canadian

Department of Indian Affairs which looked after the economic future, welfare and development of Canada's native peoples. After learning about this new job, the retired G/Capt., now reverting to his natural John Braham, became Area Superintendent for Historical Sites near Halifax, Nova Scotia. Here he purchased an old home and reconstructed it to the liking of Joan and himself. With a good pension, he had no financial worries.

His various resignations showed that J.R.D. Braham was a man of principles who had an idealistic streak. He found it intolerable to live under regimes for which he had less than full respect.

John and Joan Braham settled down well to a quite different kind of life until at Christmas 1973 he complained of nausea and headaches. After admission to hospital, an inoperable brain tumour was diagnosed and, after just over a month in hospital, John Randall Daniel Braham died, aged 53 years and 10 months.

During his career with the RAF and the RCAF he had flown a total of 5,370 hours in sixty-six different types of aircraft. It was fitting that the Canadians held a memorial service for him in Halifax. It is also fitting that the RAF museum at Hendon, which holds his log-books, now honours him with a special display. His record and decorations are likely to remain unique in the history of warfare.

Appendix A

The top-scoring fighter aces in the RAF and kindred Commonwealth Air Forces during the Second World War, compiled by researcher Christopher Shores using official records from both British and enemy sources, are as follows:

S/Ldr M.T. St J. Pattle 40 plus South African
G/Capt. J.E. Johnson 33.91 British
W/Cdr B. Finucane 32 Irish
F/Lt G.F. Beurling 31.33 Canadian
W/Cdr J.R.D. Braham 29 British
G/Cat A.G. Malan 28.66 South African
G/Capt. C.R. Caldell 28.5 Australian
S/Ldr J.H. Lacey 28 British
S/Ldr N.F. Duke 27.73 British
W/Cdr C.F. Gray 27.7 New Zealander
W/Cdr R.R. Stanford-Tuck 27 British
F/Lt E.S. Lock 25.5 British
F/Lt G. Allard 23.83 British

(The decimal points arise because of 'shared' victories. It should be noted that all these aces flew single-engined fighter aircraft such as the Hurricane, P-40 and/or Spitfire; the sole exception was 'Bob' Braham who scored all his victories in Blenheim (1), Beaufighter (19) and Mosquito (9) twin-engined aircraft. The next half dozen or so of the top-scoring aces also scored their successes in single-engined aircraft.)

Appendix B

The table on pp. 262–263 lists W/Cdr Braham's successes. The information may be summarized as follows:

Summary:

Destroyed	12	Home Defence Night
	1	Home Defence Day
	7	Bomber Support Night
	9	Intruder Day
	29	

Probables	1	Home Defence Night

Damaged	2	Home Defence Night
	1	Home Defence Dawn
	1	Home Defence Day
	2	Bomber Support Night
	6	

	Destroyed	Probable	Damaged
Messerschmitt 110	6		
Heinkel 111	5	1	1
Dornier 217	5		1
Junkers 88	4		4
Dornier 17	2		
Focke-Wulf 190	2		
Junkers 52	1		
Heinkel 177	1		
Junkers 34	1		
Focke-Wulf 58	1		
Bucker 131	1		
	29	1	6

Note under 'Aerodrome Flown From': when on Bomber Support from Wittering, Wellingore used forward airfields of Coltishall, Bradwell Bay, Ford and West Malling. When on Intruder from Lasham, Gravesend and Thorney Island they used forward airfields of West Raynham or Coltishall for operations over Denmark.

Note: In W/Cdr Braham's book *Scramble* when describing his last operation he says that he took off from Gravesend for West Raynham in an aircraft of 2 Group. Official records state that he took off from Thorney Island.

Date	Braham's Unit	Type of Operation	Day or Night	Type of Aircraft flown.	Aircraft No or Letter	A/C Sqn	Aerodrome Flown from
24.8.40	29 Sqn	HD	Night	Blenheim 1	L1463	29	Wellingore
13.3.41	29 Sqn	HD	Night	Beau 1F	R2148	29	Wellingore
8.5.41	29 Sqn	HD	Night	Beau 1F	R2148	29	W. Malling
23.6.41	29 Sqn	HD	Night	Beau 1F	X7550	29	W. Malling
6.7.41	29 Sqn	HD	Night	Beau 1F	X7550	29	W. Malling
12.9.41	29 Sqn	HD	Night	Beau 1F	X7550	29	W. Malling
28.9.41	29 Sqn	HD	Night	Beau 1F	X7550	29	W. Malling
19.10.41	29 Sqn	HD	Night	Beau 1F	X7550	29	W. Malling
24.10.41	29 Sqn	HD	Night	Beau 1F	X7550	29	W. Malling
6.6.42	51 OTU	HD	Night	Beau 1F	X7768	29	W. Malling
9.8.42	29 Sqn	HD	Night	Beau 1F	V8284	29	W. Malling
24.8.42	29 Sqn	HD	Night	Beau 1F	V8284	29	W. Malling
28.8.42	29 Sqn	HD	Night	Beau 1F	V8284	29	W. Malling
29.8.42	29 Sqn	HD	Dawn	Beau 1F	V8284	29	W. Malling
19.10.42	29 Sqn	HD	Day	Beau 1F	V8231	29	W. Malling
26.10.42	29 Sqn	HD	Day	Beau 1F	V8231	29	W. Malling
31.10.42	29 Sqn	HD	Night	Beau 1F	V8282	29	W. Malling
20.1.43	141 Sqn	HD	Night	Beau 1F	V8258	141	Ford
14.6.43	141 Sqn	BS	Night	Beau VIF	X8147	141	Wittering
16.6.43	141 Sqn	BS	Night	Beau VIF	X8147	141	Wittering
24.6.43	141 Sqn	BS	Night	Beau VIF	X8147	141	Wittering
9.8.43	141 Sqn	BS	Night	Beau VIF	X8147	141	Wittering
17.8.43	141 Sqn	BS	Night	Beau VIF	X8147	141	Wittering
17.8.43	141 Sqn	BS	Night	Beau VIF	X8147	141	Wittering
27.9.43	141 Sqn	BS	Night	Beau VIF	X8147	141	Wittering
29.9.43	141 Sqn	BS	Night	Beau VIF	X8147	141	Wittering
29.9.43	141 Sqn	BS	Night	Beau VIF	X8147	141	Wittering
5.3.44	2 Gp HQ	Int	Day	Mosq FB VI	SYE.LR364	613	Lasham
24.3.44	2 Gp HQ	Int	Day	Mosq FB VI	SYW.LR374	613	Lasham
24.3.44	2 Gp HQ	Int	Day	Mosq FB VI	SYW.LR374	613	Lasham
4.4.44	2 Gp HQ	Int	Day	Mosq FB VI	SYH.LR355	613	Lasham
13.4.44	2 Gp HQ	Int	Day	Mosq FB VI	SMB.LR313	305	Lasham
13.4.44	2 Gp HQ	Int	Day	Mosq FB VI	SMB.LR313	305	Lasham
29.4.44	2 Gp HQ	Int	Day	Mosq FB VI	SMH.LR422	305	Lasham
7.5.44	2 Gp HQ	Int	Day	Mosq FB VI	YHG	21	Gravesend
12.5.44	2 Gp HQ	Int	Day	Mosq FB VI	NS885(B)	107	Lasham
25.6.44	2 Gp HQ	Int	Day	Mosq FB VI	LR373(A)	21	Thorney Isle

Key: HD   Home Defence
      BS   Bomber Support
      Int Intruder

Radio Observer/ Navigator/ Air Gunner	Enemy Aircraft	Destroyed/ Damaged/ Probable				Area of Combat
A/C Jacobson						
Sgt Wilsdon	He 111	Destroyed	1st			Humber area England
Sgt Ross	Do 17Z	Destroyed	2nd			off Wells Norfolk
Sgt Ross	He 111	Destroyed	3rd			SW London England
Sgt Ross	He 111	Probable		1st		E Counties England
F/Sgt Gregory	Ju 88	Destroyed	4th			Thames Est England
F/Sgt Gregory	He 111	Destroyed	5th			off Dover England
F/Sgt Gregory	He 111	Damaged			1st	off Belgium
F/Sgt Gregory	Do 17Z	Destroyed	6th			off SE Coast England
F/Sgt Gregory	He 111	Destroyed	7th			off Yarmouth England
P/O Gregory	Do 217	Destroyed	8th			off Sandwich England
P/O Gregory	Do 217	Destroyed	9th			off Foreness England
F/L Jacobs	Ju 88	Damaged			2nd	off Beachy Head
F/L Jacobs	Ju 88	Destroyed	10th			off Beachy Head
F/L Jacobs	Ju 88	Damaged			3rd	off Beachy Head
P/O Gregory	Do 217	Damaged			4th	off Lowestoft England
Sgt Heywood	Ju 88	Destroyed	11th			off Beachy Head
P/O Gregory	Do 217	Destroyed	12th			off Broadstairs
P/O Gregory	Do 217	Destroyed	13th			off Beachy Head
F/L Gregory	Me 110	Destroyed	14th			Stavoren Holland
F/L Gregory	Ju 88	Damaged			5th	Schouwen Holland
F/L Gregory	Me 110	Destroyed	15th			Gilze-Rijen Holland
F/L Gregory	Me 110	Destroyed	16th			Liège Belgium
F/L Jacobs	Me 110	Destroyed	17th			Frisian Isles
F/L Jacobs	Me 110	Destroyed	18th			Frisian Isles
F/L Jacobs	Do 217	Destroyed	19th			Hanover Germany
F/L Jacobs	Me 110	Destroyed	20th			Zuider Zee Holland
F/L Jacobs	Ju 88	Damaged			6th	Zuider Zee Holland
F/L Gregory	He 177	Destroyed	21st			Châteaudun France
S/L Robertson	Ju 52	Destroyed	22nd			Aalborg Denmark
S/L Robertson	Ju 34	Destroyed	23rd			Aalborg Denmark
F/L Gregory	Bu 131	Destroyed	24th			St Jean-D'Angely
F/L Gregory	He 111	Destroyed	25th			Esjberg Denmark
F/L Gregory	Fw 58	Destroyed	26th			Aalborg Denmark
F/L Gregory	Fw 190	Destroyed	27th			Poitiers France
F/L Walsh	Ju 88	Destroyed	28th			Roskilde Denmark
F/L Gregory	Fw 190	Destroyed	29th			Herning Denmark
F/L Walsh	Shot down by Fw 190 over Denmark; both crewmen made POWs.					

Appendix C

Appendix 2 Part 1

RECORD OF ~~SERVICE~~ COMBATS with A/C.

UNIT	DATES FROM	~~TO~~	~~UNIT~~ TYPE.	DATES FROM	TO
29 Sqdn, R.A.F. Digby	Night of	24/8/40.	Heinkel 111. Destroyed.	DEFENSIVE ROLE.	
—— " ——	Night of	13/3/41	Dornier 17Z. Destroyed.		
29 Sqdn R.A.F. West Malling	Night of	8/5/41	Heinkel 111 Destroyed		
29 Sqdn R.A.F. West Malling	Night of	23/6/41	Heinkel 111 Probably destroyed		
29 Sqdn R.A.F. West Malling	Night of				
—— " ——	Night of	6/7/41.	Junkers 88. Destroyed		
—— " ——	Night of	12/9/41	Heinkel 111. Destroyed.		
—— " ——	Night of	28/9/41	Heinkel 111. Damaged.		
—— " ——	Night of	19/10/41	Dornier 17Z. Destroyed.		
—— " ——	Night of	24/10/41.	Heinkel 111. Destroyed.		
Attached —— " ——	Night of	6/6/42.	Dornier 217. Destroyed.		
29 Sqdn —— " ——	Night of	9/8/42	Dornier 217 Destroyed		
—— " ——	Night of.	24/8/42.	Junkers 88. Damaged.		
—— " ——	Night of	28/8/42.	Junkers 88. Destroyed.		
—— " ——	Dawn of	29/8/42	Junkers 88. Damaged.		
—— " ——	Day of	19/10/42.	Dornier 217 Damaged.		
—— " ——	Day of	26/10/42.	Junkers 88. Destroyed.		
—— " ——	Night of	31/10/42.	Dornier 217. Destroyed.		
141 Sqdn R.A.F. Ford.	Night of.	20/1/43.	Dornier 217 Destroyed.		
141 Sqdn. R.A.F. Wittering	Night of.	14/6/43.	Messerschmitt 110 Destroyed.	INTRUDER ROLE. NIGHT.	
—— " ——	Night of	16/6/43.	Junkers 88. Damaged.		
—— " ——	Night of	24/6/43.	Messerschmitt. 110. Destroyed.		
—— " ——	Night of	9/8/43.	Messerschmitt 110. Destroyed.		
—— " ——	Night of	17/8/43.	2. Messerschmitt 110's Destroyed.		
—— " ——	Night of	27/9/43.	1 Dornier 217. Destroyed.		

Summary of Combats prepared by W/Cdr J.R.D. Braham (in his own hands).

Appendix 2 Part 2   **AIRCRAFT FLOWN**

AIRCRAFT	ENGINE	AIRCRAFT	ENGINE	AIRCRAFT	ENGINE
141 Sqd. A.F. dittering		Night of 29/9/43		1 Messerschmitt 110	Destroyed
2 Gft Pgts.		Day of 5/3/44		1 Ju. 88	Damaged
"		Day of 24/3/44		1 Reihl 177	Destroyed
"				1 Ju 52	Destroyed
"		Day of 4/4/44		1 Ju 34	Destroyed
"		Day of 13/4/44		1 Bucker 131	Destroyed
"				1 Reihl 41	Destroyed
"		Day of 29/4/44		1 F.N. 58	Destroyed
"		Day of 7/5/44		1 F.N. 190	Destroyed
"		Day of 12/5/44		1 Ju 88	Damaged
				1 F.N. 190	Destroyed

TOTAL 29 A/c Destroyed
1 A/c Probably Destroyed
6 A/c Damaged.

Type of Aircraft	Destroyed	Probable	Damaged
Heinkel 111	5	1	1
Dornier 17	2	—	—
Ju. 88	4	—	4
Dornier 217	5	—	1
Messerschmitt 110.	6	—	—
F.W. 190.	2	—	—
Ju 52	1	—	—
HE 177	1	—	—
Ju 34	1	—	—
FW	1	—	—
Bucker 131	1	—	—

Appendix D

The following list shows the various types of aircraft flown by Gp/Capt. Braham during his flying career in the RAF and RCAF. As can be seen, he started with 1930s biplanes with a top speed of 120 mph, and ended with aircraft like the English Electric Lightning, with a maximum speed of Mach 2.1 (1,390 mph) at 40,000 ft.

The dates given are those on which he first flew each type of aircraft. In many cases he went on to fly later versions of the same type. These are aircraft in which he was the sole, or first, pilot.

Where known, the number or registration of the aircraft is also given.

30.3.1938	de Havilland Tiger Moth. G–ADXU
9.6.1938	Hawker Hart. K4970
10.6.1938	Hawker Audax. K4405
6.9.1938	Hawker Fury. K8300
20.12.1938	Hawker Demon. K5740
20.3.1939	Miles Magister. L8279
24.3.1939	Bristol Blenheim. L1507
31.3.1939	Gloster Gladiator.
26.7.1939	Hawker Hurricane. L1832
17.8.1939	Miles Master. N7719
6.9.1940	Bristol Beaufighter. R2072
29.10.1940	Fairey Battle. L5778
11.12.1940	Avro Anson. R3586
21.7.1941	Supermarine Spitfire. P8274
30.1.1942	Westland Lysander. 9795
6.2.1942	de Havilland Dominie. 7373
30.3.1942	Douglas Havoc. AA469
21.4.1942	Airspeed Oxford. 3780
25.1.1943	de Havilland Mosquito.
18.12.1943	Auster.
1.1.1944	Avro Tutor. K3456

19.1.1944	Percival Proctor. L707
25.7.1945	Hawker Tempest. SN277
28.7.1945	Gloster Meteor.
18.9.1945	North American P-51 Mustang. KH433
15.9.1947	North American Harvard.
12.1.1948	de Havilland Vampire.
25.6.1948	de Havilland Hornet.
17.9.1948	Hawker Sea Fury. 946
6.5.1949	North American F-86 A-5 Sabre. 49–199
27.10.1949	de Havilland 113 Prototype. (Vampire NF10) 3–5–3
6.1.1950	Vickers Wellington. 429
18.6.1950	Beech Expeditor G–45.
23.6.1950	Lockheed F-94 Starfire. 370
18.9.1950	de Havilland Venom. G5–5
21.9.1950	English Electric Canberra. 850
19.11.1951	McDonnell F-2H Banshee.
26.6.1952	Lockheed T-33 Silver Star. 694
29.7.1952	North American B-25 Mitchell.
22.9.1952	Avro CF-100. 18110
27.2.1954	Northrop F-89 Scorpion. 310
9.12.1954	Hawker Hunter. 900
9.1.1956	Gloster Javelin. 555
13.3.1956	North American F-1000 Super Sabre. 2073
27.9.1956	General Dynamics F-102A Convair Delta Dagger. 376
July 1957	de Havilland 110 Sea Vixen. XP828
25.5.1960	McDonnell F-101B Voodoo. 70427
9.10.1960	Douglas C-47 Dakota. 979
2.7.1962	Lockheed F-104F Starfighter. 386
13.2.1963	English Electric Lightning T4. L997
7.11.1964	CL-41 Tutor. 035
13.10.1965	Lear Jet. N805LT
5.7.1966	Northrop F-5B Freedom Fighter.
11.8.1967	de Havilland Comet. 915.

Group Captain Braham also lists a Messerschmitt 110 in his own list of types flown as at 31.12.1957. However, there is no trace of this aircraft in any of his four flying log-books. He probably flew this aircraft when he first visited Germany after the war in June 1945. His total recorded flying hours in the RAF and RCAF were 5,370 hours 50 minutes.

Index